Getting There

Manjula Padmanabhan is a writer, artist and playwright. She grew up in Europe and Southeast Asia, and returned to India as a teenager in the late 1960s. The popular comic strip character, Suki, created by Manjula, appeared in the *Sunday Observer* in Bombay and later in the *Pioneer* in New Delhi through the 1980s and 1990s. In 1997, her play *Harvest* won first prize in the Onassis Prize for Theatre in Greece. She is the author of several critically acclaimed books, including *Hot Death, Cold Soup*, *Kleptomania*, *Three Virgins and Other Stories*, *Escape* and *The Island of Lost Girls*, and a number of books for children as author-illustrator, among them *Mouse Attack* and a series of picture puzzle books.

Also by Manjula Padmanabhan

Visit to the City Market (illustrations)
Hot Death, Cold Soup
Harvest (play)
This is Suki! (cartoons)
Mouse Attack
Mouse Invaders
Kleptomania
Hidden Fires
Doubletalk (cartoons)
Unprincess!
Three Virgins and Other Stories
I am Different! (illustrations)
Same & Different (illustrations)
Where's That Cat? (illustrations)
Escape
The Island of Lost Girls
Mama, What Is the Night (illustrations)
Lights Out (play)
The Collected Plays Volume I (Blood and Laughter: Plays)
The Collected Plays Volume II (Laughter and Blood: Short Performance Pieces)

Getting There

Manjula Padmanabhan

hachette
INDIA

First published in United Kingdom in 2002 by Picador
An imprint of Pan Macmillan

This revised edition published in 2020 by Hachette India
(Registered name: Hachette Book Publishing India Pvt. Ltd)
An Hachette UK company
www.hachetteindia.com

ISBN 978-93-89253-29-0

Hachette Book Publishing India Pvt. Ltd
4th & 5th Floors, Corporate Centre,
Plot No. 94, Sector 44, Gurugram 122003, India

Typeset in Perpetua Std 11.5/14.5
by R Ajith Kumar, New Delhi

Printed and bound in India by
Manipal Technologies Limited, Manipal

MIX
Paper from responsible sources
FSC™ C043100

To young adventurers, everywhere:
Travel light. Avoid regrets.

CONTENTS

AUTHOR'S NOTE

A friend who read the first edition of this book complained that it didn't read like a novel.

I said, 'Why should it? It isn't one.' The note beneath my author bio says explicitly that it's based on my life. The friend felt the note wasn't enough to dispel the impression that I had intended to write a fictional account of my youthful jaunt.

So, for this new edition, I'd like to be clear: the book is about a journey I went on, between 1977 and 1978, to the United States and Europe. I have altered crucial details about my family in order to spare the feelings of my older relatives, and I have changed all names except mine. In every other sense, particularly after my arrival in Europe, events happened as described.

BOMBAY

BOMBAY, 1977

THEY ARRIVED OUT OF the rain on a dark afternoon in early September. Bansi answered the bell. I had glanced out of my room at the moment that he opened the door, so I saw him fall back a pace and look up, shading his eyes against the grey glare. 'Who is it?' he asked in Hindi.

Their shadows entered the house before they did. They were blocking the light so that the thin vapour blowing in around them from the street was carved into shifting beams. Bansi was asking questions. I could not hear over the sound of the rain what answers he got. But a moment later he was nodding and standing back. They entered then, two huge men, silhouetted against the light, their outlines glistening wet. They stripped off their dripping rucksacks where they stood, water streaming from them in jewelled droplets. I remained at the entrance to my room, staring at the tableau, not recognizing the shape of my own future quickening into substance, there in the hallway. Then Bansi shut the door and the light show ended. I ducked out of sight, wondering who this monumental pair were and what their presence meant in the house. Not residents, surely? Where would they sleep? Sujaya and I shared two rooms between us, as paying guests. Govinda our landlord and his elderly uncle Khushru had one each. That left the unlikely choice of the drawing room or the verandah. Telling myself that they must surely be temporary refugees from the rain, I shrugged and forgot about them till dinner.

That night, at five minutes to eight, I heard a minor commotion from around the dining area. Then Govinda, speaking in his Oxbridge accent with his voice warbling at the edges in the way it did when he was in a high good humour, said, '. . . see here – I'll strike the gong, shall I, shall I? That should bring the ladybirds out!' followed by an ineffectual *ping! ping! ping!*

He was referring to Sujaya and myself, though he knew the nickname annoyed Sujaya. She felt that he was poking fun at us, two unmarried women in our mid-twenties, living under the roof of a highly eligible bachelor.

I looked around to see if she was ready to leave the room so that we could make our entrance together. But she had just returned from work, very wet and very late, having got caught in the rain. She was in no mood for what she called Govinda's buffoonery.

So I stepped out of the room alone. Govinda turned towards me, saying triumphantly to his guests, like a magician who has successfully caused a griffin to materialize out of thin air, 'See? I told you – here's one now . . .'

The two guests were already sitting down. They were so tall that their heads were almost level with Govinda's as he stood, formally waiting till I got to my seat. In the three months that I and Sujaya had been at Palm View, our places at the elegant table with its pink marble top had been as fixed as the cardinal points on a compass. Govinda was North, Uncle Khushru East, Sujaya South, and I was West. Now, suddenly, I had been moved to North-west. I was disturbed. To be shifted without any discussion was to be reminded that I, too, was only an itinerant, with no permanent control over my position at the table.

I said, 'Oh . . . hello,' and sat, feeling oppressed by blind fate.

'Where's Ladybird Senior?' said Govinda. 'Not home yet?'

'Recovering from the rain,' I said.

'She'll join us in a moment . . .' He had turned to the two guests. 'This is Manjula, our resident artist – Manjula, meet Piet and . . . Japp?' He pronounced it with a 'j' before correcting himself and saying, 'Wait – that's with a 'y', isn't it?' And said it again, turning to me explaining, 'They're Dutch! From Holland!'

I smiled thinly and said, 'Mmm!' It wasn't just the change of seat that bothered me. It was the new faces at the table. They would be a distraction for D'Silva, the cook. For ten days now I had been planning to go on a diet. The presence of guests might ruin those plans. But I looked up in their direction anyway.

Both men were bobbing their heads in acknowledgement. Japp was fair, with bulging blue eyes darting like pale fish behind aviator frame glasses. He vaguely resembled Donald Sutherland. Piet had blocky, handspun features and might have been a dark-haired Jon Voight. They were in their early twenties. Both had recently shaved their heads and the stubble covering their scalps was less than half an inch long. Both wore T-shirts and jeans.

Bansi appeared, bearing a tureen of soup on a tray. Sujaya made her entrance just then, looking as if she had spent the whole day preparing for the event. She wore a pale green satin wrap, her skin the colour of honey on buttered toast, her thick black hair coiled in a shining knot at the nape of her neck. She said, as she settled into her seat, now at South-west, 'Oh, Holland! How nice – lovely country . . .'

Uncle Khushru wouldn't eat till later, so Bansi began his service, first to Sujaya, then me, then the two guests, then Govinda.

Govinda said to Sujaya, 'Of course, you must have been there . . .' He turned to the guests in explanation. 'Works with the airlines. Been all over the world.' He adored playing host. His heavy-lidded grey eyes were bright, and his mouth burned cherry-red against the natural blue-white pallor of his skin. His father had been English, his mother, Parsi. They were no longer alive, but in their heyday they had lived at the vanguard of Bombay's most sparkling era, in the 20s and 30s. Govinda had been born at a time when orientalism was in vogue. The 'a' at the end of his name was not an affectation. To hear it was to see hand-tinted photographs of neo-classical male dancers, their torsos bare and gleaming, their nostrils flared, peacock feathers in their hair and kohl under their eyes.

Sujaya said, 'Well . . . not really – but of course, Amsterdam, you know – cheese capital of the world!' She flashed her professional smile at the guests. 'Though I don't suppose you think of it like that? When it's your home, I mean . . .'

They smiled back with the bland expressions of people who aren't quite sure how to respond. Whether to be polite or truthful.

I said, 'Are you here for a reason? Or for a holiday?' If it was a holiday, they wouldn't stay for long. There wasn't much to see in Bombay during the monsoon.

Donald Sutherland shrugged and arched his eyebrows. Jon Voight started to say something, but Govinda answered for both of them, grinning widely. 'Yes! They're here for a reason. A special reason!' I saw now that his good humour had a specific source, an inner secret that was boiling within him. He looked from one guest to the other with bird-like movements of his head, asking their permission to reveal all. Jon Voight nodded. Govinda said, 'It's a spiritual quest!'

'A quest!' exclaimed Sujaya. 'Spiritual!'

'To meet a guru . . .' said Govinda.

'Oh, really?' I said, my spirits falling. That sounded like three weeks at the least. 'Which one?' I wasn't really interested. The question was a preamble to asking them what the term of their stay in Bombay was likely to be.

Jon Voight answered, 'Mash-Ree Hoohoo.'

I frowned. 'Excuse me?' I said. The name made no sense.

He repeated, 'Mash-Ree Hoohoo.'

Govinda intervened. 'Mahashri Guru – that's just his title, of course!' He said the correct name now and added, 'He's very well known – a sort of guru-superstar – but not for . . . well, us. Only for these chaps. Foreigners. They come from all over. Just to meet him.' Govinda was a foreigner too, in the sense that he had a British passport. But he liked to choose his moment to be as foreign or as Indian as it suited him. In this situation, in the presence of hundred per cent foreigners, he was playing his Indian role.

I said, 'How long do you think you'll be here?'

Jon Voight said, 'Sree mons.'

'Three months!' I exclaimed. 'Just to see a guru?'

It took Govinda all of dinner, including dessert, coffee and Uncle Khushru's dinner too, to explain it. The guests had come on the advice of their spiritual guide in Holland. He had been a close friend of Govinda's parents. They used to see the same guru, a little man who had started life as a bidi-seller. At the age of seventy-six he had wandered away, got enlightenment and come back. He continued to live on the outskirts of the red-light district, continued to sell bidis from his tiny stall and continued to smoke them during his discourses. He had been a great comfort to Govinda's parents in their final days. The reason that he was popular with foreigners, said Govinda, was that he pooh-poohed ritual and discredited the claims of mystics.

It was past midnight when we left the table. I still did not know what the sleeping arrangements for the two guests were. But my fear that they would get in the way of my diet had been smoothly overtaken, in the course of dinner, by my curiosity about them. In the late 70s, there was no shortage of young foreigners pounding the streets of Indian cities in search of eternal truths. I thought they were mildly insane to imagine that they would go home with anything more eternal than amoebic dysentery.

Yet here, now, were two such seekers, sharing a place at dinner with me. After a couple of hours in their company, I had to acknowledge that they seemed perfectly sane. They were amusing, cool and down-to-earth. I was fascinated. I wanted to know more. I went to bed that night wondering why I had begun the evening feeling that their presence in the house would be a nuisance.

THE DIET

TEN DAYS BEFORE THE arrival of the Dutch guests, I had been to see a doctor about losing weight. His name was Dr Shiva Prasad. He had recently opened a diet clinic highly recommended to me by a friend.

When I called to make the initial appointment, the doctor asked if I was married. I said 'no'. He asked if I had any friends or relatives in whose company I regularly ate my meals. I said I had a boyfriend called Prashant with whom I spent most of my spare time, including dinner every day. He was copy chief at an ad agency and his workday usually ended around 6.30 p.m. He would collect me from Palm View on his motorbike and we would spend the rest of the evening either at my married brother's house or at a movie. If we didn't eat at my brother's house we ate at a restaurant. The doctor advised me to bring my friend along for the first 'briefing'. According to him, the cooperation of regular eating companions was essential to the success of a diet.

So I invited Prashant to accompany me. We spent an hour with the doctor. He was a marvellous advertisement for his clinic: slender as a whip and surrounded by framed portraits of the forty racehorses he owned at his stables in Bangalore. The impression he gave was that if his 'patients' followed his instructions they might succeed not only in losing weight but in gaining racehorses too. As he put it, 'It's not about becoming thin or fat: it's about becoming successful.'

He showed us progress slides of his prize patient, a woman who, at the start of the diet, looked like a wrestler dressed in a printed silk sari. 'The first time she came in here, she couldn't walk on her own! She had to be supported by her husband!' She lost 60 kilos in eleven months. The slides, taken from the front, back and sides, were like a time-lapse film of the Michelin Tyre Man being deflated very gradually. Even Prashant, who had come with the intention of scoffing, was impressed. So I signed up.

One day later, when I went back to the clinic for the introductory session, the doctor showed me more slides of his former patients. This time, because Prashant was not with us, I saw them unclothed.

They looked terrible. We are so used to seeing pictures of female nudes who look like articulated dolls that when we see the more typical sort of woman without her clothes on, she looks diseased. One girl had a 16-inch waist and 40-inch hips. Her body was like a cartoon, wildly out of proportion. She must have wanted to reduce her hips, but the record showed that she had lost weight uniformly, including on her waist. The last slide revealed her with her middle dwindled to nothingness and her hips more prominent than ever before. She resembled a giant ant masquerading as a woman.

The prize patient, whose success had seemed so spectacular when she was clothed, looked like a sack of loose brown skin standing to attention when she was naked. Her breasts were like used tea-bags. As the weight loss progressed, the sachets deflated gradually, becoming little more than flaps of skin. There seemed to be no nipples, just two tired points aimed at the floor. The huge mound of her abdomen collapsed slowly across the months, but only the mass of it. The skin remained, hanging from her waist down, covering her pubic area. When she posed for the frontal view, the folded skin covered that area like an apron. When she posed for the slides in profile, she held up the lower edge of this fold so that you could see the extent of it.

It wasn't easy to guess her thoughts. Her face was expressionless. Her appearance suggested that she came from a deeply conservative, traditional background, yet here she was, posing naked for a doctor's unsympathetic camera. Was the lack of expression a sign of diffidence or confidence? Had she agreed out of her own volition or had her husband forced her? Was he in the room with her when these pictures were taken? Had she agreed because she imagined she was making a valuable contribution to a study of weight loss amongst obese Third World women? Had she been convinced on the grounds that she represented that rarest of breeds, a Third World woman who was yet rich enough to have weight to lose? Did she herself want to lose weight or had she done it, all of it, out of deference to her husband's wish for a slender wife?

She held her head stiffly, her expression opaque, offering no answers.

The flap bothered me. How did she relate to it, I wondered. Did she despise it? Did she pinch and prod it when she had a bath? Did she wash underneath it with revulsion? Did she sigh when she tucked it away under the waistband of her sari petticoat? Or did she regard it with a certain horrified fondness, the way, I imagined, some people regarded extra digits on their hands? I remember meeting a woman who had a second thumb on her right hand. Its nail was as perfectly manicured as the other nails on the hand. I remember thinking well of her for having accepted her irregularity, for celebrating it rather than slicing it off.

Some of the other patients whose slides I saw that day had resorted to plastic surgery to excise the unwanted folds of skin. But they had been left with scars like livid pink zippers, running across their abdomens.

I felt disturbed. I didn't want to look like a limp balloon or a surgeon's embroidery sampler. I couldn't understand why none of the patients actually looked attractive at the end of their ordeal. But I had already committed myself to being a patient. I paid my non-refundable introductory fee of 500 rupees and meekly produced a urine sample after submitting to having my blood pressure taken and my weight recorded in a clear plastic folder with my name printed smartly on its cover. The initial entry read: 65.8 kg. Height: 5'5". I wanted to add, Self-image: 0.00 – but didn't. The doctor was not easily amused, I noticed. Gaining racehorses was a serious business.

The slides were followed by a two-hour 'psychometric test'. It began with an interview with Dr Prasad's wife, Mrs Prasad. She told me that she was a practising analyst and that the purpose of the session was to determine my fitness for a course of dieting. 'Few people realize to what extent their lives can be affected by a change in eating habits,' she said. 'We have to know a little about your personality in order to adjust our method to suit your individual type.'

It sounded reasonable. She had pepper-and-salt hair and half-shut eyes which gazed at me with an expression that reduced me to a case number on a shiny plastic folder, cabinet 7b, drawer II.

We began with a résumé of family history. Yes, both my parents were alive. My father had retired from the Foreign Service as Ambassador. He and my mother lived in their own house in Calicut, surrounded by all our extended family of relatives. I had one brother, one sister, both married. Both had children.

She paused in her tracks. 'How do you feel about that?' she asked. Her expression was carefully neutral.

'About what?' I asked in return.

She may have sighed. 'It's quite normal, you know. Two elder siblings, both married, both with children. You're twenty-four, so it's not too late, of course, for you to follow their path but . . . it happens. Feelings of inadequacy, a desire to compensate – it could explain your overeating for example . . .'

As I understood the drift of her enquiry, I started to smile in anticipation. 'Oh, no!' I exclaimed. 'I don't feel inadequate – I've *never* wanted to marry – '

She cut me off at once. 'You mean, you've never had an *opportunity* to marry – '

'No.' I was very accustomed to arguing this point. It always surprised me that I faced so much resistance. 'I am opposed to marriage – as an institution. I don't believe that it's the best way for men and women to, you know, live together and . . .' I shrugged, 'raise children, whatever.' I believed that most people had children because they didn't realize that they could choose not to. If they knew, I believed, hardly any would bother having them. 'Marriage is too restrictive – it's an instrument of patriarchy, after all, a method of ensuring that property is passed from one generation to the next through the paternal line. I mean, obviously that's important, but it's only a *system*, not a law of nature – and it's used to control women's sexuality – to define it . . .'

She allowed me to carry on for a few moments in this vein. When I paused for breath, she nodded, then asked, 'Would you call yourself a feminist?'

I said, relieved to be given a chance to reveal my orientation, 'Oh, yes. Absolutely . . .'

She nodded again and said, 'Then why don't you want children? If you feel so strongly about being a feminist shouldn't that mean you want to explore your feminine nature by having children?'

I said, 'Ah – but I don't like children. I've never wanted to have any.'

I kept looking for some sign that the statements I made were having an impact on her but she didn't so much as raise her eyebrows. She said, 'I see. For how long, would you say, you've not liked children? Can you think of a specific period when these feelings began?'

I said, 'I can't remember ever liking small children. When I was small, I didn't like children younger than myself. I thought they were sort of . . . *squirmy*. And wet. Little children always seemed to be sort of damp.' She listened without comment. 'I never wanted to pick them up or have anything to do with them. I don't understand why other people like them so much. I assume that it's a survival tactic – protecting the young – raw instinct, whatever. To keep the species alive. That sort of thing – '

'Okay,' she said. 'So you don't want to get married and you don't like children. What would you say you like?'

I said, 'My work. I'm an artist, you know.' I thought it so strange that she hadn't asked me any questions about my professional life.

'An illustrator, actually. And a cartoonist – though not all the time. I mean, I'd like to be a cartoonist, but I don't get commissions to draw the sort of cartoons that interest me. I'm a freelancer, so I get paid for each piece of work I complete. No salary, and no one pays on time. It's quite difficult to keep ahead of my expenses. I stopped accepting money from my parents when I was twenty-one. I've been living away from home since then and . . . I'm not very practical. But if I could do what I really wanted, then I would just spend all day drawing and painting.'

I was gabbling, wanting her to show a response. Once more, however, she listened as if what I said was random noise. 'I also like to write. I don't get the opportunity to do the kind of work I'd like . . .' I faltered to a stop.

She asked, 'What about boyfriends?' I said I had one. At this, she made a small notation in the notepad open in front of her. I felt I had to hammer home my point, so I volunteered, '. . . Though, of course, I don't plan to marry him.'

She looked, for an instant, straight at me instead of through me and said, 'Meaning, you don't love him.' It wasn't a question, but a statement. It left me speechless. I believed the reason I didn't want to marry him was that I didn't believe in the patriarchal establishment. I tried to explain this, but she cut me short.

She asked me what I liked about food, whether it was the type of food or the quantity that I preferred. Whether I ate the same amount when I was alone or when I was in company. Whether I liked particular types of food more than others or whether I was indifferent to tastes and flavours. I said I just liked to eat, I wasn't especially concerned about rare and unusual foods, that I was quite happy with, for instance, fried eggs every morning for months on end. Hot toast and butter were what I liked best. Ice cream was good too. I had a sweet tooth.

'What about cooking?' she asked. 'What types of food do you like to cook?'

'I don't cook,' I said. 'Never go near the kitchen.'

'All right,' she said. 'Do you have any feminine interests?'

And I said, 'Oh – yes! I like jewellery and perfume!' The moment the words were out of my mouth, I knew I had failed the encounter.

The correct answer, following the feminist canon, would have been that 'masculine' and 'feminine' were outmoded concepts. As a woman, whatever I did should be considered adequately 'feminine' without requiring external reference points. But I had blundered full-tilt into the trap of sex-defined preferences. It was a rout.

For the remainder of my time with Mrs Prasad, the only thing I was conscious of was the sound, in my head, of my feminist self popping and crackling on a spit of chagrin. By the time I had slunk out of that office I was emotionally gutted. I felt like a frog that has been pegged out on a dissection board with all its vital organs on display but no gentle chloroform to spare it the awareness of this humiliating and spreadeagled fate. Mrs Prasad was followed by Dr Nalini, a psychiatrist researching the link between food habits and psychological disorders. After making a careful list of what foods I liked and the history of my 'eating disorder', she brought out her set of Rorschach blots.

It surprised me that they were coloured. I had always assumed that, being 'ink blots', they would be black. Instead, they resembled nothing more than the shape of menstrual blood stains on panties. The pinkish-red colour of many of them heightened that impression. In card after card, that's all I could see. I understood how frustrating it must be to be the needle of a gramophone stuck in a groove, as I heard myself say yet again, 'Uhhh . . . menstrual stain.' There was only one in which I felt I saw something different: little fox faces and a couple of bats hovering overhead.

The final hurdle for the day, after the blots, was to draw a picture, one each, of a man and of a woman.

I had read about such exercises. I knew that they were not meant to be tests of skill, but as a tool for digging out unconscious messages embedded in the mind of the test subject. The success of the exercise depended upon the subject's spontaneous rendering of a man and a woman. But I am an artist. As an artist, I do not draw spontaneously. I labour over my work. How could I short-circuit my natural approach to drawing in order to produce a sketch in the style of someone who doesn't draw for a living? I was completely paralysed.

I started one drawing, scratched it out, then stared at the blank page helplessly for at least fifteen minutes before finally producing two featureless silhouettes of the type used in physical fitness handbooks. I was painfully conscious that whatever I drew would be picked up for interpretation. Every line would be heavy with meaning, however much I might desire to draw something neutral. Just the desire to draw something neutral had a meaning.

If I drew the man in the centre of the page it could mean that I gave men pride of place. If I drew the man and the woman as a couple, it could mean that I believed in monogamy. Did I in fact believe in monogamy? Did I wish to be typecast as one who believed in monogamy? Did I care either way?

Should I draw the couple facing one another? Clothed? If unclothed then to what extent should I detail their sexual features? Should the woman-silhouette have long hair? And wouldn't that mean that deep in my subconscious I believed that a True Woman was long-haired and traditional? And, my own being short, did that mean that I had symbolically castrated my femininity by cutting off my hair?

Should I draw both figures the same height, even though I knew that going by averages men are taller than women? And was it honest, anyway, for me to be assessing the significance of what I drew in this manner? Was it morally right to want to influence the results of the test by trying to assess what was expected of me and doing the opposite on purpose? And what exactly was that purpose?

I apologized twice to Dr Nalini for taking so long. I explained that I was an artist by profession and that therefore I couldn't perform unselfconsciously. I don't know whether she understood the nature of my dilemma. I think she was tired and wanted to go home.

In the end, I scribbled my two pathetic silhouettes in the slapdash manner I believed non-artists approached the task. I wondered what Rembrandt would have done, what Picasso would have done. And van Gogh? He would have refused the test altogether, perhaps. Or drawn a perfectly detailed ear. Truly great artists do not agonize, they just draw, paying no attention to the petty concerns of researchers.

My woman figure was on the left, facing left, with only the barest minimum of an outline. The man was spaced a decent distance away from her, also facing left. Neither of them had any discernible hair, they were both the same height. The woman had a small breast-bump and the man an equally modest crotch-bump.

I left the clinic feeling profoundly diminished. It was eight o'clock, and the city's night was alive with the harsh glitter of neon signs, chrome-plated cars, blinding headlights, windscreens flashing hypnotically as they passed under the corner street lamp. There was a relentless drizzle. Umbrellas, slick with rain, were being borne along by a procession of weary commuters.

I saw a taxi stop 10 yards from where I stood. I willed it to remain in place till I could reach it. I willed the driver to be compliant, to be eager to please, to be agreeable to take me in any direction I wished to go. I willed the shadowy figure hurrying towards the vehicle to be stricken with doubts about the validity of his claim to the cab.

And my will prevailed on all counts.

I leaned back on the plastic covers of the taxi's seat. The despair of a few moments ago had been wiped clear, like water from a car's windscreen. Outside, the night, the puddles, the damp trouser cuffs and the muddy sari hems. Inside, the warm dry cab and the knowledge that I would be home soon.

THE PATIENT

SUJAYA'S FIRST REMARK WHEN I told her that I was thinking of going on a diet was, 'D'Silva won't be able to handle it.' It had not occurred to me to worry about this, but the moment she said it, I realized that she was right, as usual.

The diet required eight light meals to take the place of three heavy ones. The doctor had explained that so long as the dieter was never hungry, the temptation to binge on junk food could be easily resisted.

Eight light meals! The kitchen had its share of eccentricity to deal with already. Govinda was a pulse-grain vegetarian, having worked out a highly specialized diet which required him to eat mounds of wheatgerm porridge, bananas and milk products. According to him, he liked to feel stuffed after a meal, but didn't have the time to work off the results with exercise. So he had experimented with various alternatives until he found one that he could sustain with very little difficulty and which allowed him to eat four or five times a day. It meant that he could never find anything to suit his needs in a restaurant or at someone else's house, but that was of little consequence to him.

Uncle Khushru ate dhansak for lunch and steak or fish for dinner. Sujaya and I ate a combination of what was made for Uncle Khushru and anything else that D'Silva felt like making. Most of the time we ate out, so the arrangement was that we didn't pay for food unless we wanted something specific, in which case we were free to work it out with the cook.

'You can't expect D'Silva to keep track of a separate menu just for you,' said Sujaya. 'It would be completely impractical. The simplest thing would be for you to go in there and make whatever it is yourself.'

I hadn't even seen the diet yet. I said I had no idea what it might involve aside from the eight meals a day. She said that I had better find out before starting, because it would be a mess if I monopolized the kitchen every two hours, poaching eggs and boiling lean meat. 'You'll have to be a bit considerate about it, you know,' she said. 'Diets can be a big nuisance. I mean, supposing you need to eat 5 kilos of artichoke hearts for breakfast – who'll go shopping for that sort of thing? Have you ever been to the market? D'you even know where it is? Have you gone there and bargained alongside all the other housewives at eight in the morning? You'd learn a thing or two if you did!'

I stared at her in dismay. I couldn't understand why something that was so obvious to her was for me entirely invisible until she had rubbed my nose in it. I said I'd think it over, but privately I told myself that if I couldn't enlist D'Silva's cooperation, I could kiss goodbye to my non-refundable join-up fee at the clinic.

I fretted over the problem for two whole days, before deciding to take it to Govinda to solve. He grinned broadly when he heard what the matter was. According to him the answer was very simple. 'Just show your diet to Bansi,' he said. 'That's his department! He adores having someone to boss over. When my parents were alive he was an absolute tyrant with their pills and whatnot!'

I was a little afraid of Bansi. His official position was that of bearer. But he had been working in the house since he was fourteen. He had grown into late middle age within these walls, a man of medium height, his skull domed, his hair thinning on top, wide cheekbones tapering to a pointed chin. On either side of his mouth, the skin was creased into permanent smile-lines, like a pair of parentheses, though there was rarely an actual smile contained between them. His eyes were small and shrewd, with a pronounced lid both above and below. His eyebrows were strongly marked and quirked, as if in perpetual astonishment.

It was very clear that he didn't approve of Sujaya and myself. He did not think we were suitable companions for the young master and he certainly didn't appreciate the way that Sujaya took an interest in running the household. For instance, she had dismissed the laundry woman within the first week of our moving into the house. This was an absolute rebuke to Bansi's housekeeping methods because Sujaya maintained that the woman was charging three times above the industry standard. Peace was restored only when it was agreed that she could continue to do the floors and clothes for the rest of the house, while Sujaya and I made our own arrangements.

Given this background, Bansi suffered our presence with great dignity. He did not so much as permit us the satisfaction of having any complaints to lodge against him. He kept his distance. There was a younger servant called Hari who worked under Bansi. Hari's official duties included dusting and polishing. Bansi used Hari as the buffer between us and himself, while he patrolled the rest of the house, maintaining the sacred relics of his private temple.

Nevertheless, I followed Govinda's instructions, and approached Bansi. He listened silently while I told him what I proposed to do. I speak only English and his natural language was Gujerati. The medium of communication we used was an inelegant, pidgin Hindi. I wasn't sure whether he understood all that I said, but was very relieved when, at the end of my recitation, he said, 'Show me the instructions. I'll see what I can do.'

Later that same day, the Dutch guests arrived. I worried that D'Silva would not be able to manage five separate cuisines, but decided to wait till I had seen the diet before calling off the arrangements. My first appointment for 'treatment' at the clinic was scheduled for the following afternoon.

The doctor's system was to see his patients two at a time, for half-hour sessions. In the first week, we would see him every second day. If, in the initial week, we lost weight successfully, then we would be called in every third day. Then once a week. Then once in ten days. He set a target for weight loss. The aim was to reach it and be free from visits for the rest of our newly slenderized lives. If, on the other hand, we did NOT lose weight according to schedule, he threatened to call us in for daily visits. Since he charged 100 rupees per consultation, there was a powerful incentive to someone like myself, who was operating on a tight budget, to lose weight.

I reached the clinic too early for my appointment. I settled down to wait, facing a wall on which a framed drawing had been hung, showing a fat woman appraising herself in a mirror. In the mirror was a reflection of the same woman, looking slim. Not just slim: she was the cartoon equivalent of a sex goddess. Her breasts were large, her eyelashes long, her mouth was a red cupid's bow with a dot of white to suggest a highlight in freshly applied lipstick. Her fingernails were long and painted the same red as the lipstick. Her short dress was red and on her feet were red heels as high as circus stilts.

She had not merely lost weight. She had metamorphosed from a lower middle-class frump in a plain cotton sari into a glamorous, affluent sex kitten. Being thin was only one element in a complex mutation. Being sexually available was another. Being obviously wealthy was a third. Poor people, for instance, are thin but that doesn't make them beautiful. It is the slenderness of those who choose not to be fat that is admired.

There is a certain logic to it. The body stores energy as fat against times of shortages. When food intake falls short of energy requirements, the fat gets used up. Poor people look thin because they cannot afford the sort of food intake that produces a surplus of energy to store as fat. Rich people get fat because their intake of food far outstrips their bodies' energy requirements. But in order to avoid suggesting that they are storing energy against times of need, the rich of today are obliged to look thin and dress expensively. The glamour is essential. Without it, a thin person merely looks poor. Fat is an attention-getting asset, whether it is stored on the body or in the bank.

Another patient had entered the waiting room. She sat across from me, just under the drawing. She was in her early twenties. Her powdered cheeks bulged and her plump white hands terminated in sharp red nails. Diamonds sparkled from every joint of her fingers. Her air of being a human Pomeranian attached to her Lord Husband by a leash of gold chains was sustained by the obvious symbols of marriage she wore, the heavy jewellery, the red teeka on her forehead, the bangles on both wrists, the toe-rings. Every detail of her appearance bespoke wealth of the recently acquired kind, as if she had been gorging on deep-fried currency notes.

The memory of what I'd said to Mrs Prasad two weeks before was still fresh in my mind, however. I wanted to sneer at this apparition in female form sitting across the room from me, but Mrs Prasad's probing enquiry had shown me that my so-called ideology was thinner than a coat of nail varnish. I tried to imagine what it would be like to be married to the sort of hotshot industrialist who could afford a wife like this young woman in front of me. Would I, too, be weighed down with gold, my face obscured under a mask of rouge and mascara? *No!* I thought. *Never!* But I had told Mrs Prasad that I was fond of jewellery and make-up, and here I was, sitting in the same diet clinic as that other woman, seeking the same goal. How different were we, really? It humbled me to realize, not much.

The intercom on the receptionist's desk beeped. She rose to escort the two of us in.

The visit commenced with a weighing-in. The other patient had already begun her diet, so she was weighed first. The scale used was the kind which had a post with a movable bar attached to it. The bar had a sliding indicator at one end and a counterweight at the other. When the one was correctly balanced against the other, the weight of the person standing on the platform of the scale was revealed. The other patient stood on the scale as the receptionist and the doctor both conferred for several minutes over the exact location of the indicator. Eventually they came to the sad conclusion that our lady's weight had not gone down by any amount at all. It had even, said the doctor, gone up very slightly.

'Now,' said Dr Prasad, 'if you have been following what is written on your sheet this *could not* have happened.' The sheet referred to was the typewritten list of items to be eaten over the course of the two or three days between visits. It was prepared afresh for each patient to take home after each visit, each sheet being added to the red plastic file given to us on the introductory day of the diet. We were required to bring this dossier with us for every session.

My fellow patient handed her file over to the doctor. 'But, doctor, I followed the diet exactly!' She pouted. 'I ate only what is given there!' She spoke a mixture of Hindi and English.

The doctor was examining the sheet relevant to the previous two days. 'Now let's see . . .' he was saying. 'On Sunday morning, before breakfast you had a . . . coconut water . . .' He looked up. 'Is that right?' He wore gold-rimmed reading-glasses over which he peered when he looked up from the sheet.

'Haan, haan, doctor,' said the young woman, 'I had only that!'

'All right,' said the doctor, referring back to the sheet.

He might have been reading from a police charge-sheet, his expression was so grave. 'Then at . . . eight o'clock, one slice of papaya, one slice of dry toast . . . ?' He looked up.

'Haan, doctor, haan!' said the girl, wriggling forward in her seat.

He read on. 'At ten o'clock, one boiled egg, one glass of lime-juice without sugar or salt, one slice of dry toast . . .' He did not wait for confirmation. 'At eleven o'clock, one slice of papaya, one cup of tea with skimmed milk and no sugar.' Then very casually, he asked, 'Then . . . at twelve o'clock, what did you have?'

She wriggled, she lowered her eyes. Finally it emerged. 'See, doctor, I had boiled veg, two chapatis, some dry dal, skimmed milk ka lassi . . .' She trailed off. Then, in a very, very tiny voice she said, 'One apple . . .'

The doctor pounced. 'One apple?' he said, his voice steely. '*One apple?*' And he angled his glance at her over his glasses like an archer taking aim.

The fair skin with its fine down of bleached fur and its layer of powder and rouge trembled. 'See, doctor,' said the girl, 'I can't eat papaya all day long, na!' She was sitting forward with her plump hands splayed out beseechingly on the doctor's glass-topped table. Her nails, I now saw, were not quite as well-maintained as they had seemed from a distance. They showed signs of wear. *Maybe she bites them*, I thought, in the darkness of an airconditioned afternoon. Gnawing at them hungrily, peeling away the shiny red membranes till they hung in unsightly shards, like flayed animal-hide, from the carcasses of two small, five-limbed creatures . . .

'All right, all right,' said the doctor, reverting to his examination of the diet sheet. 'Then at two o'clock. What did you have?'

'One orange and one . . . one . . . banana!' She blurted the word out, belligerently. Her hands twitched.

The doctor glanced up to confirm that his victim was writhing in the grip of his inquisition. 'Then,' he said, 'at four o'clock?'

'Lassi. Papaya. Tea.' She was fidgeting as she tugged at a tendril of hair curling down from her forehead.

'Good . . . good . . .' said Dr P, absently. 'six o'clock?'

'Mosambi juice.'

'Good! And . . . dinner?'

There was a husky silence. The girl looked down at her hands. She looked away at the window. But she was beaten. In a low, still voice she said, in Hindi, 'Doctor, sometimes you have to go out, na . . .'

She was crushed, she was vanquished. Her full cheeks quivered in delicious agony. Immediately, the doctor switched tactics. He was all charm and concern. In his kindest voice he said, 'Never mind, my dear, never mind, just tell me – what did you eat?'

The girl said, her eyes downcast, 'Doctor, we went for Chinese.'

'All right, all right, don't worry! Just tell me what you had!'

So it came out, morsel by villainous morsel. Chicken and sweetcorn soup. Sweet and sour pork. Fried noodles – 'Doctor, I had only this much!' she cried at one point holding her right hand out, a tender cup fashioned from the tips of her fingers, the thumb cradled between them. Prawns in garlic sauce. Thums Up. Fried rice. Crab spring rolls. Lychees.

At the end of this confession, there was a silence. The doctor closed the red plastic file slowly. He raised his eyebrows as he removed his glasses. When he pulled in the corners of his lips, deep clefts appeared on either side of his mouth. He looked both severe and boyishly handsome. The girl was looking up at him, her slick, red-painted mouth hanging slightly ajar and her eyes wide, as if expecting any moment to be spanked. He paused a long moment. Then he looked at her, with his full, frank stare. 'So? What shall we do with you, my dear?' She burst into tears. The whole half hour of my session was taken up with the cajoling, the scolding, the advice and the reassurance the doctor had to give this lady so that she would have the courage to persevere with her endeavours to improve herself. 'You can do it, of course you can do it!' he insisted. 'You just haven't made up your mind properly yet – just you wait till I speak to your husband . . .'

Long before he was finished with her, however, my mind had been made up. I would eat grilled air and broiled water for a year rather than be reduced to the level of that pathetic plumpness who shared the room with me that day.

I had realized in the course of this first session that the doctor was not the dandified lecher I had mistaken him for. He was suavely intelligent and deviously cunning. In each patient, he discovered a weakness. Then he customized a goad to poke into that weakness. With me it was pride. He had positioned me alongside one of his weakest victims, making me witness her total disintegration. In the clearest possible terms, he had revealed what lay in store for me if I did not follow his formula for weight loss. He had guessed that I would not permit myself that shaming experience.

When I looked at the diet sheet I saw that there was nothing exotic or impossible for D'Silva to create. I began to feel the way a caged animal might, when it sees that the door to its prison has been left ajar: a soaring sense of my ability to flee the Dungeon of Body.

I left the clinic feeling powerful and unleashed. There was a powder-fine drizzle of rain outside, but its wetness did not bother me. I found a cab easily. I glided into my room and I sniffed at all the familiar artefacts from my past life of tame, cage-bound domestication. Sujaya was not yet home. I sprang onto my bed in the darkness, spread my shining whiskers and purred.

THE DIET BEGINS

TWO DAYS LATER BANSI informed me that he was ready to start my new regimen. The first course for the day was scheduled for 6 a. m. I am not an early riser, so I decided to spend the night at Palm View rather than at Prashant's place.

The following morning I was awake half an hour before the alarm went off. The moment it sounded, I leapt out of bed, threw on a caftan, brushed my teeth and strode from the room. I was just in time to see Bansi placing a glass of tender-coconut water on a silver coaster, with a matching coaster above it as a lid, out on the marble-topped table. I felt rare and privileged to be starting the day with such a drink. It tasted as if a small sweet pearl had been dissolved in dew and chilled overnight.

I put on my jeans and sneakers to walk across to Prashant's flat. He lived close by in an apartment block called Jujube Towers. I had arranged to wave out to him at 6.20 a.m., standing in the car park from where he could see me from his window.

He came down, laughing to find me so serious and determined. We walked briskly for an hour, then he saw me back to Palm View. It was 7.30 a.m. I made my bed, chose clothes for the day and had a shower. Sujaya had not so much as removed the eye-mask she wore against the morning's light, while I was already at my desk in the front room that we shared as a study, wanting to roar with the knowledge of my own competence.

At eight, Bansi knocked on the door of the study, to call me out to breakfast. The dining table was set for six but Govinda was the only other person present. At my place, I saw that Bansi had arranged two slices of dry toast on my quarter plate. The toast was made from the home-made fat-free bread that D'Silva had created just for me. The butter dish, which would normally have been close to my plate because Bansi knew my weaknesses, had today been placed on the far horizon of the table, near Uncle Khushru's plate. A glass filled with recently poured water sweated coldly on its coaster. I sat down feeling cherished.

Govinda smiled a greeting at me, while digging into the mound of his wheatgerm porridge with the automated movements of someone who is used to eating alone. He wielded his spoon like a boiler-room attendant shovelling coal into the maw of a furnace. 'I hope you like D'Silva's bread,' he said. 'Ladybird Senior tried it last night and said it was too hard on her teeth!' He regarded my quest for slenderness with the amused indulgence of the constitutionally thin.

Bansi appeared from the kitchen. On his tray was a boiled egg, pointy end up, in a dainty blue and white Wedgwood cup. After placing the cup in front of me, on my plate, Bansi stepped back but didn't leave the room. I had the impression he was waiting.

I raised my teaspoon and tapped the egg, expecting to make three or four dents before chipping away the shell to uncover the firm, white flesh beneath. But the instant the spoon made its first dent, a dark mist rose in front of my eyes. The lack of resistance under the shell revealed that the egg was not hardboiled, but soft.

My loathing for soft-boiled eggs is something I need to explain. It was a revulsion dating from early childhood, when all food was classified into Slimy and Non-Slimy categories. Slimy food was to be abhorred, eaten only by slugs and deviants. By my definition, raw eggs were unthinkable abominations, while soft-boiled eggs, with their quivering, semi-solid, snot-white slush were not only slime, but *sneaky* slime: an egg's shell gave no indication of what it contained until the would-be consumer had cracked it open. Refusing a boiled egg that has been cracked open was often difficult. As a child, I had learnt very early that if a boiled egg was placed in front of me and if it proved to be soft, then the only way to avoid eating it was to throw up at once.

Yet here, now, directly in my path, placed there by Bansi, on the introductory day of my diet, was exactly such an egg. It was clear why he was hovering. The egg was a test. He had told himself that if I could face a runny egg, I would be worth the attention and effort expected of him in the weeks ahead. If, however, I insisted that it be removed to the kitchen to be transformed into something safe and harmless, a scrambled egg, a sissy egg – well, then. I wouldn't be worth his effort, would I?

I had only a few seconds in which to make a powerful decision.

The stream of my life seemed to slow down, pause and separate into two distinct elements, each one to be weighed in its own balancing scale. On one side was the whole mass of my life's experience, shaped roughly like a snowball rolling down the slope of my time on earth. In early childhood, the ball was tinier than the smallest marble, but very sticky. Everything it came in contact with remained fast to it. As I aged, so did the ball grow larger, but also less sticky and its outer surface less dense. Already, the outer layer was starting to shed bits and pieces that it had picked up. I could see how, as the years increased the surface area of the sphere, so too would the rate at which the ball shed what it had picked up increase.

I could see, looking at this time-ball of my life, that my aversion to soft-boiled eggs was something buried deep within my whole substance. In itself, I now saw, the disgust I felt was childish and whimsical. Yet, to cast it out, I needed to reach deep into the core of that sphere of myself, where it was hot and dense, where logic did not rule over raw sensation. I needed to justify such an effort. How could I be sure that by changing something, even something so insignificant, buried close to the heart of my life, I would not risk disturbing the truth of myself? Just to be asking myself questions of this nature was causing alterations in my understanding of who I was.

By contrast, on the other pan of the balance scale in my mind's eye was just one overwhelming item: my desire to lose weight. Contained within that desire was the combined weight of the doctor, the other patients at the clinic, the transformation that awaited me at the end of the dieter's rainbow, the fame and fortune that were the natural due of slender people. The desire to lose weight, I now saw, with my teaspoon poised above the plain white dome of the egg, was really about becoming someone else. Someone efficient and industrious who could fight minotaurs before breakfast, someone who would succeed in her quest to be financially independent and ideologically pure, someone whose illustrations would soon be the talk of the town, be sought after and valued. Someone of consequence, taste and wit.

All of this was available for the price of . . . one soft-boiled egg.

The scale in my mind tipped decisively.

I tapped another dent in the egg. I picked away triangular sections of shell, till the aperture created was wide enough to admit a spoon. I dipped the spoon in and brought out a mound of undercooked bird-embryo. Even as I felt the blood shrink from my mouth, I forced my whole being to submit to a new imperative. Twenty-four years of revulsion were swept away in that one act of will as I ate the egg.

The foundation of the diet was powdered skimmed milk. It was permitted in any of four forms: as milk in tea and coffee, as dahi, as lassi and as paneer. Every day, Bansi made up two versions of milk. One was a paste-like concentrate of the powder which I could scoop out and stir into hot beverages. The rest went into a large glass bowl out of which was made the dahi. Half the dahi was made into paneer, and a quarter became lassi by mixing the dahi in water.

Bansi had a gadget for performing this feat, a stainless-steel cylinder with a disk-shaped plunger at the end of a thin rod. The plunger was perforated and fitted the inside of the cylinder snug enough that it could be moved up and down like a piston. Every morning and afternoon, Bansi would stand just out of sight of the dining room, mixing the lassi. The sound of the plunger tinkling within its steel container and the shoosh of liquid swirling in and out of the perforations soothed him. He would remain at this task for long minutes, tinkling slowly and languorously.

In order to eat D'Silva's toast and keep pace with the tide of Bansi's skimmed milk products, I had to alter the way I structured my day. Before the diet, I used to drift back and forth across town, eating with friends or with my sister-in-law at my brother's house, or at their club. After the diet had started, I found myself less and less inclined to spend any time away from Palm View. It was only under Bansi's watchful eye that I could maintain the strict rotation of boiled eggs, slices of papaya and fat-free soups. Even spending the nights at Jujube Towers with Prashant was a problem because of the 6 a. m. dose of coconut water.

Mrs Prasad's words had been prophetic. By controlling what I ate and where I ate it, the diet changed the whole course of my life.

THE DUTCH GUESTS

ONE WEEK AFTER THE diet had started, I was sitting alone at the table eating lunch. The monsoon had been very active for several days at a stretch. The drip-drip drizzle with which the morning had begun had abruptly escalated into a roaring deluge. Shadows flooded the house as I tackled the main course of broiled chicken. By the time I had reached the finale of the meal, a slice of papaya that looked and tasted like boiled, sweetened tongue of ox, the dining room was under a thick shroud of rain-inspired gloom.

I could have turned on a few lights, but preferred not to. The darkness around me matched the darkness within me. I wasn't hungry, but at the same time, there was a spare, bewildered feeling inside, very different to the sense of sleek satisfaction with which I ended meals in the pre-diet days. All the sounds and laughter of earlier feeding patterns had dimmed down. What remained was the bare fusion of nutrients within the reactor of my body. I was coming to understand that for all the years before this diet, I had regarded food as a form of entertainment. In fact it was just fuel. It was gasoline, it was electricity, it was an arrangement of molecules which were required to keep another arrangement of molecules in running order.

Dim light filtering in from the verandah touched accents in the silverware, in the silent crystal in the sideboard, in the water in my glass. The heady sense of being at the helm of my ship of destiny had dissipated. In its place was a dreary consciousness of having once been a pirate's galleon bursting at the seams with worldly treasures, now filled with a sensible cargo of nicely balanced calories, sailing with steely determination for the fabled port of Reduced Girth. I regarded my past with loathing and my future with Hermesetas-flavoured tedium.

There were two more places at the table. Uncle Khushru was at the Club, Govinda and Sujaya were out at work. Piet and Japp, for whom the places at table had been set, normally returned home from their guru too late to eat lunch at the same time that I did. This afternoon, however, just as I dug into the fruit on my plate, the doorbell rang. It was the two Dutch guests. They were in a boisterous mood. They entered the house in great sloshing strides. 'Hullo! Hullo!' they yodelled. 'We haff had a loffly schwim!'

'Such *awful* weather!' I said.

Outside, the rain continued pounding down, the distilled essence of the Arabian Sea emptying itself upon the city. Bansi closed the door behind Piet and Japp, looking down with his eyebrows arched high in disapproval at the muddy footprints left on the floor.

But Piet was responding to my remark. 'Oh, nonononono!!' he exclaimed. His clothes were plastered to him, his ravaged umbrella tucked under his arm. He was powerfully exhilarated. 'You forget – Holland is ffery wet! For us, thees weether is – HOME!!!'

Simultaneously, Japp was pawing the air with great energetic gestures, like a swimmer carving his way up through a waterfall. 'It woss like schwimming!' Rain-water sprayed in every direction from the force of his movements. He was like a St Bernard coming in from the original flood.

Bansi wriggled behind and around Japp, narrowly escaping being brained. He had a pained expression on his face. He disappeared towards the kitchen to organize their lunch.

'It woss like schwimming,' continued Japp, 'like schwimming through peeple!'

'It woss fonthasthique,' said Piet. 'The water, some places, it woss *dis* high.' He indicated about mid-thigh. 'And the road? It woss a reever!'

Japp said, 'We saw, at von place, a whirlpool!' He made an obscene slurping sound. 'And, and all kinds of *theengs* disappeering into eet!' Further slurping sounds, then a long slow burp. They both burst into gusty laughs. 'A child . . . two cows . . . von car!'

Piet said, 'We saw dogs, you know?' and he looked suddenly at me, to make sure I was following all this. He made gestures to suggest a dog swimming frantically, arms and legs churning. 'Schwimming and schwimming to get away from the whirlpool . . .'

Japp took it on. 'And then the bus would come, and this beeg – ' his arm described a tidal wave – 'you know, and all the poor peeple, you know, the peeple waiting for the bus, you know.' He ducked, his large features distorted wildly to show the compound fear of patient commuters faced with the prospect of sudden death by drowning.

'. . . and, and then, the bus would schtop, you know, and the peeple would fight to khet on to the bus . . .' said Piet.

'. . . and the umprellas koingk up and down . . .' said Japp, pumping at invisible umbrella shafts.

'. . . and the peeple fighting to khet off the bus . . .' said Piet, battling a vigorous horde of would-be passengers. In the twilit dining room of Palm View, his huge arms described great sweeping circles. Bansi, who had just reappeared with a steaming dish, ducked nimbly once more.

'Lunch ready,' he said, sternly.

They disappeared, then, pulling at their clothes and peeling them off as they went. I had always thought of Palm View as roomy, but they dwarfed it. The light fittings were in constant danger of being smashed by their smallest movements. The queenly furniture seemed cramped and fussy.

They returned, wiping themselves with what seemed in their hands to be furry handkerchiefs but were in fact bath towels. I had finished my papaya and was drinking a cup of unsweetened coffee. Bansi appeared once more, with the dish he'd had to reheat because of the delay. It was moussaka, the speciality of the house. It had been made in a large, deep, rectangular Pyrex bowl.

He offered it first to Japp, who turned to me and said, 'Are you eating dis?'

I would have thought it was obvious that I wasn't, since I was drinking coffee, but I shook my head anyway. Japp took up the serving spoon and, as Bansi watched with his eyes starting from his head, dug up exactly half the moussaka and deposited it *plotch!* on his plate. Then he turned the handle of the spoon to where Piet sat, on his left, expecting that Bansi too would simply swivel around to where Piet sat. But, for Bansi, the habit of serving from the diner's left was hard-wired. To serve Piet on the wrong side was causing severe distress. He did it, nevertheless. I glanced at his face and saw that he was suffering. When Piet had helped himself, Bansi stared at the now empty dish. I knew what he was thinking. His training demanded at least two expeditions to the dining table with the main dish for the meal. The fact that the dish was empty now meant that he could no longer perform in the customary manner. He stood there, immobilized, his permanent smile drooping. He caught my eye. I smiled in sympathy. Piet suddenly looked up. Intercepting the exchange he said, 'Some-fing is wrongk?'

I said, 'No, but . . .' Bansi left the room shaking his head slowly. Japp had raised his head too by now and both guests were looking at me, puzzled and a bit hurt. I had the absurd impression that I was speaking to two giant condors, perched on the edges of their chairs. They were holding toy cutlery in their huge hands and inclining their heads this way and that, enquiringly.

I said, 'He likes to be able to make two trips.'

Why? For what purpose? Hadn't they lessened his labours? Shouldn't he feel grateful? Wasn't it unfair? Should they apologize to him? How foolish to want to come on two visits when one was good enough! Should they do their own cooking? While we discussed the sensitivity of a well-trained butler, it came out that the reason I had not eaten the moussaka was that I was on a diet. 'Diet?!!' exclaimed Piet. 'An *Eendian* – on a diet???' He and Japp could not get over this, their faces cracking open with great astonished grins. After all, India was a country best known for its starving millions, wasn't it? So how could anyone want to be on a diet? Merely to be Indian was to be on a state-imposed diet!

We talked late into that afternoon, about dieting Indians, about the guru, about Hermann Hesse's *Siddhartha*, about Fellini's *Amarcord*. There seemed to be so much to talk about. Japp didn't stay for very long, but Piet and I remained at the dining table, talking, talking, talking. Like the rain cascading down outside, we talked compulsively, as if unable to contain within us conversations soaked up in the course of several years' worth of collecting.

HOUSEKEEPING

SUJAYA WAS UNHAPPY WITH me. Her unhappiness expressed itself in the sharp-angled movements she made when we were alone in a room together, as if she wished to avoid even looking at me directly. Something I had said or done must have upset her but I knew from experience that it was better not to ask her what it was.

The reason we were living together was that we had been friends in a nearby women's hostel. Sujaya had found these rooms at Palm View but could not afford the rent on her own. So she proposed that we room together. Sujaya was down-to-earth and fastidious. I was woolly, unreliable and extremely lazy. Given a choice, I would rather be buried alive under a pile of unwashed laundry than ever do it myself, particularly since the option of using a washing machine didn't exist in those days. I had promised her when we moved into Palm View that I would do my best to be considerate and that she was within her rights to chivvy me into doing whatever she thought was necessary for the two of us to live in harmony. If only we could have occupied the two rooms separately we might have got on better. The room in front was a glassed-in portion of what had once been a verandah. It had wonderful light, and was ideal for an artist. It did not have access to the bathroom, however. So even if Sujaya had the cavernous and gloomy bedroom all to herself, we could not have lived in a truly independent manner. At the time that we moved in, we both believed that our equal need for pleasant, reasonably priced accommodation would see us through our differences. But as young married couples soon discover, even the grandest passions wane in the presence of the daily drip-drip-drip irritations of toothpaste tubes squeezed the wrong way or shoes which are not neatly lined up. Sujaya and I, without even the excuse of passion to sustain our tolerance, were very quickly at the point when our tempers frayed in the mere anticipation of an argument involving whose turn it was to change the cushion covers and whether the dust-mice were breeding faster under my bed than under hers.

After dinner on the day that I had spent talking to Piet, I lay down on my bed, wanting to think. My mind was whirring with the ideas ploughed up by my long conversation. Sujaya had changed for the night and was sitting at the dressing table that we had agreed she could have, since it was clear that it was Sujaya, not I, who took pains over her appearance. I wasn't looking in her direction, but knew that if I did, I would see her seated in front of the tall thin mirror, as if posing for an advertisement for elegant nightwear, methodically completing her pre-slumber toilette. At her command was a battery of tall and short, fat and thin containers, a Manhattan skyline of cosmetics. The clacking sounds made by these myriad jars as she opened and closed them were something I associated with the close of a day.

We continued thus, she at her skin-cleansing ritual and me in my reverie until she said, with no preamble, 'I don't suppose you have the *least idea* how selfish it is?'

I surfaced unsteadily from my thoughts and rolled over on my side to face her. 'What?' I said.

'No! Of course not. You – you don't even know what I'm talking about, do you!' said Sujaya. She was scrubbing her skin with a small pad of cotton.

'No,' I said, 'I don't . . .' And would have liked to add that judging from the tone of her voice I probably wouldn't want to. But according to Sujaya, my reluctance to face unpleasantness was itself a problem. So I refrained from adding my spark to her fire.

She was silent as she passed the cotton over her face with those brusque, unhappy movements I had been noticing for a few days. I waited.

'It's your trip,' she said, finally. 'I heard you talking about it . . .' She discarded the wad of cotton, now mauve-tinted with end-of-day facial debris. From the plump glass bottle in which she stored individual puffs of cotton like tiny captive clouds, she snatched up a fresh pad and shook astringent into it with the vigorous movements of a terrier that has caught a rat. 'Of course you wouldn't dream of telling me your plans! Oh no. I have to hear about them like a – a – spy! Listening in while you talk about them to someone else on the telephone!' She slammed the bottle of astringent back on to her dressing table and turned her head towards me. 'Really – it's so . . . *humiliating*!'

'The trip?' I said. 'But it's nothing, it's just . . . barely, I mean – we're just talking about it . . .' I could not understand what there had been about the conversation she had overheard to anger her so.

There was another charged silence as she dabbed her face with cleansing strokes. 'And – and what about the room?' she began afresh. 'While you're away? I don't suppose you've thought about that, have you? Even for a moment?'

Prashant and I had been planning to go abroad to the US on a holiday. My sister Radha, or Radzie as we called her, lived in the US. She came to India on annual visits, staying for two hectic weeks in Calicut. I generally planned my own visits to Calicut to coincide with Radzie's so that we could all be together. The previous year had been a benchmark of sorts. My brother Raghu, his wife Gayatri and their two children had come with us as well. And so had Prashant. He was meeting my parents for the first time and, though no one had voiced the thought out loud, it was a significant event on the horizon of our relationship. It meant that he had gained access to the heartland of my family.

We had slept in separate rooms, behaving more like cousins than partners in a relationship. But it was during this holiday that the idea of visiting Radzie in the US had been initiated.

I had never been to the US. The thought of travelling there in the company of a man whom I could flaunt as a boyfriend, not a spouse, appealed to me. It would confirm my own view of myself as a counter-culture revolutionary, living outside the confines of social acceptance. It would help me ignore the fact that in my family's eyes Prashant had already achieved the status of in-law, a fact that troubled me but to which I had not yet found an acceptable solution.

Our plan was to go in October–November. In July Prashant applied for leave from his agency. In August he confirmed his dates and wrote to one of his cousins in the US for the affidavit of support he needed, to apply for a visa. And now it was mid-September. He had taken a loan from his office to buy his ticket and was getting ready to buy the 500 dollars of foreign exchange, which was what Indians travelling abroad in those days were legally permitted to buy. I, meanwhile, had yet to locate my passport.

Whenever Prashant brought up the subject of the trip, I said I was preoccupied with the illustrations of the book I was working on and until they were finished I couldn't make any plans. But the book was refusing to get finished. The conversation that Sujaya had overheard had been a call from Radzie in the US, asking me when she should send the affidavit of support for me. If Sujaya had been listening closely, she would have heard me say that I was too depressed about the illustrations to proceed with them and yet, without finishing them, I wouldn't have enough money to afford the trip.

Radzie was sending me a prepaid ticket, but I would still need money to pay my rent for the two or three months that I planned to be away. I needed enough to see that I wouldn't be completely broke when I got back. Most of the publishers I worked for were skunks who paid very little and never on time. It was part of everything that was wrong with my life, that my drawings were appreciated because I took a longer time over them than my fellow illustrators, yet no one was interested in paying me a price that acknowledged that extra effort.

Sujaya said something. But I missed it. 'What?' I asked. 'You know perfectly well I'm talking about the house!' she said.

I sat up now, scrambling to reconstruct the possible provenance of her remark. The house referred to had to be Palm View. 'What about it?' I asked, even as I guessed that she was referring to the threat of eviction. The monsoon was the season of house collapses. At the time that we moved into Palm View, Govinda had explained that the six-storey building was owned by a landlord who wanted to clear his tenants from the building in order to sell the land to developers. As a tactic to force the tenants out, he had ceased to maintain the building. It was a standard ploy on the part of landlords all over the city.

So far, no tenant had moved. Over the years of neglect, the building had become seriously weather-beaten. Now the municipal inspectors had come around, threatening to declare the building unsound and have it cleared. This did not suit the landlord, as he would not get the price he wanted for the land if this were to happen, so he had been paying bribes to keep the municipal inspectors at bay. Meanwhile with every monsoon, the building deteriorated further. No one could predict exactly when it would happen, but some day not too far in the future, the rains or the government or the landlord would see to it that Palm View would be no more. 'You mean, having to vacate?'

'What else!' said Sujaya. She had finished with the astringent and was undoing the knot in which she confined her long hair. It rippled out and she passed her fingers through it a couple of times before taking a brush to it. 'I've told you before: I'm *not* going to be responsible for all your STUFF if we have to move out while you're away!'

Now I understood why she was angry. 'You mean my desk,' I said. It was an enormous piece of furniture, made of teak and covered with dark green leather. It could be dismantled in three pieces not including the unbroken sheet of glass, half an inch thick and emerald green at the edges, which covered its full extent. Its working surface was the office equivalent of a football field. The two supporting members had drawers on one side and cabinets on the other.

I had bought the desk for 100 rupees from my brother and thought it was a wonderful bargain. But Sujaya considered it a personal insult that someone with whom she was sharing rooms should be so impractical as even to desire such an unwieldy piece of junk. She thought it was rude, inconsiderate and tasteless to admire furniture which was big enough to house a whole family of slum-dwellers.

'It's not just the *desk*!' snapped Sujaya. She put her brush down and turned towards me. 'It's *everything* . . .'

I was sitting at the edge of my bed, feeling like a child who is being scolded, not because it has done wrong but because its mother is in a bad mood.

'It's the desk, it's the diet, it's the passport, it's the book that's never going to be finished on time,' she said. 'It's your whole attitude of waiting to do things till *you* want to do them, not when it suits other people!'

'Sujaya – ' I said, feeling shocked at her harsh tone.

'I bet you've not done anything about your ticket or your visa, or your cholera shots or – whatever it is you need in order to go. And in the end you'll look helpless and get everyone else to run around for you!'

'What's that got to do with my stuff?' I said, wanting desperately for the unpleasantness to stop. Sujaya was always telling me that I must make myself face conflicts, not run away from them. This included confronting her if we had differences, rather than pretending to be meek by accepting whatever she said.

'Oh, for God's sake!' she said. 'It's not just your stuff, it's your childish, selfish, careless attitude to life! You say you don't like to get angry so you leave other people to get angry! Other people to pick up your clothes, other people to take care of your desk, other people to look after your ticket. It's in everything you do! And *Palm View* – I mean, do you think I'll find a new place for you, pay your rent for you, shift all your mountains of books and clothes for you and . . . and art materials and . . . you know! – while you're away? Well, I *won't*! I just won't do it!'

She went back to brushing her hair for a few strokes, then paused. 'And another thing,' she said as she turned to face me again, her eyes throwing fire. 'What about the rent? If you leave Palm View now, I won't be able to pay the full two thousand on my own, you know.'

She gathered her hair together and twisted it once more into a neat, gleaming knot. Then she picked up the pale blue jar of Elizabeth Arden night cream. In a calmer tone, she continued. 'I mean, just think if you were in my position,' she said. 'Just think how it would be if you *didn't* have Prashant to run around for you or if you *didn't* have your brother and sister to pamper you – what would you do?'

Inside my mind, a continuous stream of soothing counter arguments had been unspooling right alongside Sujaya's bruisingly honest speech. *But I DO have my family and I DO have Prashant*, I heard myself whine. *How can I behave as if they weren't there, when they are?* Each person adjusts herself to the reality of her own life. I could no more conduct my life as if I did not have a supportive family than Sujaya could conduct her life as if she did.

But I had to say something, so I offered, 'Supposing I postponed my trip to the States?'

Sujaya shot back with, 'And Prashant? What about Prashant?'

Prashant isn't your business, I wanted to say. *Leave him out of this!* To buy time, however, I said, 'What about him?'

'You're not travelling alone, you know!' said Sujaya. 'It's not just your trip. You have to think about Prashant's convenience too!'

'What's convenient for me will be convenient for Prashant,' I said coldly. There was an edge of politics in my remark. Sujaya had recently separated from her boyfriend of many years. He wanted to get married, but she had wanted him to live separate from his parents. He had refused. When she threatened to leave, he told her to go right ahead. The wound was still fresh and it was easy for me to sprinkle pepper in it.

Sujaya refused to let up. 'You can't treat him like a pet dog! Supposing it's not possible for him to go later on? Supposing he doesn't get leave when it suits madam to go on holiday?'

I said, 'Listen, Sujaya, what do you want from me? I'll postpone my trip – isn't that enough?'

Sujaya picked up on the first part of this speech. 'What I want from you,' she said, turning towards me, her face as white as a Kabuki dancer's with the cream, 'what I want from you is . . . *responsible behaviour*! It's not a question of *suggesting a solution just to keep Sujaya quiet*,' she flashed, revealing that she knew exactly what had motivated my response of a moment back. 'It's a question of figuring out what suits everyone's convenience and – *growing up*!'

I was silent. I knew that there was a full granary of truth in Sujaya's argument.

Yes, I was inconsiderate, incompetent and self-indulgent. I was fat, after all. I was a person whose intake of fuel exceeded her body's needs. Fat stored as unsightly wads of flesh was the physical expression of greed, black money in the body's fuel-efficient economy. Time is also a kind of fuel except that it can't be stored. Nevertheless, I could feel the rolls of unused hours lying in unsightly heaps across the sagging belly of my days. In the time that it took my fellow illustrators to complete a whole book I might get one small drawing done. I could not force myself to produce anything if I wasn't in the mood and getting into the mood might take hours or days of just lazing about, waiting for inspiration to dawn.

I lay back on the bed, feeling like a papaya-flavoured jellyfish in an ocean swarming with slender, efficient, vertebrate life forms. I needed a different ocean, or a different time zone. A different life.

A BROTHER SPEAKS

THE NEXT DAY I went over to my brother's house in the morning. I was very close to Gayatri and often spent time with her. I had packed a sandwich of D'Silva's toast and paneer with me so that I had something to eat when it was time for lunch. My brother, who usually came home from his office in the afternoon, was also at the table.

He was sixteen years older than me, nervy and domineering. He had left home for college by the time I was born, so I hardly saw him for most of my childhood. I was a little scared of him because he had a sharp tongue and did not shrink from using it. He was a successful corporate lawyer. His life revolved around following rules and ferreting out obscure definitions of the law. In his early years, setting up practice while my parents were still travelling abroad, he'd had to struggle to keep his head above the tideline. This had caused him to become obsessed with security and social approval. In his view, our parents had made a gross mistake in allowing me to grow up like a weed, unruly and unchecked. No doubt he believed it would have been better if I had not been permitted to sprout at all. I knew that he considered my life to be a monument to self-indulgence. But since I was not dependent on him, nor lived in his house, there was nothing he could actually do to prevent me from being what I was.

I saw his eyes flicker in the direction of my plate when I got out my sandwiches. He said nothing, however, until he was almost through with his meal. While the cook was out of the room, fetching one last paratha for him, he said, 'What's the matter? Our food's not good enough for you?'

'She's on a diet,' said my sister-in-law.

'A diet!' said Raghu. 'Only fools need to diet! Stop making a fuss and eat like the rest of us!' He pushed the bowl of chicken curry towards me.

I said, 'No thanks.'

Gayatri said, 'Don't force her! She's free to diet if she wants – '

My brother said, 'Then why come to our house to eat?'

I said, 'I'll sit somewhere else, if it bothers you – ' and started to get up.

'No!' said Raghu. 'The food's already on the table! If you don't take it, it'll go to waste.'

'I told the cook that I wasn't eating,' I said, 'so if there are leftovers it's not because of me.' Raghu didn't touch leftovers, believing that food became unclean the moment it was cleared from the table.

'Enough, enough,' said Gai, not wanting the disagreement to escalate.

'Unlike you, the cook has eyes in his head and brains between his ears,' said my brother, addressing me. 'When he sees three plates on the table, he cooks enough for six. If you don't eat it, he will – and why should I subsidize the cook's lunch just because my sister's a fool?'

'Stop it!' said Gai. 'The cook gets his own food, he doesn't need our leftovers – '

'Okay – but then who eats what we leave?' my brother wanted to know.

'I do,' said Gai, looking defiant. It wasn't a lie. Whatever didn't get eaten in one form generally came back to the table recycled in some other form, so that Raghu wouldn't recognize it. But she added, just for credibility, 'And the dog too,' she said, referring to their dachshund, aptly named Rasputin.

Raghu turned to me and said, 'D'you see what you're doing? Forcing my wife to eat dog-food!'

'It's not me doing that,' I said, '*you're* the one who has the hang-up about food – ' But I stopped, realizing that the hissing sound in the room was the steam coming out of my brother's ears.

Just then, the cook reappeared with a fresh paratha. He offered it to Raghu. My brother pointed in my direction and said, in Malayalam, 'To her.'

I looked the cook in the eye and shook my head. The cook, whose name was Pillai, was a small-built man with Groucho Marx eyebrows. He was extremely highly strung and was known to collapse in hysterics if the milk boiled over or a dinner guest came late.

My brother said, in an awful voice, this time in English, 'GIVE IT TO HER!'

I said, to no one in particular, 'I won't eat it.'

Raghu snatched the paratha from the plate and sent it flying like a frisbee across the table to where I sat. But I ducked, and the dog, who had been paying close attention to these events, leapt up and caught the unexpected snack in mid-air. The cook gave a howl, dropped the plate and fled from the room in tears. The plate broke. My sister-in-law began to laugh.

Raghu was breathing hard. He shoved his chair back so that it shrieked, and stood up. He was a short man, but he grew a foot for every moment that he stayed angry. He was shooting up now, at the rate of knots. 'I haven't interfered much in your life so far,' he said. 'And I don't intend to waste my time interfering in it now. But the bare fact of the matter is, you have a bad influence on this house.' I opened my mouth to defend myself but he said, 'Shut up!' So I shut up.

'I'm not talking about this afternoon any more – or your stupid diet or your stupid opinions. I'm talking about what you're doing with your *whole life*! It seems to me that I am the only one who notices that everyone else we know – all our cousins, the rest of our family, all the people of our class and background – are in some respectable job or married, with children. But you? What are you doing? Scratching a living from your miserable drawings, living in some third-rate brothel with a landlord who looks like an albino mongoose and screwing around with some boy whom you tell the whole world you're not going to marry!'

There. It was out in the open. Gai rolled her eyes up and arched her eyebrows.

'I haven't said anything so far. It's your life. No one can help you if you want to make a bloody mess of it. You want to waste all the opportunities you've been given, your education, your childhood abroad, all the things that other people don't have and won't have even in ten lifetimes? Fine. That's your choice and welcome to it.

'But I see you coming into this house every day, twice a day sometimes. You sit at my table, you eat my food, you enjoy my house and all the comforts that I have worked hard to afford. And what do I get for all that? I'll tell you: nothing. Worse than nothing. After all, you might be contaminating my house with your whatever – friends, wrong ideas, germs . . . after all, I have young children – your nephew and niece – and what impression will they get of life when they can see you, their aunt – their father's sister! – roaming the streets like a bitch on heat?' I could feel the skin on my face blistering and peeling away with embarrassment. But since I couldn't think of what else to do, I continued eating my paneer sandwich.

'And now I hear that you're planning a trip to the US with this boyfriend of yours – what's his name? – this Maharashtrian fellow you're running around with. And my stupid sister in the States is going to pay for you and no one's going to say a word – but what is the meaning of all this expenditure? What are your intentions towards this boy? I mean, are you going to marry him or not? And if not – then why this public spectacle – ?' He broke off, shook his head as if to clear it. The cook, who had sidled back into the room to sweep away the fragments of the broken plate, leapt aside to avoid being stepped upon.

'Anyway, frankly, I don't care,' continued Raghu. 'You might be my sister but I can't control what you do with your life. All I'm saying is, in this house, under *my* roof . . .' He paused as if considering whether to go ahead with what he intended to say. He decided he would. 'I don't want it. You can ask my wife or our parents or your sister in the States. I've talked to them all before this, about you. I have asked them to warn you about the consequences of what you're doing with your life. Apparently they have all chosen to be silent. Too afraid to voice their thoughts, too afraid to *harm your feelings*! Huh! But what about my feelings? Or our mother's feelings? Or my children's feelings? No one talks about that! And it seems that you don't care. So – I don't care either,' he summed up, not looking at me, turning around instead to the bar just beside the dining table.

A small glass bottle of digestive saunf was within easy reach. He picked it up and unscrewed its top. 'One day, you'll thank me for what I'm saying now,' he said, shaking a small quantity of the aromatic seeds out on to the open palm of the other hand. He closed the bottle and transferred the saunf to his mouth. 'I know how much this house means to you. I know how close you are to my wife – after all, she came into the family when you were just a child. But from now on, if you want to meet her in this house, in my house . . . you'll have to change your ideas about life. Marry that boy or let him go. Bring your life under some control or . . . live it somewhere else.'

With this, he switched himself off and swung away towards the bedroom, his and Gai's. He normally had a half-hour nap before going back to work.

My sister-in-law and I waited till Raghu was out of earshot before speaking.

'Foof,' I said, holding my head. I had finished my sandwich by then.

'You know what he's like,' she said. 'A lot of sound and fury . . .'

'Signifying quite a few things, though,' I said. A silence passed between us.

'Don't worry,' said Gai. 'He can't stop you from coming here . . .' She smiled and added, 'It's my house too!'

'But I'll stay away a few days anyway,' I said.

'Just a few,' said Gai.

SUNSTROKE

THE MONSOON HELD ITS breath over the weekend and the sun came out. Piet and Japp went on a trek with Govinda in the low hills around Kurla Caves. Govinda wore a hat, a loose, long-sleeved shirt and covered the back of his neck with a handkerchief. The two guests wore string vests and shorts and returned looking as if they had been grilled in a tandoor. That evening, a Sunday, the three of them sat around the dining table regaling Sujaya and me with the tale of their adventures. Frequent halts had been made because of a runny stomach, leaves had been used as toilet paper, dancing peacocks had been sighted, scorpions had been successfully warded off.

The two Dutch were sitting at the table wearing brilliantly coloured lungis they'd bought on the train from Delhi to Bombay, to use as bedsheets on the way. They had tied the lungis loosely at the hip. Vast tracts of skin scorched carmine by the sun were thus exposed, criss-crossed with fine white lines where the string of their vests had protected them. I found myself noticing the smooth hairlessness of the skin, the muscles on the upper arm, the regular fluting of ribs.

Japp's torso was constructed out of straight lines which bent unwilling into the contours of a body. Piet, on the other hand, was handsomely proportioned. His chest was deep where the ribcage curved up to meet its breastbone, falling away gracefully to the waist. The navel lay on the stomach wall like a shallow thumb-print in smooth clay.

The next day, Piet came home from the morning session at the 'guru's' saying he felt strange. He attributed it to the metaphysical energy pouring into him. 'There is a wind blowing through my brain,' he said. But by the end of the day the wind had turned into a typhoon, threatening to blow his mind clean out of his skull. His eyes were dim and his skin was grey underneath the layer that was already peeling off. He didn't have an appetite. His hands were clammy to the touch.

The doctor was called. He declared that Piet had severe sunstroke. Govinda was unsurprised and unsympathetic. His guests hadn't taken the least precaution against the assault of the heat, he said. 'No, no! It has to happen! How else do they learn?' Japp grinned and looked sheepish as everyone congratulated him for having escaped unscathed.

Piet was advised complete bed rest, as much fluid as he could hold down and spoonfuls of glucose.

For two days he did not appear at the table for his meals. Japp went to the guru alone, had lunch and then vanished again, exploring the city, he said. In the afternoons, there was no one else in the house besides Bansi and me. On the third day, Piet came out to breakfast looking pale and bewildered. He had a cup of weak tea before returning to his room.

That afternoon, I paid him a visit.

Behind the dining room, a narrow, dark corridor spanned the breadth of the house, trailing off towards the kitchen on one side and admitting two doors on the other. I had never explored this part of the house before and wasn't sure which room Piet was in. I guessed that the farther door led to Uncle Khushru's room which meant that the nearer one, whose entrance was obscured by a limp curtain stirring in a faint current of air, must be Govinda's. I had been told that Govinda was sleeping in his uncle's room on a mattress, while Piet and Japp slept in his room.

I paused before tapping on the shutters of the open door. I didn't have anything in particular to speak to Piet about. It annoyed me to realize that already, for no reason that I could name, I was behaving coy and uncertain. It was as if there was, in the innocent act of paying a fellow guest a visit, a hidden agenda. I brushed these ideas aside and tapped on the door.

There was no response. I tapped again and said, 'Piet?'

I heard the sound of bed sheets being stirred and a voice like a candle that has gone out, leaving a flickering after-image of itself, say, 'Yes?'

I asked if I could come in. He said, 'Of course,' in his phantom voice.

The room was unlit, a spartan space, maybe 15 feet square. The height of its ceiling gave the impression that it was sunk deep into the earth, like a chamber at the bottom of a well. There were two camp-cots on either side of the room. In the overhead dusk, a ceiling fan rotated sluggishly. Piet lay on the cot to the left of the door, looking like a felled tree wrapped in a loose white shroud of bed sheets.

I knelt by the side of the bed and asked him, in whispers, whether he wanted to be visited or to be left alone. He said he felt he was speaking through a telephone from an astral plane, but aside from that he was feeling all right. He said he would tell me when he was tired.

He wanted to talk about the guru. 'He's really good,' he said, in his ethereal voice. 'He knows a lot. He sits there, with his bidi and he's not doing anything until suddenly he looks at you and *paf!* he gets through.'

'I don't know what you mean,' I whispered back.

'It's hard to explain,' said Piet. 'But it's something like . . . we go to him because we want him to get through. But when we're with him we can feel that our minds have become like lead, maybe. Completely solid. Nothing gets through. And then suddenly – '

'*Paf!* Yes – okay,' I said. 'But I don't understand what you mean when you say you want him to get through – get *what* through? And why him? What does he have that everyone doesn't have?'

'It's hard to explain,' repeated Piet. I had to strain to hear him, his voice was so soft. I had noticed for some days that I could no longer hear his accent except in occasional words. 'But it's like . . . there's a lot of rubbish stuff inside our brains. I don't know how it gets there. It's maybe, like, mental shit, huh? Sort of sticky and slippery and full of kind of lumps. So we can't get it out ourselves. And it gets in the way of real thoughts. So we need help. And people like the guru can do it – they can just punch holes in the minds of other people and the rubbish – some of it – just pours out. And the mind feels clean and relaxed. And we can think clearly, suddenly, for the first time, maybe.'

He told me that he was studying psychology – he pronounced the 'p' when he said the word. He said he was hoping to develop his extra-sensory powers so that he could cure his patients using traditional methods while also applying the *pafl* approach. 'But it's a lot of hard work,' he said. 'A lot of things come up that no one wants to see.'

'Could I come to the guru some day?' I asked.

'It depends on you,' whispered Piet. 'Is there something special you want to know?'

'No,' I said. 'Can anyone come?'

'Of course,' whispered Piet. 'But it's better if you have a question – you know, like it's easier if you go to a doctor and say, *I have a pain in my head – I need a lobotomy please!* Instead of, *Sir, you see, I just wanted to look at your instruments, you know, and your degrees and maybe if you could tell me why my life is a mess that would also be good!*'

I laughed, saying, 'I could ask him about God. The existence of, I mean. Is it something he deals with? Does he say there's someone out there or . . . not?'

Piet paused before he answered. He turned his body around carefully as if conscious that he was filled with crystal objects that would shatter if he moved too fast. He bent his outstretched right arm until he could prop his head up on the fist of his hand. 'I don't know,' he said reflectively. 'You could ask, but I don't know what he would say. When he doesn't find a question interesting he just sort of laughs and lets his deputies answer.' The guru spoke exclusively in Marathi, so he had a couple of interpreters who sat beside him, translating into English and Hindi.

'And you?' I asked. 'Do you believe in God?'

He allowed a smile to visit his features for an instant before shrugging. 'It's hard, huh? To talk about things like this.' He shook his head slowly and said, 'I don't know. Do you?'

I said, 'I used to.' I was being serious, but he laughed, a brief bark of sound which took more effort than he could afford just then, so his head sank down for a few moments before he explained what he found funny.

'It's the way you said it,' he said. 'You know, like . . . *I used to collect stamps, but then I stopped –* '

'It *was* like that!' I explained. 'I really used to believe, you know? Till I was sixteen and a half. From the time I was eleven, twelve – I *prayed*, really, every day – at night, just before sleeping.' It was strange to recall this fact. It wasn't something I had thought of for a very long time.

'What kind of prayers?' he wanted to know.

I explained that I had spent eight years in Catholic schools. The Lord's Prayer was the one I knew best, so I said it, followed by a list of petitions. I permitted myself five petitions on any one night. If one of these was of special significance, I gave myself leave to repeat it five times. Sometimes I would repeat the entire cycle five times just to make sure that my communications were getting through to the celestial office.

Piet found it very funny. 'Like the Post Office here!' he said. 'Like filling a form in triplicate!'

'I'm a bureaucrat's daughter,' I said. 'For me, God was a combination of the Central Government, the Post Office and the Supreme Court.' It opened up a line of enquiry. Perhaps each person conceived of the divine in the image of the line of work they were most familiar with? Doctors might think of God as the Divine Healer; bus drivers might think of Him as the Divine Conductor; prostitutes might think of Him as the Divine Customer. 'Praying is like posting a letter – an act of faith. You write your message on to a piece of paper, then fold it within another sheet of paper. On that you write a formula of words and then you throw the whole package into a box. You don't see how it reaches the person you send it to and you don't see that person send something back, but when you get a reply it's like your prayer has been answered.'

'Why did you stop believing?' he asked.

'Because there was one special letter He didn't deliver.' It was a real letter, something I had been waiting for, for weeks. I was at that age when every moment has the weight of a sovereign more precious than gold. As the weeks stretched into months, my belief in post offices, both of this world and the next, thinned out and vanished.

Though I wasn't brought up as a Christian, my Catholic schools had ensured that the God I believed in was Christian. This meant that I believed in the Christian Devil as well. I didn't consciously realize it until I stopped believing in God.

His infernal counterpart, like a bad tenant, refused to vacate my consciousness. At nights, and especially during power failures or thunderstorms, I could sense the subliminal snickering of his minions. It seemed wholly hypocritical to pray at times like this, though I did, feeling guilty and craven. It was terrible to feel that my immortal soul was at risk even though I had ceased to believe I had one.

Werewolves, vampires and others of their persuasion were all potential hazards. How did a non-Christian defend herself against Christian fiends? Would I or would I not be privileged to use a crucifix in my defence? And who would decide? I tried to reassure myself with the thought that none of these monsters could possibly be so pedantic as to demand proof of a victim's faith. But troubling questions remained. Surely such creatures were themselves in opposition to God and to faith! In which case, were they believing Christians or not? And what about pagan vampires – were there such things? And what protection was effective against them?

Piet was amused by these urgent questions. He said he didn't have any clearly formed beliefs about God. He couldn't remember when he'd stopped believing in a divine consciousness. The unquestioning beliefs of childhood seemed to have gradually grown thinner, less substantial and less consequential until suddenly one day they were simply no longer there for him.

He thought that my loss of faith was rather abrupt. 'It seems a bit hasty,' he said, 'though sometimes it can be like that, I know. You believe in something or someone and then – one day, one small thing happens and – *paf!* It's over.'

ENERGY

PRASHANT WAS AS CLOSE to being a perfect boyfriend as anyone could hope to find. He was exceptionally good-natured. He enjoyed work and he enjoyed play. He was attractive in a rugged masculine way, and yet there was also a roundedness to him, a softness of skin, a daintiness of hand and foot, which was endearing.

He was an inch or two taller than me, which is not saying very much. He had tightly curled hair, cropped close to his head. He had a moustache of the kind which clings to and curls over the top edge of the mouth. And though he was otherwise clean-shaven, I was always very conscious of his beard-line. It started from his cheekbones and continued right down till the base of his neck.

It grew very industriously, that beard. He shaved his chin satin-smooth every morning. By evening, the same chin was stubbled through with little bristles. The ceaseless vitality of Prashant's facial hair delighted me. I considered it on a par with the seasonal migration of geese and other natural phenomena. Governments might rise and fall, but twelve-year cicadas would continue to emerge on schedule from their underground incubators, bears to hibernate, Arctic hare to change the colour of their pelts in spring and . . . the stubble to poke out of Prashant's skin by evening.

We were happy together, in the way of children with their favourite cuddly toys. When I was over at his place, we shared a single bed. If we were not actually working, we were always together, on our own, or at my brother's flat, or with friends.

We saw a lot of films together, we read the same books. We played endless games of Scrabble and Mastermind. We talked about our thoughts and ideas for the immediate future.

But I did not call this love.

I believed that love was a condition too fine and rare to be within my reach. I had come to this conclusion because of my appearance. All the stories I had read as a child stressed the importance of beauty in a heroine's life. A girl might make her entrance in a story looking deformed or wretched but by the end of it, if she was a heroine, she would miraculously become beautiful. And the whole point of her beauty would be to attract a mate of the dragon-slaying, glass-mountain-scaling class, who would provide her with a secure palace in which to raise a brood of children.

Yet when I, as the main character in my own life's story, stared into mirrors, I did not see a heroine's face. Quite obviously, then, I would not enjoy a heroine's fate. As a child, I was pudgy and cross-eyed. At thirteen I wore braces and at fourteen was condemned to eternal short-sightedness. I felt certain that the only role left to me in stories was as the goose girl who volunteers to be the dragon's first victim because she's too plain to be anything else.

At fifteen and sixteen, I grew frontally while my friends grew vertically. I had pimples to contend with and frizzy hair to be quelled with curlers soaked in beer. My only feature that could be counted as an asset was that I didn't need to wax my arms and legs, because they were naturally hairless. It seemed an unlikely foundation for romance, however. I could not think of a single fairy tale, myth or fable in which the supreme hairlessness of the heroine's limbs was named as one of her sterling qualities.

Then came sixteen and a half and there was a radical change in my perspective. My features continued to be unremarkable, my body was shaped like an inverted pear and I was neither charmingly short nor gloriously tall. Nevertheless, I fell in love. It happened with all the inconvenient suddenness with which a goose girl, while waiting to experience the melancholy satisfactions of becoming dragon-fodder, discovers that there are categories of men other than 'prince'. In this case, it was one of the visiting Catholic priests, an Italian, at my school. His very unsuitability and the abstract, spiritual nature of the contact was wildly appealing to my schoolgirl sensibilities.

The period of bedazzlement lasted a mere three months. When I finally recognized that it had just been an adolescent fixation, my pride could not bear the strain. I imploded with chagrin, wanting to flush every last particle of emotion out of my system till nothing remained, no trace of the debilitating weakness known as romance. But of course it was futile. It was like calling out 'Silence!' in an echo-chamber. The louder I shouted, the less silence I heard.

Teenagers tend to find radical solutions to situations of this kind. My solution was to get off the bus. Not immediately, because that would have been ridiculous and dramatic. I wanted a quiet, dignified and well-planned death, one which would cause my family as little trouble as is possible under the circumstances. In particular, I did not want to leave behind a gory corpse or a juicy story for the newspapers to linger over.

I had two schemes to consider. One was to buy a ticket on a luxury liner and then, on a moonless night, vanish into the shark-infested infinity of the ocean. I didn't believe in suffering, so the plan included a handgun and an inflatable jacket with a small leak in it. Once I had shot myself, the jacket would gradually deflate, my remains would sink, sharks would be attracted to the blood and *voilà!* curtains. The other scheme was even simpler. It was to visit a game sanctuary and shoot myself in the vicinity of a tigress with cubs. Either way, I would be fully recycled, with no tiresome remains. I would leave letters explaining my absence, so that my friends and family would be spared the bother of a protracted search.

At sixteen, I didn't have the means to explore either of these avenues of demise. So I told myself that I must postpone my plans till I could afford a tasteful annihilation. Fourteen years seemed a reasonable time. I would, at thirty, have aged only just enough to know that I was glad not to be aging any further. My family would not feel that I had died tragically young.

Planning to die at thirty meant that I did not need to make arrangements for security in the long term. I would pay no taxes, make no investments, buy no life insurance, own no property. It was a fine thing to be so definite about the very matter that for other people was so obscure. In the same way that terminally ill people focus on getting the most out of what remains of their lives, even including pain and suffering, I too could train myself to concentrate on enjoying the time left to me.

Being beautiful was no longer an issue, because there was no 'ever after' to worry about. What I did need was to make a lot of money. I certainly did not want to end my days by leaping off the deck of some nameless dhow lurking in the shallows off Dubai. I wanted to go out in style, over the side of the *QE2*, filled with caviar to give my sharks a treat. I wanted to leave lavish bequests to charities and handsome inheritances to my siblings' children. Since my family was not rich I had no capital on which to build. All I had, from early childhood, was a small gift for drawing. By the standards of the classical European painters who were the stars in my private cosmos, I knew that I barely qualified as a meteorite. But that was all I had.

I worked hard at enlarging my talent and at creating a persona for myself as an artist. I believed it was necessary to dress for the part so I studied the appearance of talented and successful people. Many were remarkably homely but they made up for this by dressing in an eye-catching manner. I tried to do the same. I wore the kind of bright, clingy T-shirts that caused men in the street to breathe in sharply, waggling their tongues. My daily-wear ornaments were four gold bangles, a half-sovereign made into a finger-ring, two gold necklaces, diamonds in my ears, one diamond in my nose, silver anklets at my feet and silver rings on my toes. When I wore a sari I added a heavy silver belt that jingled as I walked.

I used gold shadow on my eyelids, coated my lashes thick with mascara and stuck sequins at the corners of my eyes. At an age when everyone aside from certified losers wore contact lenses, my cruel, unfeeling parents refused to buy a pair for me. So I rarely wore my glasses, preferring to wander the city streets in a myopic haze, giving alms to fire hydrants and hailing lampposts as long-lost friends.

At eighteen feminism caught up with me. It forced me to realize that there were problems far worse than being frizzy-haired, bespectacled and fat. It enlarged my horizon of conflict. It gave me a sense of community and purpose. It gave me a point of view and a vocabulary of complaint. It empowered me to buy my own contact lenses. In the name of feminist solidarity I toned down my clothes and stopped wearing makeup. But for all that it did for me, feminism could not give me a reason to live beyond thirty.

At the time I met Prashant, I was almost twenty-two. Eight years remained before I bought a one-way ticket on the *QE2*. Very little had changed. I hadn't managed to be successful in my work and was often discouraged by my prospects. There were times when I wondered why I was bothering to wait till I was thirty. I explained to Prashant that there was a limit on the term of a relationship with me. Marriage and children were out of the question. I said that I was serious about my plans to recycle myself and requested him not to try to dissuade me.

It was part of what I liked about Prashant that his first response was, 'Okay – but we have till thirty, right?' His state of mind was like a cool, wrinkle-free, drip-dry shirt. I got the feeling that nothing I did or said would ruffle him.

In the two and a half years that we had been together, we'd had very few disagreements.

Now, suddenly, we began to argue about the diet.

According to Prashant, since the time of my first visit to the clinic, I had changed. He couldn't explain exactly what it was. He described it as a kind of hardening, a turning away from the interests that we shared together. When I told him about the confrontation with my brother, his response was, 'What did I tell you? That wouldn't have happened if you hadn't been on the diet.'

'I can't stop now,' I said. 'I've lost half a kilo!'

I had just returned from my fourth visit to the clinic. I told Prashant that the doctor had wanted to take the first of my progress slides. He asked me to remove my clothes.

But I had made up my mind in advance to refuse. After the session during which I had seen the nude slides of his other patients, it had occurred to me to think that I did not want to be just one more exhibit in the doctor's freak show. I felt it was disloyal to my body to expose it in that fashion, with my face obscured, to the gaze of who-knew-what audience. The slides might be stolen from the doctor's clinic, for instance, and be sold to men whose taste for perfect bodies had grown jaded. Or the doctor himself might be making a roaring business in the 'alternative' nude-photo market. Whatever it was, I didn't feel the need to relinquish control over the sight of my body, flabby and unglamorous though it was.

I didn't explain my reasons to the doctor, saying only that I wouldn't go further than my underwear. He said, 'My dear, you don't understand! These pictures will be an invaluable aid to your will power!' I wrinkled my nose and shook my head. He said, 'Okay, never mind. There's another approach.'

He took pictures of me in my undies, then put the camera away. He told me to remove my bra. Then he directed me to stand in front of the full-length mirror in the room, to review myself. This was called the Mirror Test, he said, in lieu of the slides. He recommended that I try it myself at least once every day.

I stood in front of the mirror. He stood behind me. 'Look closely and critically at yourself,' he said. 'See that sagging belly there, this unnecessary flesh here,' he said, pinching the relevant portions. 'And here –' reaching around me – 'the looseness!' He picked up one of my breasts, then let it flop back down. There was nothing lewd about his actions. I could have been an interested student audience to whom my own reflected image was being revealed. I looked to my own eyes like one of the slide-victims, shapeless and ungainly. If, at that moment, he had suggested carving it all off with a potato peeler, I would have agreed.

Prashant was outraged to hear of this incident. 'Bastard!' he said. 'Feeling up his patients!' He said he would gladly go across and bash the doctor up on my account. Of course, I must never go back to him.

'Don't be silly,' I said.

It was late at night. Prashant and I were lying cuddled under a cotton sheet, while the heavy rain rattled on the pane of the open window just behind our heads. Cool wet air was being chased around the room by the ceiling fan. I was sleepy and unwilling to argue. We were spending an evening together for the first time since I had started the diet. We had gone to see a film and had dinner together, even though the only thing I could find on the menu to eat was thin soup. We returned to Prashant's place in time to avoid being drenched in the rain. The evening had been pleasant but I found myself thinking that in all that time, lasting some five or six hours, we had talked of entirely superficial matters.

Prashant said, 'Who's being silly? You're the one who says that you stopped using buses because of all the jerks who made passes at you. What's the difference now? Just because he's a doctor he can get away with it?'

I said, 'Of course not. It's . . . uhhh . . . something to do with *energy*.'

'Energy!' exclaimed Prashant. 'What energy?'

It was very difficult to explain. I told Prashant about the conversation I had with Piet while he was recovering from his sunstroke. Piet had talked about the vital energy that each person has at his or her disposal. According to him, it could be likened to an electrical current. There were people who could transmit it, he said, adding that he was one of them and was learning to develop his skill. More typically, however, were people who drew energy off from others, because of their own unstable or depleted resources. The effect was the same as draining a battery.

I tried explaining this to Prashant. 'The guys on a bus *get* something – something like energy – from touching a woman. Maybe there's a resistance that increases the charge, I don't know. When it happens to me, I can feel it like a surge of power – *pow!* Gone from me, snatched away without my consent and I *hate* it. I want to slaughter the guy who does it and all the guys who even think about doing it. But the doctor's touch was completely different. He took nothing. He was neutral, like a piece of wood. There was no loss of energy – '

Prashant said, 'I don't want to hear this crap – '

The warm light of the reading lamp beside Prashant's bed belied the tension in the room. I was anxious to undo it. I said, 'Listen. Why don't you come to Palm View some day? Then you can ask Piet all about energy yourself – '

'I don't want to know,' said Prashant, 'and I don't think you want to know either. He's just filling you up with bullshit ideas like this one and before you know it, half the city's doctors have got their hands up your bra – and you're even paying to let them do it!'

I reminded him coldly that he had no right to tell me what I did or did not want to know. I said that he was being childish and stubborn about something I found interesting. I assured him that if he came to the house and met Piet, he might change his low opinion of him. The two of them might even share an interest, I said. 'He rides motorbikes too.'

Prashant made a rude sound and said, 'Oh, of course! I'll bring my bicycle chain along and swing it around his *energy*!'

I said I was sleepy and didn't want to discuss the matter any further.

TRANSFER

TWO EVENINGS LATER, HOWEVER, Prashant did come over to Palm View for dinner. According to him, Piet and Japp had appeared so frequently in my conversation that he felt he had to check them out.

He came at eight o'clock. The Dutch guests, Govinda, Sujaya and myself were already sitting together in the drawing room, talking companionably. Within five minutes of Prashant's arrival, the evening began to deteriorate. He accepted his drink from Govinda, he lit his pipe and then, sitting down beside Piet like a general about to fire his first salvo at the enemy, he said, 'So? I hear you're on a religious quest?'

Piet's face emptied itself of expression like water vanishing from a mirage. 'Yais!' he said, his accent suddenly manifesting itself at full strength.

Japp, sitting in the armchair opposite Piet's, on the other side of the room, reacted immediately to the charged atmosphere in the room, by jumping to his feet and going outside to the verandah.

And then there was a long silence.

We five of us sat, like puppets in the hands of a malicious puppeteer, unable to move or to speak, knowing that whatever we did, our joints would squeak, the words in our mouths would taste like sawdust. The fact that we all knew this, and knew that all the others knew it too, made it impossible to break the spell of the situation.

Sujaya was smiling broadly in embarrassment. Govinda was coiled like a spring come loose from the seat of the cavernous armchair in which he sat, his grey eyes sparkling from the unaccustomed currents vibrating in the normally quiet air of his home.

A year or two may have passed before he ventured the remark, 'They're here to be with their guru, you see.'

I said, desperately, 'He was a bidi-seller before he became a guru!' And I glanced at Piet hoping that he would see that I had thrown him a conversational gambit. But he was busy impersonating a smooth rock cliff.

'He's eighty years old,' I said, 'and he still smokes bidis . . .' I looked over at Piet again. He merely smiled and nodded.

'Isn't it extraordinary!' Sujaya now exclaimed. 'A bidi-seller becoming a guru!' She seemed almost to yodel.

'And what does he look like?' said Prashant. He had an expression on his face of indulgent contempt. He was in that mood that children sometimes get into when they want to smash whatever it is that their parents find precious. 'Sitting on nails and all that stuff?' I had never seen this side of Prashant before.

'Of course not!' I said hotly. 'He looks like anyone else!'

'You've not seen him, have you, Manj?' Prashant said to me. 'So how would you know?' Turning back to Piet, he said, 'I meant, what does a bugger like that look like? Does he wear robes? Long hair? That sort of thing?'

Piet pushed his mouth out in a European pout and said, 'Chust . . . a ffery h'old man.'

Govinda turned to Prashant and said, 'You don't understand. These gurus are quite different to the kind that you and I know about!'

Prashant ignored this remark to ask Piet, 'How long are you here for?'

Piet said, 'Tu and a haff mons more.'

'And that's all you'll do while you're here? Go to the guru?' asked Prashant.

'Yais,' said Piet.

'And what do you do when you're in Holland?' asked Prashant, his tone implying that someone who could spend three months running after eighty-year-old lunatics couldn't possibly have much of a life elsewhere.

'I'm studying psikhologhi,' said.

'What?' said Prashant. 'I couldn't get you.'

'Psikhologhi,' repeated Piet.

'Psychology,' I said through clenched teeth.

'So you're a student, huh?' said Prashant, tamping down the tobacco in his pipe. 'How come you're interested in religion?'

'I am *not* eentrested in relighion,' said Piet simply. 'We came to meet the ghuru. Dat ees owl – '

Govinda said, 'They have a friend who recommended him.'

'Just like that, huh?' said Prashant. 'Hear about a guy, jump on a jet and fly down, huh?'

There could be no answer to such a question, so another dreadful silence thundered down upon the room.

Uncle Khushru entered from where he had been sitting, on the verandah, doing the *Times of India* crossword puzzle over his evening drink. Having finished the crossword, he was now on track for his dinner. He transited the drawing room without acknowledging any of us, making for his personal barracks at the back of the house. He was small and spare, with a big beak of nose, beetling eyebrows, bushy white hair and a starched white moustache. He held his left elbow stiff against the side of his body, a phantom swagger-stick permanently in place there. In half an hour he would sit down to dinner, eat it and retire.

Uncle Khushru's passage through the room loosened Piet's reticence. 'Een de West,' he said suddenly, 'we don't haff ghurus. So for us, eet's reely *worth* eet to come heer. Eet means reely a lot to us – we reely look forwort to eet.'

Prashant said, 'Now that you've seen him, how do you find him?'

The alchemy of language cannot easily be explained. One instant Piet spoke like an African grey parrot with swollen adenoids, and the next he was human again.

'Oh, he's wonderful,' said Piet, 'exactly as I thought he would be. It's . . . it's hard to give you an example . . .' He looked perplexed for a bit. 'It's like, the chakras – you know the chakras?' Prashant shook his head. 'You know, the kundalini? The kundalini force?' said Piet. Prashant nodded. 'Yes, well, it's like the kundalini, you know, they say like it's coiled down here,' and he patted the base of his spine. 'The thing is to get it to rise up . . .' Here he brought his hand around to the front, raising it theatrically upwards and over his head. Then he looked across at Prashant, searching for signs of comprehension.

It was Prashant's turn to look inscrutable. From his expression Piet might have been talking about pixies.

Piet continued. 'There are nine sort of, you know, like, stations, that the kundalini has to pass through to reach the top. They are called chakras.' He said chakras like a kindergarten teacher explaining the spelling of 'lighthouse' to an incredulous child. 'Well. Most people, you know, their kundalinis are blocked at one chakra or another. Mine, for instance, was blocked here' – he patted his chest – 'I've always had troubles with my chest, you know,' he said, solemnly. 'But one session with the guru here in Bombay and *phwitt*!' He grinned. 'It was gone! It was fonthasthique, huh?'

Prashant nodded to acknowledge that he had enjoyed the story and then said, 'Can you imagine doing an ad campaign about a guy like your guru chap?'

I said to Piet, 'But how do you know the cold went because of the guru?' I spoke in what I hoped was a tone intense and rapt enough to cancel out Prashant's boorishness. 'How do you know it wasn't just the weather or something like that?'

'Oh, it's not only the colds,' said Piet earnestly. 'I used to feel these' – he broke off to contort his face expressively – 'tensions, all the time. I felt there was like a block or a stone in my chest. I just knew there was a problem. But my – our' – here he waved his hand towards the verandah where Japp was still sitting – 'friend, the one called Kay who Goveenda was talking about, he told me that I had a problem centred in the chest chakra and that I had to do a lot of meditation to get rid of it. So then I started really thinking about it and working on it and then I could feel the block.'

Prashant said, 'But what did the guru do? How did he do it?' He leaned forward so that his elbows rested along the tops of his thighs, his pipe in one hand. He gave the impression of being deeply involved, but I knew him well enough to know it was a charade. I felt embarrassed for him and for myself. I knew that the moment we were alone, I would be treated to a hilarious reenactment of all that had been said and done here, with various embellishments and side-remarks. It seemed to me then that we had never talked about anything more consequential than the plots of the movies we saw or the books we read. In our conversations we actively derided anything bordering on the metaphysical. Yet with Piet, that's all I talked about. I realized that the discomfort I felt at this meeting between Piet and Prashant was something specific to me, to the different person I became when I was with the one or with the other.

'It's . . . difficult to explain,' Piet was saying again, his brow creased from making the effort. 'Do you, for instance, understand energy?'

Prashant must have nodded.

'It's like, the guru, he has TREMENDOUS energy. So when he encounters other people, and if they are, you know, open to him, he can just reach in and *khphoww!* Get rid of all that stuff inside. You know?'

'How does he know where to . . . strike?' asked Prashant. I could hear the silent laughter in his voice. I looked down at my hands. I was thinking that I had to get us away even though it was raining heavily again and the street was flooded. I felt it would be better to risk drowning in the effort to get Prashant out of Palm View than to permit these two very separate spheres of my life to collide again. It was strange that I had known Piet for just a little under two weeks and yet could already regard the time I spent with him as constituting a sphere as whole and as massive as the one I had assigned Prashant.

'Oh,' Piet was saying, 'he can see, just by looking at a person, what their state is. Everyone has a kind of *aura* around them, you know, and the quality of the aura depends, you know, on many things. Like energy . . . it's . . . how to describe it? It's a sort of, ahh, cosmic electricity, you could call it.'

'Ah-haah,' said Prashant, nodding. 'Like static energy, only different, huh?'

'Yes, exactly,' said Piet, a little uncertainly. 'Except that . . . this is, you know? – more personal. I mean, each person has a different level . . . and one person can . . . I mean, like I can, for instance, transfer energy, you know, from me to . . . someone else, you know.'

In the presence of Prashant's, to me, transparent contempt, I began to feel a counter-charge of recklessness rising inside me. Govinda and Sujaya were watching the scene with polite interest. Before I'd had time to ask myself whether what I was about to do was wise, I had leaned forward to bring myself into the current of the conversation between Prashant and Piet.

I said, 'Can you transfer energy to anyone?'

'Yes, of course,' said Piet, turning to look at me directly for the first time that evening. I noticed that his pupils were dilated to black pools around which the olive-green irises had become slender golden halos. I wondered whether it was the effect of the dim overhead lights.

'Even to me? Now?' I said, feeling breathless.

'Sure!' said Piet. Meanwhile, around us, I could feel the other energies in the room coming to a standstill. 'You have to put your hand out . . .'

I did so, my right hand, palm up. Piet placed his own right hand, palm down, over mine, but not touching it. 'Now. I'm going to start transmitting energy . . .' he said. 'I must concentrate, so I won't talk, all right? . . . You must also concentrate . . .'

'On what?' I asked. I felt I was walking a gangplank suspended over an abyss of disapproval from the others in the room. What was happening wasn't sociable. It was a private transaction taking place in full view of the public world. But there was no way out of it. I had asked a question and the answer had resulted in this situation.

'Think . . . of the space . . . between my hand and . . . your hand . . .' said Piet, speaking in between pauses. I looked at him. He looked straight back at me. I wondered how it was possible to see with pupils so hugely distended. A part of my mind wondered coldly whether the sparks in the air were after all only tendrils of some chemical substance escaping from his mind to mine. *Does he smoke?* I wondered. *Cannabis or tobacco?* I felt uncertainty crackling about me. I felt exposed and unlaced.

I averted my eyes, unable to hold that dilated gaze any longer. *He can't do this*! I thought. *He doesn't have permission to look at me that way!* Especially not in that setting, in that drawing room, with three other people looking on. It felt bizarre. It felt perverse. My face was hot.

All the while, my hand was glued to the air beneath Piet's palm. I could feel Prashant next to me, a glowering, sneering presence. But I turned my attention away from him.

I asked myself if I felt anything, in my hand.

It was a small area after all, perhaps seven square inches. I closed my eyes. It's not as if one actually feels one's hand, when it is not in contact with anything, when it is held suspended in space, with its fingers loose so that they are not even in contact with one another. Its presence there at the end of my arm was nebulous, a fog of dim sensation in the shape of a hand.

I could feel the weight of the ring on my third finger, with its heavy gold sovereign. I could feel a mild tension from continuing to hold the hand out, unsupported. There was a sort of warmth, which may have been the result of the tension. And then there was a . . . sensation.

A brightness tickled the inside of my hand. But it was very fine, an ion-feather lightly freckling the inside of my palm. I tried to clutch at it with my mind, to hold it there, to confirm its presence. In doing so, I lost it.

My forearm began to ache from keeping it steady and unsupported. Silly thoughts were forming like soap bubbles in my mind, drifting and popping inanely. I wanted to say something that would undo the seriousness inhabiting the space between my hand and Piet's.

Piet said in a low voice, 'Do you feel . . . something?'

I said, 'Yes. A sort of . . . warmth.' Then I opened my eyes and saw the room around me. Nothing confirmed the possibility of that ethereal tickling on the inside of my palm. I didn't dare look at Govinda or Sujaya. I could sense Prashant hot beside me, like a grizzly bear which has eaten a bowlful of chilli peppers.

Piet said, 'Yes! You should feel, you know, like a sort of ball rolling?' He was completely unaware of the others in the room. His face was lit up.

A profound misery was invading my spirit. I was going to kill the moment.

I could not continue this public spectacle. *We are not merely ourselves,* I thought. *We are also a composite of who our friends think we are.* None of the three others in the room knew me to be the sort of person who either sought or received invisible energy pulses from large Dutch men. Every social being is caught in a web of expectations, each thread woven by one or the other family member, friend or acquaintance. I could feel the pull, not merely of Sujaya, Prashant and Govinda but of my brother, my sister, my parents, my cousins, the whole constellation of aunts, uncles and assorted relatives, exerting their influence upon the palm of my hand, insisting that I should snatch it away, that it was not characteristic of me, of the person they thought I was, to be sitting in this way, in this room, with this foreigner, doing this thing. There was nothing forbidden or distasteful in the thing itself, except that it was unfamiliar. It belonged to a society different to the one to which I belonged.

Yet there I was, doing it. Did that make me a stranger to all those who knew me? Or did it make the person I was at that moment, an impostor, masquerading in my skin? Was I someone who ate soft-boiled eggs? Or not?

I knew that it was in my power to end the exchange. All I had to do was to pull my hand away. But I didn't want to. I wanted to explore this other dimension of experience with which Piet seemed to be so familiar. I wanted to find out for myself if it was an elaborate confidence trick or whether there really was another reality twinkling just outside the reach of ordinary knowledge. It angered me to feel that while Piet could explore any realm he chose, I was held in check by an invisible halter, which had nothing to justify itself other than a distrust of the unknown.

It seemed to me that I owed it to myself to throw off this halter. I was twenty-four. According to my private agenda, I had six years left to live. If there was something I needed to know about reality, I needed to know it now. So long as I allowed myself to wear the blindfolds that others around me wore, I couldn't know anything aside from what they told me.

A complex idea flickered into shape in my mind. While I struggled to resist the conflicting pressures working on me, with my palm locked in place under Piet's palm, the idea became an aperture through which my mind could find release. I would have to examine it later. Meanwhile in response to Piet's question I said, 'I do feel something – but I have to stop now! My arm's hurting!'

The light in Piet's face snapped off. 'Sure!' he said as he drew his hand away.

THE THREE STEPS

PRASHANT WENT HOME TO his room that evening while I stayed back at Palm View. I needed to think. The idea that had twinkled into existence during the so-called energy transfer took a long time to unfold, its consequences becoming bigger and more difficult to accept the more I looked at it. I told myself not to make the mistake of thinking that it had anything to do with Piet or his energy. Nevertheless, he had been the catalyst. He had punched a hole in my view of reality, just by being who and what he was. Like an animated cartoon in which a character bursts through a wall leaving a cut-out of itself behind, there was now a cut-out of Piet in my understanding of reality. Through the shape of him, I could see a very different landscape to the one to which I was used. I felt a violent need to explore that landscape.

If I had never seen it, I may not have permitted myself to feel the dissatisfactions of my life as keenly as I did. But a door had opened and the confines of my life had been flooded with the light of other possibilities. I had to explore what existed beyond that door or risk the disappointment of knowing that I did not deserve anything better than what I had.

The basic idea involved taking a vacation from my life. It couldn't be just a change from the city I was living in or the people I knew. What I needed was to step outside the skin of known associations that the people I knew had of me and to walk around a bit like that, skinless, waiting to see who I became and what would happen when there were no constraints upon me. So long as I was in the company of even one person who knew me, it would not be possible to achieve this effect because that person would remind me of who I was or at least who they thought I was.

Piet had told me already, several times, that his family was well off and that he lived with his mother, three younger brothers and a sister, in a big house. He talked about the house with great affection, as if it were a living being, a large, generous-hearted relative perhaps, in direct contrast to Palm View with its impersonal fellow tenants, its vicious landlord and its impermanence. He had on several occasions assured me that I would love this or that feature of his house and that I must come to visit. Well, I thought to myself, that's what I would do. I would go to Holland, spend one month there in Piet's house and come back.

There were very many obstacles in my way.

It wasn't just that I did not have the money to afford such a project. It was also that I could not tell anyone amongst my friends and family about my intentions. Even at a distance, I would be monitored by my family and I would feel restricted by their attention. I deliberately had to cut myself off from them, without alerting them to the fact that I was planning to spend a length of time amongst strangers in a country far away, with no better reason than that I wanted to, with no visas or scholarships or job offers to explain my desire to be away.

I had a partial solution. I had a friend living in Germany who, I believed, would agree to help me without revealing my whereabouts to my family. Her name was Mallika, Micki for short. I knew that I could trust her and that she would respect my desire to be left in limbo if that's what I wanted. The fact that she would know where I was would create a slight strain on the perfect skinlessness that I was planning for myself. On the other hand, she wouldn't actually be in the same city and I believed that her knowledge would not be of the kind that would limit me.

Piet was the portal through which I would enter this other space. It seemed to me logical that in order to pass through him I needed to arrange a physical encounter with him. That was how I stated it to myself. It should have amazed and rather shocked me that I could think like that, so coolly and without a pause to worry about the moral and social dimensions of such a campaign. But from the moment the thought first entered my head, it seemed perfectly at ease there, as if it had been a long-time tenant.

I did not ask myself whether it was right or wrong, or even whether there was any special attraction or affection involved. Such notions were completely irrelevant. I felt I was being shown a path and like a sleepwalker, or someone under a spell, I could either follow it even though it seemed to lead straight through a pit of live coals and into a brick wall or I could flinch and draw back. All the imperatives of childhood fairy tales suggested that I should walk on. So I walked on.

Three steps were required. The first was to visit the guru.

I had already talked to Piet about the guru so it was easy to ask if I could be taken along for one of the sessions. Piet readily agreed. He and Japp went twice a day, early in the morning and then later, at ten o'clock. Piet suggested that I come for this second session. His directions were to get to the Grant Road bridge on the 103 bus. 'Before it gets to its stop there is a traffic light – the one where five hundred roads meet at the centre,' he said. 'Get off there, cross all the roads and get to the other side. That's the bridge. I will be waiting.'

We decided to make it the first Wednesday in October. It had been raining all night, so in the morning, under a weak sun, the city smelt of earth and damp laundry. When I reached the foot of the bridge, I could see Piet standing at the summit of its arc, so much taller than the crowds of pedestrians around him that he was visible from a distance. He was staring over the side of the bridge, down towards the tracks of the suburban commuter rail system below. He seemed unconscious of the noise and the chaos of the traffic thundering over the bridge behind him and of the swirling non-stop parade of people around him.

I assumed he was still mulling over the early morning session at the guru's. But when I caught up with him, the first thing he said, his voice husky with excitement, was, 'There!' Pointing downwards. 'Do you see it?'

I was taken by surprise. I didn't know what to expect. I looked down at the gleaming tracks, seeing nothing that could be worth pointing to. I shook my head.

'No, no!' scolded Piet. 'On the side! The right side!' There was a shoulder of loose dirt beside the tracks and then a low huddle of grimy residential buildings. They weren't what Piet wanted me to see. He pointed again and only when it was clear that I wasn't going to pass this test, did he say, 'The Harley!' in a hushed voice. 'That's where it lives!'

A Harley Davidson. I knew the name because Prashant was a biker.

'I've been looking at it each time I pass this way,' said Piet. 'The owner leaves it outside in the rain – a *Harley*!' He had noticed it at first glance, the first day he crossed the Grant Road bridge en route to the guru's. He had known instantly what it was.

I looked towards that sooty front yard, but saw nothing there which resembled a motorbike. Other people on the bridge, moving around us, noticed that we were looking at something over the side of the bridge and began peering over it themselves. Seeing nothing there, they were now staring openly at us. Actually 'staring' is the wrong word. It does not convey the quality of being raked by another person's vision, as if one were a slab of stone being scraped hard in order to understand its true nature. I could feel cold eyes assessing me, assessing the companion towering beside me, passing the two of us through their collective wisdom and spitting us out again with no recognition of shared humanity to dull the edge of that corrosive scrutiny.

'And you're sure it's what you think?' I asked, hoping that by talking about the bike I would conceal the fact that I still hadn't seen it.

He said he had already been down to meet the owner to ask about its price.

'You're *not* thinking of buying it!' I exclaimed.

He shrugged. 'Well,' he said, 'it's so cheap, you know? I mean – a *Harley*!'

I felt a knot of anxiety form within me. Here was something alien. I could not imagine wanting something so big and so unwieldy to bring home from a foreign trip as the rusting hulk of an antique bike. I would absolutely never want anything enough to go knocking on the doors of strangers, to haggle over the price and at the end of the exercise be willing to face the tiresome rigmarole of getting the thing crated for shipping out to Holland.

If we were so different in something so simple as material desire, how much more different must we be in other, less obviously defined areas? I felt like an inexpert swimmer who has strayed from a paddling pool out to the open sea and in a moment of sharp clarity brought on by fear recognizes that she is out of her depth and must act immediately, *now*, before the tide sweeps her beyond recall, to get back to the well-defined shore.

But the morning crowds on the bridge were pressing around us, making movement difficult. I wasn't sure which bus would get me back to familiar territory, or where to find it. I hadn't brought enough money for a cab. Piet glanced at his watch, noticing the time. 'Oh!' he said, taking my arm and propelling me forward. 'It's getting late!' The carousel on to which I had stepped was in motion. Lights were flashing, wooden horses were starting to sway. It was already too late to get off.

We continued on our way, with Piet talking enthusiastically all the while. The more he talked, the more disorientated I felt. The city in which I had lived for six years, relating to it as a neutral grey backdrop, was vanishing. Through Piet's eyes I began to see a manic carnival where the street signs were in gibberish, the people were dark-skinned clowns, and the local ethics impenetrably hilarious. Everything that I took for granted or dismissed as being of little importance Piet gaped at and reacted to, without qualifiers or contexts. It was like focusing on each separate tile of a mosaic to the extent that the composite picture was lost.

The penultimate section of our path took us through an arcade of tiny stalls packed tight along the narrow pavement, their goods arrayed in steep displays. Sunlight stabbed down through holes in the overhead canopy, glinting in cheap plastic toys decorated with glass and tinsel. Freckles of reflected light cannoned dizzily in the shadows, glistening in the eyes of watchful stall owners. Piet stopped and pointed. 'These little suitcases, you know?' he said, picking one up from a stall. It was about the size of a coffee-table book and as sturdy as a potato wafer. 'I thought it might be good for packing an LP, you know? Then I could send it home to my family!' He meant that the sheer exotic craziness of a tiny suitcase, complete with hinges and miniaturized clasps, would be an amusing device for his family to see.

The owner of the suitcase stall had snapped to attention from the moment that Piet had shown an interest in his stall. 'You like?' he shrieked in the falsetto voice he reserved for talking to these freaks from other planets. 'You buy? Yes! You buy! See? Very best quality . . . come . . . I show you . . .'

His tone acted like blood in a shark's pool. Within seconds the other stall owners were swarming around us. It didn't matter that Piet, in his recently acquired cotton kurta–pajama did not look particularly rich. It was enough that he belonged to that breed of human which was known to buy ordinary objects at prices that only the incurably insane would consider paying. So any sort of miracle was possible. Little children stretched their hands out, grinning hopefully. Beggars hobbled towards us with their palms extended. Even the street dogs, exhausted and threadbare with mange, looked at us with brightening eyes. Piet waded with good humour through it all. He said, 'It's funny. I've been walking this way every second day for three weeks now. And they still say the same things!' What did he expect? 'They don't give up! That's fonthasthique, huh? Every day, I say, 'No-no-no!' But they never stop hoping – '

At this moment, a stall owner bounced up and pushed a pair of cheap lace panties in Piet's face, saying frenziedly, 'Yes . . . yes. . . yes . . .'

Taken by surprise, Piet bellowed, 'NOOOOOOOO!' and flung the man off, so that he fell on the pavement in a loose pile of spindly limbs.

There was sudden, stunned silence. The dazed stall owner lay on the cracked flagstones of the arcade, his big moist pop-eyes starting from his head. For a moment it looked like he was going to burst into tears. But a titter broke from one of the other merchants. Then another and another. Soon they were all roaring and hooting and slapping one another's shoulders. It was a rout, a festival. The tall stranger had been made to lose his composure! The big white ox had honked like a she-donkey impaled by a stallion! The would-be panty-salesman subsided in a giggling heap, delighted to have triggered such a sterling event.

Piet turned to me, smiling uncertainly, 'I didn't want to be rude, but' – he shrugged – 'what else to do?'

I shrugged too, but for different reasons. I was burning with embarrassment. I saw Piet's point of view, but I could also hear the comments of the merchants around us and the snickering tone that didn't need translation. How astonished they would have been to hear that Piet wondered why they didn't recognize him from one day to the next. It would have been like asking them to distinguish one ripe mango falling from heaven from any other ripe mango. Ridiculous!

At the end of the bazaar-arcade, the road bifurcated. We took the right turn. The guru lived just above the bidi-stall from which he had earned his livelihood before gaining enlightenment. The stall was still visible, perched on the ledge of a window on the side of a long, low building, two storeys high. Both margins of the narrow lane were defined by the decaying, tile-roofed habitations built as mass-housing for cotton-mill labourers in the early years of the century. The pavement had been so encroached upon that it had virtually disappeared. No actual walls were visible, because every available space was crammed with narrow, shuttered windows and doors. The road was tight with handcarts, vehicles, cyclists, cows and pedestrians. There seemed very little through traffic. Overhead, racks for laundry were suspended outside the frames of windows on the first floor, on both sides of the street, shutting out the sky. Wet garbage from countless kitchens poured directly into the gutters bordering the street.

Only one front door had been recently painted. It was bright blue and standing open.

That was the place.

THE GURU

WE ENTERED THE DOOR. Inside was a room just high enough for Piet to stand up straight in, and about as wide. The floor had once been the open pavement, but was now swept clean and dry. A shallow bench jutted a foot into the room, rimming three sides. Under this bench was stored the footwear of those who had already settled down in the audience chamber overhead. To one side, I could hear a monotonous rhythmic sound, which halted as we paused to remove our sandals. The air smarted with the smell of raw onions.

In the right-hand partition, a shutter flicked open. The face of an elderly woman was framed by the aperture. She examined us impassively. Then the shutter closed once more. From the other side of the partition, the sound of onions being chopped resumed. Across from the door through which we had entered, a wooden stairway angled steeply upward through an open hatch. We climbed this, Piet behind me.

I surfaced within a bright, airy space, not more than 15 feet square, in which about thirty people sat on the coir-matted floor, awaiting the guru. Most were Indians, though there was a scattering of Westerners, including Japp. A few heads had turned in our direction as we appeared, then turned away again, incuriously. Japp looked through me, as if he didn't recognize me. I wondered if that was because I had already been so altered by the ordeal of arrival that I was actually looking different.

Five or six women were sitting with their backs to the single window overlooking the narrow street. I had been informed that male–female segregation was encouraged so I chose a seat beside these ladies. Piet and Japp, on account of their height, sat with their backs to the wall, a short distance away, amongst the men.

I glanced at the women around me. From their clothes and their faces, it was clear that they did not belong to the neighbourhood in which the guru lived, but instead might well share a street or an address with me. We avoided eye contact. It was as if the effort of coming to see a guru was enough to peel away the veneer of civility that would have required us, in any other situation, to exchange names or at least the minimum of greetings. We sat close enough that our knees overlapped, yet behaved as if we had not noticed one another.

There was a muted murmur and that air of breathless expectation which heralds a performance of some sort. I was staring at the floor, trying not to prejudge my situation. I had been with my parents to sit in the presence of holy men often enough before this, as a child. I had never felt anything profound during those sessions, mostly a type of boredom tinged with the fear that I might never be able to straighten my legs out again from sitting cross-legged or might need a toilet before I could get to one. The air of piety annoyed me. The incense choked me. I used to long to run away.

With this background, I was finding it difficult to justify my presence in that room. I told myself to stifle my thoughts. In a relatively short while, the audience would be over and we would be free to go home. I felt quite sure that it had been a mistake to come and that I would return to Palm View completely unaltered by the experience. I worried about what I'd say to Piet and whether I could still justify following the difficult path laid out before me if I couldn't even take this first step with true conviction.

As I was thinking these thoughts, I became aware of a brilliance beside me. From the corner of my right eye I saw that the man closest to me was dressed in a white chikan kurta starched so bright that he was throwing light. I could smell his aftershave. He sat in an expertly coiled lotus position, the undersides of his feet raised up to reveal the perfect pinkness of one who bathes in Polar Bleach and wears socks to bed. I looked around to catch Piet's eye, asking a silent question in his direction: *Is this the Actor?* He smiled and nodded, then looked down, blushing, because at that moment an electric current trembled through the room. The guru was ascending the steps. He was spare in the way of someone who has reduced his material needs to the minimum, including his body. A rumour of hair clung to the edges of his dome-like head, otherwise bald. His skin was the colour of clove tea. He had a pronounced nose, a mobile, active chin and clean-shaven sunken cheeks. He moved in swift, economical jerks, like a severely censored film. He spread a square white handkerchief on the floor. Folded himself down in a neat double spiral. Tucked his right ankle under himself, curled his left ankle over the opposing thigh. Faced forward into the room. Ready.

His eyes darted quickly about, touching every person. I looked down before he reached me, feeling self-conscious. Beside me, the actor stirred. He obtained permission to speak.

'Maharazh . . .' he began. His accent proclaimed that he was English. I had seen him in a couple of movies. He had been paired with a famous fashion model, then she had famously dumped him. Despair, desolation. Piet and Japp had already described him to me, saying that he had been present every day for a week, each time with a new question.

This morning, his query related to temptations of the flesh. 'I have been meditating for three years now,' said the actor. 'I have practised all the austerities.' He enunciated beautifully, as if he had been practising what to say. 'But I am still not able to silence . . . *desire*.' He set this last word down as if it were a rare and fragile gem.

Beside the guru sat a portly man, a retired income tax official. Piet had told me about him. His name was Mr Sukhatme and he was one of the interpreters to the guru. He whispered to the guru, as the actor spoke, while the guru stared sharply at the foreigner, nodding once or twice. 'I have been a vegetarian for three years,' declared the actor in his rehearsed voice. 'Strictly. No eggs. I have given up alcohol. And cigarettes. All forms of intoxication. I recite my mantra four times a day. Five times on Sundays.' He paused dramatically. 'And I have had . . . no sex. For seven months now. No sex.' He paused again, as Mr Sukhatme translated. The room was very still.

'And yet,' the actor continued, 'when I sit in the lobby of the hotel where I stay, and I watch the women moving back and forth' – he trailed his hand gracefully in the air, suggesting the passage of butterflies – 'I feel . . . *desire*. Uncontrollable . . . *desire*,' I looked at him. His profile was calm. His cool grey eyes betrayed none of the heat that his words described. 'Please tell me, Maharazh. What am I doing wrong?'

Mr Sukhatme whispered. The guru drew back and gave out a short hard bark of laughter. His face seized up with mirthful wrinkles. He spoke in Marathi, in energetic rat-a-tat bursts. 'Tell him,' said the guru through his translator, 'tell him – I pity him! I feel sorry for him! I sympathize! He has suffered, poor man!' The audience began to snuffle with pious laughter. 'But it will do him no good!' The room fell silent again. 'He will not approach enlightenment this way.' The guru was a small man but his gaze stalked the room with the confidence of a lion tamer. No, the lion itself, in a roomful of would-be tamers. His toothless smile had dazzle, had charisma. He was grinning now.

'Because there is no way to *approach* enlightenment. Because there is no *path* to enlightenment!' he said. 'Meaning, there is no PATH. Meaning, it is not a cinema that you can buy tickets for! Meaning, it is not a mountain that you can go on pilgrimage to! There is no address, where it is written "Enlightenment Available, 50 paise per head!" So there is no "closer to", there is no "distance from". There is no here, no there. No almost, no maybe, no halfway or quarterway. Not even three-quarters way. Not even *ninety-nine per cent*.' He winked towards some favourite in the audience, some private joke. 'There is only –'

his hand chopped down on the coir floor – 'Unlightenment –' *chop!* – 'Enlightenment –' *chop!* – 'Nothing in between!'

Afterwards, Piet, Japp and I wandered slowly through the bazaar, in silence. Not the crowds or the merchants, or the beggars, or the slow thick heat, or the dirt attracted my attention any more. We stopped at an open chai-shop and had glasses of coarse, salty buttermilk. The other two did not seem to worry about amoebas so I didn't either. The morning's hesitant sunlight had faded by the time we decided to pool our money for a taxi home. Clouds bore down upon the city, the air thinned out. It was drizzling before we reached the house. In the few feet between the door of the taxi and the entrance to the building, cataracts of water poured down upon us. Bansi was standing sternly at the dining table, glaring at the puddles we left on the floor. I told him I didn't want lunch and turned to go to my room. Piet leaned towards me and whispered, 'How did you find it?'

'Fonthasthique,' I whispered back, surprised to realize that I meant it.

THE MOVE

THE GURU HAD IMPRESSED me. He had a sense of humour. The power of his personality showed in the way he held the room, in the tautness of his attention. He seemed to need nothing, not the audience, or the fawning remarks of his sycophants, or any part of the clutter of ordinary beings. He offered no formulas or magic potions. He had little respect for organized religion. He just *was*.

I could not dismiss or belittle him, or find silly jokes to make about him. I could not, for instance, talk about him to Prashant, or to Gai, except in the vaguest possible terms. I did not like revealing that I had been shaken out of my complacency. I felt that my life up to that point had been a pale and shallow one. Now there would be no turning back. I had taken the first step, and now the next two steps of the path before me beckoned.

The second one was to move out of Palm View.

I said to Prashant that I was ready to plan our trip to the US. 'But I'll have to move out of Palm View right away,' I said. 'And I'll need to make enough money to pay the advance rent before I leave. And I'll need to finish the work I have on hand.' I estimated that it would take me at least one and a half months before I could afford to fly out of Bombay. I already knew that Prashant's office had sanctioned leave from the first week of November till the first week of January. I told him that he would have no choice but to go on ahead of me. 'I'll join you as soon as I can – but please don't try to argue about it, because if I get upset now I won't be able to finish my work and then I won't be able to go away at all.' He was angry and disappointed, but saw the logic of my argument. It was either that or no US trip till a year later.

Prashant had a friend called Zero Mehta. Zero was only his pet name but it suited his anaemic personality very well. He had an elongated mantis-face, a Frank Zappa moustache and thick glasses. He was Parsi and he worked in the Mercantile Bank. Prashant did not know him intimately, but they had recently met at one of Prashant's office parties. Zero said that he lived across the road from Jujube Towers, in a building called El Paradiso. He had a two-bedroom apartment on the twelfth floor. He said he was looking for a paying-guest to occupy one of the bedrooms.

I went across to see him.

'I need a room for one year, Zero,' I said. 'Prashant and I are planning a trip to the US. I need a place to store my things till I get back.'

'You'll be away for a whole year in the US?' he said, looking impressed.

'No!' I exclaimed. 'Of course not. I'm flying on an excursion fare so – you know, three months, four at the most . . . whatever. When I get back, it'll take me a few months before I can find something more permanent.'

He told me that the bank gave him a rent allowance but it wasn't quite enough. 'It's not a big flat but . . .' He shrugged, looking around. 'You know what it's like. Nothing this size in South Bombay is less than twenty a month. I'm getting it for sixteen, bank pays twelve. I thought, okay, four from my side and if I can get a friend to stay as a PG – beautiful.'

I had to agree that the flat was worth what he was paying for it. It was airy, with balconies on either side of the drawing room. It had twin bedrooms, both around 20 feet square, with attached baths. Zero had the West room and I, if I accepted the arrangement, would have the East. I told him that my priority was to store my belongings in a secure place in case Palm View needed to be evacuated in my absence.

Zero said that the only reason he'd have for wanting the room back was if he got married while I was away and, 'There's no one in sight!' he sighed.

'Are you sure?' I asked.

'Oh yes,' said Zero, 'I'm sure.'

I should have asked him how anyone could be so sure that he wasn't going to marry in the next three months, but I wanted to trust him because I wanted to have the room. It was crucial to my plans. Besides, Parsis were known for their honesty. I had worked for two years with a Parsi community magazine and I knew as well as any non-Parsi could that their high standards of integrity were locked into their chromosomes. It was the reason for which they were trusted as bank tellers, chartered accountants, lawyers and moneylenders.

The terms we discussed were that I would pay Zero 1,500 rupees a month, with two months' rent in advance as a deposit. If I moved in, it would be on 1 November. I said I'd talk it over with Prashant but that from my side it was a deal. Zero smiled happily and said, 'Let's hope it works out for both of us!'

I got back to Palm View and called my sister-in-law to tell her of this development. Since my brother's ban on visits, we had taken to speaking on the telephone or meeting during the day at the gym, where she was a member. I called Prashant at his office and told him his friend's place looked like a good proposition. Then I marched on the spot for forty-five minutes. This was the exercise routine recommended by Dr Prasad. 'There are no excuses anyone can give me for not being able to march on the spot,' he said. 'No *Doctor, doctor it was raining so I couldn't walk!* or *Doctor, doctor I don't have enough space in my house to exercise!* If you don't have enough space to march on the spot,' he said, 'you can't afford to be one of my patients – so swing those arms, raise those knees and march, march, march!' One and a half hours was what he demanded on a daily basis.

I marched twice a day for three-quarters of an hour and memorized poetry as I pumped my legs and arms. By the end of my third week at the clinic, I had lost two and a half kilos and gained 'The Lady of Shalott' and 'The Walrus and the Carpenter'. Now I was starting on 'Kubla Khan'. Then I had a bath, went to my desk and worked industriously till lunch time.

The children's book I had been struggling to complete had 64 pages in full colour plus the cover and endpapers. The outright fee without royalties I would be paid for the whole thing was 4,000 rupees. This was such a miserable sum that the only way I could justify the effort was to finish the book in a fortnight. But my style of drawing is detailed and painstaking. It was already over a year since I had started. I had spent twice or thrice the amount of my fee in materials and in travel expenses to and from the editorial office. A more experienced illustrator would have refused the work or given up halfway through. But I wasn't experienced, I needed the money and I didn't have the confidence to complain.

The visit to the guru changed me. The quality of authority he projected, of being able to control not only his own destiny but that of those who came in contact with him, was enough to charge me with purpose. Telling myself that the 4,000 rupees that completing the book would bring was necessary for the plans I had for my immediate future, I put my head down and attacked the remaining pages of the book like a bull turning on its matador. In a few days I was able to accomplish what I had been unable to do for months. I was on my final two-page spread on the day I met Zero.

Bansi called me to lunch.

When I got there, I found Piet alone at the table. Japp had gone off 'exploring'.

'You look tired,' I said to Piet.

He said he had just returned from Govinda's boss's home to which he had been invited on an 'energy mission'. Apparently Govinda's elderly boss had a young wife who was desperate to conceive. 'She called me over,' said Piet, 'because Govinda had told the boss something about my energy transfers. So I went. The boss was also there and he was this *businessman,* you know? In his little tie and his business suit. And I could see that he hated everything, me, the session, he didn't believe in it, nothing. And he just sat there and had his whisky and said nothing, while his wife explained. She said she didn't have babies yet and she wanted to be a mother and all that stuff. I said I have no experience in this field.' He shrugged. 'I can't give wishes. The energy is just *something* that I can transmit – it's not like a ray gun or anything!' He grinned suddenly. 'But I felt really sorry for her. So I just sent her that. Just my feeling of pity.'

He was not surprised to be consulted in this way. 'If I can become really good at sending energy,' he said, 'I'll be able to do it at a distance. I'll be able to call you, for instance, and say, "At 12.47 exactly – " he tapped his wrist in the place that a watch would be, though he wasn't wearing one that day – "I will send you 600 milligrams of super deluxe energy!" And – *whup!* You'll get it!'

I said, 'How would you know if it reached me or not?'

'I'd know,' he said. 'I know when it leaves me. I can feel it.' At times like this, I had to suspend judgement. Some of the things he said sounded to me like fairy talk. Yet his face was absolutely tranquil. He was not attempting to convert me to his view. It was just a statement. 'We can do an experiment. I will send you energy, but I won't tell you about it; I'll make a note of the time. When you get it, you can also write down the time. Then when we meet, we can see if you got it at the same time when I sent it . . .'

I said, 'But you can write down *any* time and say that you sent me energy – '

'But then the time won't be same as what you write down,' he countered.

'And if I don't get it?' I asked.

'Then there won't be anything to check, of course,' he said, laughing.

Conversations of this type made me feel as if the ordinary air had been replaced with helium. My voice began to sound distorted to my own ears and I felt light-headed and giggly. Nevertheless, I persevered, saying, 'But look! You could be lying! You could tell me that you had sent me energy at such and such a time, and maybe I would feel nothing and then if I said I felt nothing, you would say, "But I sent it at such and such a time – and if you didn't get it, too bad!"'

He shrugged and said, 'Yes. Maybe. I could.' He looked at me. His eyes were full of light. I couldn't tell if he was laughing at me or just laughing in general. 'And so what?'

I said, 'But . . .'

He shrugged again. 'It *is* subjective. Everything. If I say this table is made of – of' – he shrugged reflexively – 'cream cheese, then . . . it is!'

I looked at him unhappily, starting to shake my head.

He said, 'I create the world when I wake up. I destroy it when I go to sleep. Or – okay, I don't destroy it, because I don't do anything with it. It stops, when I stop. It starts when I start.' He spoke with simplicity and an absolute lack of guile.

I shook my head. 'No!' I said. 'That's ridiculous! You don't *create* me,' I said. 'I exist on my own, outside of you – like everyone else, like the rest of all reality – '

He said, 'You can say that to me. But you are just a part of *my* dream and in *my* dream, I let you say it. And when I am in a deep sleep – you vanish, with the rest of all reality. If I don't know you exist, then . . . *you don't exist*!'

I drew myself together to speak, but before I could, he said, 'The point is . . . *you* can say all of this too. To yourself. About me.' He smiled. 'I am part of your dream and you are part of mine.'

'No,' I said, 'we share reality and have our private dreams . . .' Bansi had cleared the lunch dishes, leaving behind only the sugar bowl from the coffee service. It was a graceful object, the belly of a silver teardrop, hollowed out and filled with sugar. I could see a dim reflection of myself in its curved surface, and of my hands, distorted, as I reached towards it. I pushed the bowl with the tips of my fingers, just outside my range of comfortable reach, trying to position it at the centre of the table.

Piet's attention was drawn to the sugar bowl. He reached towards it while thinking out his next statement. He pushed the sugar bowl a little to the side, making micro-adjustments. He gazed at the bowl, frowning very slightly. 'I'm going to tell you something,' he said, finally. 'It's very simple but it goes . . . very . . . *far*. So I'm just going to say, it – huh?' And here he looked up, as if to reassure himself that I was in the correct state of receptivity. 'It's this . . .' He paused. Speaking with slow deliberation, without placing stress on any one word, he said, 'There . . . is . . . no . . . experience . . . without . . . desire.'

I remember feeling disappointed. That was *all*?

He continued to concentrate on the sugar bowl. 'It takes some time to see the point of it,' he said. 'You have to think about it, slowly.'

I said, 'You're saying that desire is a necessary ingredient of experience?'

'You won't get it at once,' he said. 'It took me months. You can fight it but when you really, really, think about it, you *know* it's the absolute truth.'

I said, 'I don't believe in absolute truths. Any truth is relative to what can be known given a particular set of circumstances . . .'

He smiled and shrugged. As if to say I was welcome to hold these views but that didn't make them true.

Just then, Bansi, entering from the pantry area and finding the dining room in darkness, turned on a switch. Piet and I must have made an odd sight, facing across a table, with our arms outstretched, reaching towards a sugar bowl in the centre. We weren't touching, but our hands shared the surface of the bowl. They didn't touch there either. They merely curved towards one another, like bashful sea anemones, on the silvery skin of a teardrop.

JAPP

ONE WEEK LATER, I had begun to pack my things in readiness for the move to Zero's place. I had finished my drawings for the children's book, much to the publisher's astonishment. I think they had secretly hoped that I would give up so that they could get it illustrated by someone else who would not complain so much about them. To my astonishment, they assured me that my cheque would be ready by the end of the month. I had been dreading the battle of getting the money out of them.

Sujaya now said, rather ruefully, that she was going to miss me. Govinda had laughed out loud when I asked him whether Sujaya would need to pay double if I left. 'Of course not! Ladybirds would be welcome to stay free if I could afford it but I can't and so . . . it's only to cover basic costs. Don't worry – and come back whenever you like if it doesn't work out.' He said I could keep the front-door key for however long it took for me to feel at home in the new place.

Sujaya worried that I would never be able to manage on my own. 'You can have all your meals here, you know,' she said, 'if you want to keep up with your diet. And what will you do about laundry? Is there a place to hang clothes? Is the water supply steady? Have you thought about those sorts of things?'

I hadn't especially, but was grateful for her concern. I said that I would certainly stay in touch. If for nothing else, at least to use the telephone, because Zero didn't have one. I wasn't sure what I was going to do about food. Zero's cook seemed a rather moody fellow who looked inclined to resent the fact that there would be a female presence in the house all day long. His independence would be seriously curtailed. But I had decided that he would calm down when he realized that I wasn't going to interfere in his life.

I no longer consulted my diet sheet because I hardly ever felt hungry. A slice of papaya in the morning and D'Silva's bread with paneer was all I needed in the way of food and I drank the low-fat lassi to avoid dehydration. Whenever I met Gai now, she narrowed her eyes and said that I would dwindle out of sight. I gave her the smug, 62-kilo smile of a successful dieter and said, 'No worries! I'm fine – just a little lighter, that's all!'

At the time of my last visit to the diet clinic, I had lost 5 kilos. It was six weeks since I had begun and the latest little dumpling in human form to share my session with the doctor looked up at me, round-eyed with respect. The doctor himself seemed a little diminished. 'Well, my dear,' he said, 'you can manage on your own, now, I think – but come by when you feel like it, just to have a chat . . .'

I returned to Palm View from the clinic feeling thoughtful. Winning the doctor's approval had been one of the primary incentives in the first week of the diet. Now it was of small concern. I almost had the feeling that I had failed him by succeeding because I was no longer in his control. It was a new perspective. To be nostalgic for my image as a fat, incompetent loser!

It was 4 o'clock by the time I got back to the old house. The rain had eased over the past few days. Mellow sunlight touched the verandah, though it did not penetrate the gloom that hung over the dining table. Japp was standing there, a huge figure dressed in white cotton. A tray had been set out on the table, with the teapot under a cosy and five porcelain cups turned upside down on their saucers. Japp was frowning as he looked at the tray. He began lifting up each cup one at a time, looking under it, then replacing it on its saucer with a crash. I watched him a moment and then said, 'Are you trying to break them?'

He glanced up, startled. 'Oh!' he said. 'It's you!' Another fragile cup was smashed back upon its saucer, remaining miraculously intact.

'What are you doing?' I asked.

'Looking,' he said. 'Looking for something I can't find.' He had run out of cups now and was turning his head this way and that, his pink rubbery lips compressed in frustration.

'For what?' I asked.

'The truth,' said Japp, abandoning his quest suddenly and sitting down. 'I thought, maybe – it might be hiding under these cups, you know. And maybe some cookies. They sometimes have cookies here, no? With the tea? Or only the truth?'

I turned down the corners of my mouth to acknowledge his little joke and, pulling back a chair, sat down myself. I thought I might as well have some tea now that it was there. 'Is this tea for us?' I asked. 'Or are there going to be guests?'

Japp sighed heavily. He stared at me a moment and then said, 'I don't know!' his voice yodelling in mock-seriousness. 'I don't know-ooooo!' He laid his head down, with his cheek flat on the surface of the table, then switched sides and placed the other cheek down. 'It's *kühl*, huh? The table is *kühl*. Cold.' He was taller than Piet and the effect of folding himself over the table brought his head practically to the centre of it. Then he said, with his head turned on its side, so that he wasn't looking at me, 'I think some guests were supposed to come. But they haff not. And now, anyway, their host is not heer also. Piet. He has gone out.'

We sat in silence a few minutes. Then he held his head up to look towards me, supporting his chin on the folded fist of his right hand. He twitched his nose in a characteristic gesture he had, to make his glasses ride higher on the bridge of his nose from where they customarily slid down. 'So tell me,' he said. 'What did you think of the session, you know? At the ghuru's.'

Ten days had passed since that visit.

I said, 'It was . . .' I stopped and looked away. I still couldn't find the words to say what I had felt about it. I hadn't described the visit to anyone. It was in a place beyond description. To say that it was good or bad or indifferent would have been to force a value on to something that was too unique to be assessed. He waited a few seconds, then laughed.

'It's like that for you too?' His face changed completely when he smiled, losing its manic expression. 'I thought it was only . . . us. Becoss we're . . . how you say? Mad Westerners.' He made the universal screw-loose sign by the side of his right temple with his hand. He repeated, 'Matt Veshternersssss!', exaggerating his accent. He did not speak as fluently as Piet, but there were times when it seemed to me that he chose to be that way. He looked at me with his head rolled over to one side. 'Do we seem mad to you?'

I shrugged, saying, 'No. Not mad. But when you first came. . .' I paused to pick my words tactfully. 'When you first came, I couldn't understand *why*. Why anyone would come so far just to see a person they had never met before . . .'

He seemed to lose interest, because he was looking away again, squinting his eyes slightly in the gloom of the dining room. There was no one in the house besides ourselves. The smile faded from his face. His hair, now a bleached-straw stubble half-an-inch in length and his pale eyes combined to give him an ethereal look.

I thought he wasn't going to answer, but then he did. 'It's becoss we *are* mad,' he said. '*That's* why we come.' He looked back at me. 'Do you know wot Piet is studying in college? His subject?' I said, yes, psychology. Japp smiled very slightly. 'Do you know why?' I shook my head. He nodded, saying, 'Becoss of . . . madness. You ask him. His whole family is mad. All his friends, too. Me – especially. I'm *completely*' – he made a comic face, crossing his eyes and extruding his tongue from the side of his mouth, grinning like a lunatic – 'mad! We're all mad.'

I sipped my tea thinking that I didn't like Japp much. There was something disturbing about him. Disturbed, perhaps, just as he said.

'And you? What do *you* do?' I asked. 'Are you also studying something?'

He said, continuing to smile faintly, 'No. I'm doing nuffing.' He was bent over the table, holding his head upright against his left forearm, so that the loose skin on the left side of his face was distorted upwards, giving his features a rakish expression. His mouth was like a pair of fat, wet, pinkly naked slugs wrestling slowly to the sound of the words created by their movement. 'In Holland, mad people don't have to work, you know? It's one of the prizes the government giffs us for being mad. That's why we're all mad. It's becoss if we're mad, we don't haff to do no work.'

I assumed he meant that Dutch social welfare schemes provided for the insane.

Just then the phone rang. He went to get it, evidently expecting a call from Piet, because when he spoke, it was in Dutch. Returning from the call he said, 'Some people woss coming to see Piet,' contriving a foxy look, as if he knew he should not say more. 'For a – a – *konsultation*!' He snorted again but without humour. 'You know?'

I nodded. The boss's wife. Japp contorted his big wet mouth into an exaggerated sneer then looked away again and laughed. There was an unpleasant edge to his laugh. 'So . . . I don't haff to tell you no more, then!' He got up and shrugged with his whole loose frame. 'You like Piet, huh?' When I tried to be noncommittal, he said, 'Oh, *ja, ja* – you do. Effryone likes Piet. He talks so goot, you know? Better than me.' He sat down again. 'But I know Piet more,' Japp continued. 'And he *iss* goot, yes. But he iss also . . .' He made the screw-loose sign.

I felt I was being disloyal when I asked, 'Why? In what way?'

Japp shrugged, wrinkling his spectacles up the bridge of his nose. 'The energy transfer,' he said. 'It's bullshit, I think. Do you belief it?' Japp's eyes, when he focused acutely upon a subject, were like blue searchlights.

'Yes,' I said, though my voice sounded insincere even to my ears. There was a silence.

I said, wondering to what extent they shared their observations, 'He was talking to me yesterday about *experience* – ' I didn't finish my thought. Japp nodded quickly and said, intoning the words in his exaggerated way, 'You mean, There iss no experience wizout deesirrrre?' And he gusted a short laugh. 'Ja. I know it.'

'And?' I said. 'What do you think? Is it true? Do you believe that too?'

Japp was starting to lose focus. He said, 'Errm. Ja. Iss true. I belief it.' Then he shook his large frame all over and stood up so suddenly that the chair tipped over behind him, though he caught its seat in time and said, 'Also but I don't belief it! Also – it doesn't matter! Becose, becose, becose . . . there is NO experience wizout desire!' And then he left the room.

EL PARADISO

GAI HELPED ME MOVE into my new room. It took just one morning, with a handcartwallah to transport the heavy desk in three bits from Palm View to El Paradiso. A couple of days later, Prashant left for the US.

The next morning, I went to the guru's for a second session. I got there on my own this time, taking a cab till the point where the road bifurcated. I no longer felt self-conscious walking through the bazaar. I barely noticed I was there. I felt as if the person I had been at the time of the first visit and the person I was now were as different as an insect which has emerged from its pupa and the empty, dried-up shell in which it had lived until that moment.

Upstairs in the audience chamber there were more foreigners this time. The first half hour was entirely taken up with the guru ticking off the newcomers for wearing shorts rather than long pants. No discussion was entertained. Limbs and torsos were to be decently covered. After this, one of the foreigners began to talk about his previous births. My attention wandered away from the room. I felt an extreme warmth, especially about my face, as though it were enveloped in a gauzy balaclava. I was so overcome with a desire to sleep that I may have nodded off.

When my attention returned, I heard that the guru was dismissing queries about past lives. 'Forget about past lives,' he was saying, through his interpreter. 'If you believe in past lives, how will you account for what happens when the municipality sprayer comes around and kills one million cockroaches in the locality? Does it mean there will suddenly be one million births in some other place? And what happens when there's a flood and hundreds of human lives are lost – are there suddenly more baby donkeys?' He shook his hand, palm outward, disparagingly. 'No. There is nothing. Don't waste your time thinking of past lives, future lives. Think only of this life in front of you. Concentrate on it. Ask yourself: are you alive?' The room was still. He looked around. He looked in my direction. I looked back at him. His gaze was direct and intelligent, though not especially friendly. It was neutral, as if he were talking to a plant or a stone. 'You,' he said to me, 'can you say why you have come to see me?'

I did not hesitate with my reply and said, 'No reason.'

He stared at me a moment and said, 'No reason! I see! And are you dead, already? Or alive?'

I said, 'Dead.' I knew from my conversations with Piet that this was the correct answer. Being dead was the equivalent of being in a deep sleep, being indifferent, being unmoved. It was the ideal state, because it was changeless. I felt the satisfaction that comes from being a good student, even as I scolded myself for being dishonest. After all, if I were truly dead, I would not feel satisfaction either.

He stared at me another moment and then moved on, saying nothing more to me.

Soon the session was over and we were descending the narrow stairs, relocating our shoes and looking for a taxi to take us home. Piet and Japp were pleased with the exchange between myself and the guru. 'You were very lucky,' they said. 'He doesn't notice most people. Or he laughs at them and makes them look foolish.'

There hadn't been anything profound about my answers. I had not gone to see the guru because I had a question to ask of him. It would have been too complicated and undoubtedly very rude to explain that my motivation for seeking an audience had to do with my own agenda involving Piet, Holland and stepping out of my skin.

To Piet and Japp I said, 'I went to see him because I happened to meet you and because you spoke about him. It was curiosity. . .'

Piet said, 'It doesn't matter. What you do *is* what you want to do.'

I said, 'That's not true. I do all kinds of things I don't want to do.'

He shrugged and asked, 'But – why?'

'Because I have to,' I said. 'Because it's expected of me.'

'Who expects it?' asked Piet.

'My family or my friends – ' I said.

'You choose to let these people decide what should happen to you,' said Piet.

'No!' I said. 'We don't choose our families – so we don't *choose* the ties we have with them – '

'We start making choices from the first few seconds of consciousness,' said Piet. 'Some babies lie quietly in their mothers' wombs and other babies kick and squirm around and make their mothers uncomfortable.' Piet contorted his huge frame in the cramped backseat of the taxi, briefly transforming the tiny Premier Padmini into a makeshift metal womb in which the three of us plus driver, fellow quadruplets, hurtled across the city's belly. 'And when they grow up, some children are quiet and other children cry all the time and need to be spanked. They choose to do what they want to do even if it means they must get hit. In a sense, if you think about it, they *choose to get hit*!'

We were en route to Palm View, but just as we passed the Colaba Bandstand, Japp, who was sitting in the front seat, tapped the driver's shoulder, signalling him to stop at the next corner. 'And now,' he said, 'I choose to get off! Goot-bye!' He sprang out of the cab and loped off, almost running.

I turned to Piet and asked, 'Why did he do that? Is he angry about something?'

Piet shrugged non-committally before volunteering, 'He says he needs to be alone.'

When we reached Palm View I got down and went in with Piet instead of continuing to El Paradiso.

Piet sat down to lunch. We were alone at the table. 'Japp isn't happy here,' said Piet. 'I mean, living in this house with me.'

'Do you know why?' I asked.

'He says I . . . disturb him,' Piet replied. 'He says I make him feel tense. Or . . . something. I don't really understand. Maybe it's because the room is too small, you know?' He looked back at me. 'In Holland we . . .' he groped for diplomatic words, 'we don't spend so much time together. But here, we're in one small room, breathing the same air all the time. He says I make him nervous.' He laughed. 'He says, I talk at night, that I make too much noise and he can't sleep. But I say he doesn't bathe enough and he doesn't smell so good. And he . . . farts. It's like, it's like he does it on *purpose*, very loud and very . . .' he made a face, 'disgusting,' he finished lamely. 'I can't explain. It's like he wants to say something, but he can't say it in words, so he says it like this. By farting. It's his body speaking. Or maybe his aura. Maybe his aura and mine are' – he brought his hands together in an explosion – '*paf!* – in conflict.'

'How did you become friends?' I asked.

'He was my sister's boyfriend,' said Piet. He looked far away, as if seeing Holland around him. 'He was always in the house.' He paused, then shrugged. 'When they broke up, my sister got so depressed, she got anorexia nervosa. Do you know anorexia nervosa?'

It was the first time I had heard the term. He explained what it was. 'It's an illness that is common in rich countries – almost exclusive to women. They stop eating, they starve themselves completely. Sometimes to death. Juliana, my sister, had to leave the house and go away before she got better. She's studying psychology now, to help herself understand her problem. But Japp would still come to see me. He became my friend. Then we both went to see – you know, the person we talk about – Kay?' He gestured to the space around ourselves. 'The one who introduced us to India, the guru, everything. Well, Japp does everything I do. So when I decided to come to India, he came too.'

Piet's father died when he was sixteen. 'But he never liked me. So . . . it was good in a way,' he said, shrugging sentiment and emotions out of the picture. 'And I didn't have to do military service because I could say that I was the head of the family! Though I had to sign up anyway. I came home in this fonthasthique uniform, black, you know? It was really beautiful, all the buttons shining . . . I felt . . .' he shrugged, 'it's hard to explain. Really – *powerful*. But my baby brother was very unwell, he was born blue, with this congenital heart disease. So they exempted me from service . . .'.

Listening to these stories about Piet's life was like watching a film of another world of experience. I knew from a conversation I'd had with Japp that Piet had a girlfriend. But he wasn't happy with her, or so Japp indicated. 'She wrote him some kind of stupid letter,' Japp said to me. 'She wrote on the cover, "I love you!" It made Piet really mad.' I had seen this letter, when it came in. A blue aerogramme with the words '*Ik hou van je!*' written in place of the sender's address. I hadn't understood what the words meant but had intuited that they were not from a mother or a sibling.

There were some newspapers on the dining table, including a copy of the *Times of India*, crossword-side up. Piet pointed to it and said, 'I have a friend who is absolutely clairvoyant. He did one of these one day, in front of me, just completely, start to finish, without stopping. Amazing, huh?'

I said, 'But . . . there's nothing special about doing crosswords. Anyone can.'

He was staring at the crossword in front of him. 'Sometimes, when my energy is working well, I can do them. *Paf.* Other times, it makes no sense. Like this one – it makes no sense!' He handed the paper to me.

I thought it was obvious that the reason the puzzle made no sense to him was that it was in English. I said so. He looked faintly amused and said, 'When my energy is right, I can do anything!'

It was my turn to look sceptical. The puzzle was a cryptic one and I was familiar enough with its style to put on a little demonstration. I wanted to show him that even someone such as myself, with no claim to energy fields, could perform the trick. 'Well, here's the first word,' I said. 'The answer to One Across is "territory".'

He frowned and said, 'But – '

I said, 'The clue is "*Almost dogged, party patch*", nine letters. "*Party*" often stands for the word "Tory" so that's the main hint. Then "*Almost dogged*", well, that could be "terrier" with the last two letters missing which explains the "*almost*". And the word itself is a "*patch*" meaning a patch of land – territory.' I paused. He was looking blank. 'Then – well, you look at Four Down and it says, "*Period of longing, up to a point*" so that's "Yearn". Get it? "Year" is the "*period*", the "*point*" is "n" for north, and "*longing*" is the solution of the clue, meaning "to yearn". So then I can feel sort of sure that One Across is right, because it ends on "y" and Four Down starts with "y" – do you see?'

Piet was looking at me with an expression between disbelief and respect. 'The ones we have in Holland are different,' he said. 'The clue is just one word, and the solution is another word just like it and all the words are interlaced. You can read them up and down, in every direction. Not like this one,' which had not more than three crossings on any one word. 'Even so,' he said, 'you must be clairvoyant too. You got it without thinking at all, it was instantaneous.'

'No,' I said. 'I'd like to be, but I'm not.'

Bansi had cleared the things from lunch. Piet folded himself down over the table in his favourite position, chin cupped in his hands and said in a lazy, teasing voice, 'If you *really* wanted to be, you *would* be – '

'Piet.' I said, 'life doesn't work that way. It would be nice if it did, but it DOESN'T.'

'For example . . . ?' he asked.

'Okay,' I said. 'For example, I'd like to come to Holland. I'd like to visit you. But – I can't just do it! In the first place, I don't have the money – and in the second place, even if I *did* have the money . . .' I shrugged helplessly. 'My family wouldn't *let* me!'

He shook his head. 'No, no, no,' he said. 'You still don't see how this thing works. What you do *is* what you want to do – otherwise you won't do it. If you say you want to come to Holland, it's fine – but unless you come, it means to me that you don't want to come because – you didn't.'

'Okay, then,' I said, 'Okay. I want to come to Holland. Really. Now what?'

'So – come!' he said, his expression placid.

'Would I be able to stay in your house?' I asked. I felt like an ant at the edge of an ocean of possibility, wondering whether the transparent, uncertain surface would bear my weight or collapse under me.

'Of course,' he said, shrugging as if it were self-evident.

'I wouldn't be able to pay for my stay,' I said, wanting him to know the worst right away. 'I'd need to find some way of making money while I'm there – '

'You should come. It would be . . . interesting,' he said. 'I could take you to meet my friend, Kay. You can tell me what you think of him.'

I said, 'Well, I'll have to look for some way to sell my drawings. That's my main reason for going. I know that the work I do here would earn three or four times as much abroad. If I could just establish a connection, I could sell my work there and live here, but earning well for once.'

From his folded-over position, Piet looked up, arching his eyebrows and said, 'I don't know anything about how you would find work, huh? We would have to think about that once you come there. Maybe it won't be so easy . . . but you can always stay with me, and find out.'

'Anyway,' I said, 'it's probably just a crazy dream. Right now, I don't have the money to get there, or a ticket or a visa – '

'You'll find those things,' said Piet simply, 'if you want to enough.' He paused and then he tapped the crossword puzzle still lying face up on the table. 'Just like you can solve the puzzle. Because you *want* to.'

THE CARDS

GAI CALLED TO SAY that my brother had relented about the ban on my visits. She said she'd talked him out of it. I went over at once and was happy to be back in the flat that had been home to me ever since I had left boarding school to enter university in Bombay.

At the same time, looking around at all that was familiar, I felt that in the two short months for which I had been absent, the house had moved away from me. Or maybe it was I who had moved away from it. Gai saw that I was quiet. She asked what was wrong. 'Is it because of Raghu?' she wanted to know.

I said, 'It's his house. He has a right to decide who enters it.'

'It's my house too,' she said. 'I told him that if he wouldn't let you visit me, I'd leave him – '

'You didn't!' I said, staring at her. I knew that she'd been upset on my behalf at what he'd said, but I didn't think that she would consider it worth the tension of challenging him head on. 'Really? And he wasn't angry?'

She grinned and said, 'Well . . . I think he was so surprised he didn't know what to say!'

I laughed at that and we talked about loyalty. But a silent track of thoughts ran alongside our conversation, in my head, as we talked. However much my brother had insulted me that day, I was also grateful to him.

He had done me a favour. He had performed a social version of the Mirror Test on me. With his brutal, bruising words, he had held up a mirror to me of what my behaviour looked like in the eyes of other people, people like himself, for instance, people who lived squarely in the middle of Indian reality. I could see how ungainly I looked, in that unsparing gaze, how utterly out of joint with the world in which I lived.

Raghu's crudeness got through to me in a way that nothing else would have. Staying away from Gai's house and missing the luxuries that I took for granted in it, I recognized that I was getting a taste of what it was like to live outside the sphere of my brother's well-heeled existence. In a dozen lifetimes as a freelancing illustrator I would not make enough money to afford the spacious apartment in an upper-class Bombay neighbourhood like the one in which he lived. I hadn't even thought of it in that light until it was no longer available to me.

I had been living so deeply immersed in my illusions that I hadn't recognized the extent to which I sponged off his attractive lifestyle. I had allowed myself to imagine that it was mine too, until he gave me a crash course in the kind of psychological Siberia I would face if ever I had to fend for myself without the privileges of money. His money. I didn't have any of my own to speak of.

The larger society that swirled around me without quite touching me was one in which I would be expected to want nothing more of life than a conventional marriage, where having healthy children would be considered the height of achievement, where sexual intimacy outside of marriage was considered an abomination known only to subhumans, screen idols and foreigners. Raghu's words had registered like whiplashes upon my self-image but I told myself that I was foolish to allow his harangue to rattle me. Adversity can be turned to use as a toughening agent. I needed to think of what he'd said in that light.

I had grown up wearing the jewelled harnesses that kept me and others like me in our place within our social class. The only time we ever felt our bondage was when we strained against it in the direction of some forbidden pleasure. But eating frugally had apparently caused a change to take place. I had shed weight, literally as well as metaphorically. I was now loose within the harness. My scheme to seek a short-term asylum in Holland was an attempt to slip it off altogether.

According to Piet, most of us experience life as tourists in a museum created by our elders and peers. We record our lives as a succession of blurred and ill-composed snapshots. We are not taught that we can choose what to focus our desire upon. We are rarely allowed to understand the skills of perception and consciousness which is our birthright as human beings.

But applying Piet's ideas to my life was not easy. It meant reversing the habits of self-indulgence and passivity with which I had grown up. I kept wanting to sit back and allow chance to have its way with events. Pushing myself to take the first two steps, going to the guru and moving to El Paradiso, had been difficult enough. Now there was a final step, and I found myself baulking.

In this mood, I made a compromise. I consulted my Tarot cards.

I had a curious relationship with the cards. I had studied statistics as part of my BA in Economics. I knew that according to the elegantly simple laws governing probability, chance was something quantifiable. So whenever I consulted the cards I did so with half my mind sneering and the other half waiting with bated breath. If the results did not appeal to me, I ignored them. If I liked what I saw, I put the cards away, feeling a secret, happy glow.

I took them out now and spread them in the only pattern I knew, called the Mystic Cross. I read them once, twice, thrice and each time I got the same depressing message: GIVE UP THIS PATH! So I put the cards away again, feeling the cool breeze of rationality calm my confused nerves. It was nonsense of course, as I had known all along. Then I asked myself what Piet might think of the cards. Would he approve or disapprove? The side of him that believed in cosmic energies would be attracted. But the side that believed in self-determinism might be contemptuous. The more I asked myself what he might think, the more I felt I needed an immediate answer.

I was in Zero's apartment and it was late in the afternoon. As there was no telephone, if I wanted to speak to Piet, the simplest option was to walk across to Palm View. I entered the quiet lane on which the old house sat, just as Piet also turned into it from the other side. We smiled and greeted one another as if we had planned to meet.

I told him about the cards and he was immediately interested. He saw nothing unusual in believing in probability theory as well as Tarot cards. It was no different, he said, from the way in which mathematicians continue to make accurate calculations despite being aware of irrational numbers such as pi, which do not have a precise value. We made a date. I told him how to find El Paradiso. Then I went back to my twelfth-floor eyrie feeling as if I had accomplished a great deal.

THE THIRD STEP

AT THE TIME THAT I moved to El Paradiso, I had borrowed a cheap cassette recorder from Prashant's room and hooked it up to speakers with the sound quality of 500-gram Nescafé tins. On this machine I played an 'Indo-fusion' tune called *Snowflake* in an endless loop. It had the shallow, boneless quality of music that is created with no context to ground it and it depressed me to acknowledge that I could never hear it, but I wanted to hear it again. I told myself that it was a tune in transition, just as I was a personality in transition. I felt like a yolk sac of ideas, not yet solidified into the substance of a living being. It seemed acceptable to be attracted, in this fluid state, to music which was as artificial as it was sweet.

I deliberately had this music playing in the background on the day that Piet came to have his cards read. I didn't want any false pretences. If audio-saccharine was what I currently wanted to listen to, then I didn't want to hide behind something more sophisticated just to impress my guest.

I read the cards and we talked a bit about fortune-telling. But I wasn't paying much attention to any of what we said. I had a question to ask. I had been rehearsing it in my mind since the time that I invited Piet over. When I finally asked it, I felt like a tightrope walker of the kind who balances three tiers of tutu-clad girls, each bearing a full glass of water on her head, on a pole that he holds in his teeth. 'Piet,' I said, with my own teeth clenched tight to stop them from chattering, 'would you be interested in going to bed?'

He nodded quickly and said, 'Yes!'

It couldn't be right away, of course. We needed to discuss logistics. I asked him what he did about birth control and he blushed to confess that his girlfriends so far had always been on the pill, or claimed to be, anyway. I said I preferred the barrier devices available at any chemist's shop because they were protection against disease as well. We discussed these matters calmly, as if it were the route of an overland journey. In a sense, for me, it was.

I told Piet that there was a chemist's shop in the nearby five-star hotel. I suggested that he should stop by there on his way back to El Paradiso, whenever next he came on a visit. We agreed upon a date.

A few days later Zero gave a party for his friends. The occasion, I realized in some dismay, was Diwali. The sound of exploding firecrackers was building slowly towards the crescendo of unbelievable noise that marked the festival. One of the few ways of surviving it was to throw a party at which the music could be turned up loud enough to drown out the carpet-bombing going on outside. Zero invited me to attend the party, but I declined. It was of course the date assigned for my encounter with Piet. I fretted about this briefly, before deciding that it may even suit my purpose. With a party going on, Zero would hardly have any attention to spare on wondering how I was spending my evening.

I was extremely edgy on the morning of the day, the way I might feel before a tooth extraction or brain-transplant surgery. I had no appetite. I didn't know what to wear. I thought of all the movies in which the heroine dresses up for a special evening and I felt ridiculous just to consider the idea. I believed it was dishonest to pretend to be anything other than what I was, so in the end I wore whatever came most readily to hand, which was jeans and a loose cotton top. I had a brief struggle with perfume: after all, that was also a deception. But I decided in its favour in the end, telling myself that I wore it for my own satisfaction.

The more difficult decision was whether or not to wear my contact lenses.

It comes as a shock to most normally sighted people when they discover what an extraordinary piece of engineering a contact lens is. The hard variety, which is what I wore, is an inflexible plastic cap placed directly upon the front of the eye. In theory it is shaped to suit the precise curvature of the individual wearer's eyes and is supposed to adhere to the moist surface of the cornea snug enough that it cannot be felt. In practice, the first fitting for a lens feels as if a transparent quarter-plate has been clamped down tight upon that most sensitive and delicate portion of the human anatomy. It is a sensation so exquisitely close to pain that only advanced masochists would know the difference.

And yet, within a couple of days of wearing these instruments of refined torture, the sensation fades from consciousness. The twitching jerk which is caused by each blink of the eyes' lids ceases to be noticeable. I got so used to my lenses that I often fell asleep with them on. I normally wore them for fifteen hours at a stretch. The only trouble they gave me was in combination with dust. If a speck of something lodged under a lens, that eye would feel as if it were being raked by a steel spur. Under such circumstances, there was nothing to be done but to tear off the lens, wash it and put it back in, praying that the eye had not been permanently lacerated.

The question of whether to keep my eyes on or off during an encounter of the intimate kind was therefore an important one. Wearing lenses was a risk, because they could so easily slip off, ship dust and get swallowed or inhaled. The option of keeping them on until a general disrobing was in progress was also not attractive. There is nothing seductive or alluring about removing lenses. It is a brisk, mechanical activity on a par with, say, flossing or gargling and I could not, in my endless mental rehearsals of the evening, work in a casual moment when I could lean back languidly and say, 'Ahh . . . excuse me! Mind if I take my lenses out?' – squeeze, pop, squeeze, pop, followed by the washing and storing routine.

In the end I opted for removing them early in the evening so that

I didn't have to think about them again. My eyes had already adjusted to being lenseless by the time I heard the doorbell over the din of the party. I was able to see well enough to find my way across the drawing room and through the crowd of around thirty young people milling about with their drinks and their plates of dinner, to reach the front door and let Piet in. On the way back, it was a relief not to be able to see clearly the startled expressions on a few of the faces as I led my huge guest back across the darkened space, to my room.

Shutting the door was like sealing the airlock on a space capsule, leaving all of the universe to rage outside. It was just after 9.30 in the evening and the sound of the festival was approaching that critical phase when the combination of crackers and the so-called 'atom bombs' formed a continuous wall of violent sound. The air at ground level was sulphurous, but on the twelfth floor it was still relatively clear.

It was the vogue that year for the residents of high-rise buildings to go up to their roof-top terraces and toss lighted bombs down from there. The devices would burst in mid-air, right outside the bedrooms and balconies of other tenants, with a force strong enough to knock canaries off their perches. So after locking the door, I went over and shut both sets of windows. The silence was surprising, like going suddenly deaf. Piet grinned. 'You are nervous, huh?' he asked.

I said, 'It's so obvious?'

He said, 'Not really, no. It's just . . . the situation.' He looked around, shrugging in perplexed amusement. 'The bombardment, the party, the world, the universe . . .' He grinned, again, his expression friendly and familiar. 'It's fonthasthique, huh? Life.'

I told him that this nervousness today was nothing compared to the time when I had asked him. 'I couldn't be sure what you'd say. If you'd said "no" I would have felt like a complete *idiot*!'

He said, 'But it's always possible to tell if someone's interested or not. Just look inside their eyes, huh? If the pupils are dilated, they're interested.'

'But that can happen because the room is badly lit!' I protested. I was looking at him and could see that his pupils were hugely dilated, the same as on the evening of the energy transfer. My room, however, was bright with light. It embarrassed me to look at him now. It was like staring directly into his brain, his every thought exposed and vulnerable.

'It doesn't matter,' he said. He was smiling in a reflexive way, as if the corners of his mouth had been fitted with springs. 'If the pupils are dilated, then the person is feeling receptive, you know? It's the correct state of mind.'

I was starting to feel as if my blood were gradually being transfused with champagne, a light, bubbly sensation, the way I felt when I wanted to giggle uncontrollably. We were both sitting on the floor, leaning against the bed, a respectable distance between us, *Snowflake* was tinkling tinnily in the background. Outside, the muffled detonations of atomic bombs rent the air at ten-second intervals. Piet covered my hand with his and whispered, 'You've heard of atropine?'

I started to giggle. 'Of course. It dilates the pupils,' I whispered back.

He began to giggle too, so that his voice emerged in breathy gurgles. 'So – so I always thought, you know, when I was young, how romantic it must be to be an eye-doctor, you know? Because of all the patients who must feel so relaxed with the atropine in their eyes . . .'

We were both shaking with laughter. It was hard to breathe. He reached around me and put the lights off. 'I think it'll be easier to see when the light is dark,' he said.

We had both read Carlos Castaneda's account of his experiences while training to be a Yaqui sorcerer.

'Did you believe what he said? In that book?' I had read only one, *Journey to Ixtlan*, having picked it up to read on a train journey from Bombay to Calicut, thinking that it was science fiction. But it was weirder than science fiction, it was hallucinatory. By the time we reached the terminal stop, I was ready to float off the train and drift across to my parents' house in a fit of transrational magic. It was extremely annoying to find that I had to use my feet to get down from the train. Peyote and a teacher were both necessary to enter the world described by the author. I had felt vaguely cheated.

'It doesn't matter,' said Piet, 'even if he is making it up. It's fonthasthique. I really like what he says. It's very . . . free.' He wasn't finding the word he wanted. 'It pulls the edges of the mind this way and that. You read it and you feel *yes*! *Very yes!*' He grinned. His face opened up hugely when he smiled, like a great light.

DEPARTURE

I WENT FOR ONE more session at the guru's. I had accepted a commission to copy a portrait of Mumtaz Mahal from a Mughal miniature as an oil painting for some nameless restaurant in Dubai. I never normally agreed to do such work, but it was the only way I could earn the 5,000 rupees I needed to buy foreign exchange for the journey. I botched the painting, but was paid for it anyway. I had just been to the bank and withdrawn the cash in crisp 1,000-rupee notes, as large as doll's house bedspreads, on the morning that I went to the guru.

It was a quiet session, that last time. I stared at the old man, guessing that I would not see him again, but he did not look back at me or notice me in any way. The topic for the day was 'watching the cobra'.

The translator Mr Sukhatme was in form that day and did most of the talking. I found him an annoying man, smug with his own self-importance. According to him, the correct way to address the distractions that arise in life is to imagine that one is sitting in front of a swaying cobra, within its strike range.

'You must neither run away from nor towards the cobra. You cannot. If you move so much as one single hair, it will strike. It will neither move an inch nor take its eyes from you, because then you might strike it. So there is nothing to do but' – here he held up his right forearm, with the fingers of his hand cocked forward to mimic the hood of a cobra, and waved it hypnotically from side to side – 'watch the cobra. Watch it. Don't take your eyes from it. Your whole life will depend on the attention you give to that moment. Surrender yourself to that moment.'

Sitting in that room, trying to interpret this idea literally, I found myself sitting in front of not one but two cobras. The first was the money downstairs in my handbag, lying unprotected amongst all the pious footwear of the guru's audience. The second was an event that had taken place a few days after Piet had visited my room. We were together in a taxi and I had reached out to hold his hand. I let it go after a few seconds because it seemed to embarrass him, though he said nothing. It was as if there was an unspoken contract that whatever occurred in the privacy of Zero's should be confined to that space and that space alone. By holding his hand in the cab, I was breaking the contract.

Why should I mind? I believed that my friendship with Piet was above such petty, earthbound conventions as emotion. But listening to Mr Sukhatme drone on about cobras, with his forearm swaying hypnotically, I had to recognize that I was feeling unhappy. A grey depression had been seeping into me for a while, brought into focus by this talk about cobras.

I refused to think that it was because I was feeling rejected or marginalized. I told myself that the reason I minded being kept a secret was that it loosened my claim to reality. If no one except Piet and myself knew about the time we spent alone together, it would mean that those passages of my life would vanish from the record of fact as completely as the pedestrians who fade out from a time-lapsed photograph of a busy city street. Just thinking of it made me feel myself becoming transparent. Was this the reason that secrets are so rarely kept? Because one or other of a pair of conspirators does not suffer the cloak of invisibility gladly?

It annoyed me to see that however I rationalized my dissatisfaction with the situation, I could not accept it lightly. The aim of all meditation is to clear the mind of distracting thoughts whereas I found that the more thoughts I cleared out, the less control I had over the few thoughts that remained inside. By the end of the session, my mind was writhing with cobras, time-lapsed photographs and slender brown hands reaching into my handbag in the room beneath the one in which we sat.

When the session was over, I rushed downstairs to check my handbag. The money was intact.

On the way home, in a taxi, we offered one of the other members of the audience a lift to his hotel. He was from Mauritius and spoke English with a strong French accent though from his appearance he could easily have been mistaken for an Indian. He was wearing shorts and had been ticked off by the guru for exposing his legs. He said he thought it strange that an unworldly man was concerned about such trivial matters as clothes and exposed skin. He couldn't believe it had any relevance to the search for eternal truth.

Japp said, 'Ah – but there *is* no relevance! To anything!'

Piet said, 'It's just *maya*, of course – including your discomfort. Don't hold on to it.'

I said, 'If clothes are really trivial, then it shouldn't matter to you either way.' The Mauritian looked unconvinced and got off, still shaking his head.

I met Piet once again, over tea at Palm View. I had gone over to say goodbye and we took leave of one another in a friendly, non-committal way. I promised to write to him from the US. We exchanged addresses and I told him I would inform him of my dates and travel plans, once I had a better idea of them myself. He said he would look forward to meeting me again. My last sight of him in Bombay was of him poring over the forms in multiplicate for shipping his pre-war motorcycle to Holland. We laughed over the spelling of Harley Davidson. 'Harvey Davior-ghem ROLL!' said Piet.

I met Japp once more too, walking moodily back towards Palm View.

He had taken temporary lodgings in a seedy nearby guest-house in his effort to escape Piet, he said. 'He's too much sometimes. He makes his teeth to . . .' grinding his own alarmingly, 'so, at night. He keeps me totally awake. I had to get away.'

Then he grinned. 'But from the big Dutchman I fell into the arms of the liddle brown rats!' Japp said that whenever he walked in a crowd of Indians, he felt he was surrounded not by humans but little brown rats. I knew that Japp liked to solicit strong reactions to what he said, but I did not feel like obliging him on that occasion by saying that I found this description insulting. In any case, I didn't particularly. Rats are warm-blooded mammals just like us. They are also sociable like us, and live in teeming, congested colonies. Like some of us. Despite their small size, they could wreak terrible damage and they were, in their own way, invincible. It wasn't difficult to see why a very tall man might feel that swarms of short brown people were rat-like and why they terrified him, which he said they did. 'But I must *confront my fears, ja?*' he said. 'I must *watch the cobra*. So I must live amongst the liddle brown rats. I must DROWN in them.'

Here he imitated the expression of someone vanishing down the drain of a sink, his watery blue eyes bugging out, the vast tongue extruded like a chunk of ham. 'I am getting used to it. Almost, I enjoy it.' He smiled again and shrugged. 'When you come in Holland I can tell you if I survive or not!' I had told him of my travel plans. Neither he nor Piet could know how precarious these plans were or how differently conceived from the excursions they made when they travelled.

When I bade him goodbye he hugged me with an unexpected show of emotion and said that he was glad to have known me, adding, 'For a liddle brown rat, you are . . . not too bad!'

I bought my foreign exchange, got Emigration Permit Not Required stamped in my passport to distinguish myself from the uneducated labour seeking highly paid enslavement in the Middle East, and had my booster shots against cholera, typhoid and deportation. Late one Saturday night, I boarded the Air India jumbo that would take me to New York.

NEW YORK

ARRIVAL

IT WAS A BAD FLIGHT. Either the aircraft was under-pressurized or my sinuses were over-filled. Whatever the reason, the result was that as the plane began its descent towards its halt at Dubai, a sensation like forked lightning cracked across my skull. Just a flicker and then it was gone. I was inclined to pay no attention to it, hoping that it was a temporary spasm. But it wasn't. Each time it recurred it lasted a little longer and became a little worse.

I didn't know what to do, because I had no precedent to follow. I had been on long flights before this one with no previous experience of pain. Now my skull felt as if it were coming undone at the seams. The seat-belt sign was on, and everyone around me was facing forward with that expression of rigid attention which air passengers adopt when they wish to convince themselves that only by remaining at full psychic alert will they be able to bring the cigar-shaped flying coffin in which we all sat safely to the ground. Meanwhile I could only wonder whether blood would start seeping through the cracks which were undoubtedly developing under my scalp or whether it would gush directly out of my ears like twin scarlet fountains. By the time we landed in Dubai, I was surprised to find that I was still alive. My ears felt as if they had been stopped up with huge wads of cotton. While the rest of the passengers twinkled about the duty-free shops on wings of greed, I clutched my head and fretted about the remainder of the journey. It annoyed me to think that my scheme for dying at thirty and being recycled by sharks or tigers was being sabotaged by the incompetence of some anonymous aircraft maintenance crew.

We reboarded the flight and took to the air once more. The pain had receded, but I guessed that it was connected to descent. That meant that the landings in London and New York were going to be grim. When the hostesses came around with a pre-dawn snack I fell on mine with the hunger of one who understands that this may be her final meal. Pushing aside all memory of my diet, I ate the styrofoam eggs and the leatherized sausages, washing the lot down with three cups of the scalding dishwater which went by the name of coffee. At the end of this feast, I felt a cola-hued depression settle upon my spirit.

Suspended here, between my recent past and my immediate future, I finally felt appalled at the unseemly twists I had introduced into my otherwise sedate and placid life. I couldn't account for the shifts in my behaviour. Perhaps if I had always been a tempestuous character, given to wild and unpredictable rages against conformity, it would have seemed less surprising. But I thought of myself as an even-tempered, easy-going, harmless sort of person with only two minor quirks in that I was opposed to marriage and was planning an early death for myself. I believed that any quirk was minor if the only person to be affected by it was the one who had it. Having decided that I, being plain of face and figure, should not expect entanglements of the sensuous or romantic kind in my life, I could not understand what had overtaken me in the past few weeks.

I tried reminding myself that I was pursuing a philosophical enquiry into the nature of reality. But here, up in the air, disengaged as I was from earthbound illusions, I saw that by any independent observer's reckoning I was immersed in a sleazy romance complete with self-delusions, deceitful behaviour and a tall, dark – well, relative to Japp – stranger. I couldn't even point to a lecherous villain: I had not been seduced or victimized. I had acted out a plan devised entirely by myself, and it was idiotic, witless, worse than any fiction.

It was painful, from this perspective, to recall that there was a time, not so long ago, when I seriously believed that private lives could be conducted with the same sense of responsibility and decorum as, say, a business partnership. Individuals entering a relationship had only to define their terms and sign on a dotted line. Based on the understandings contained within each private contract, partnerships could be as sedate or as racy as their partners wished to make them.

I had heard of people who had worked out legal contracts to include multiple relationships within the terms of their otherwise conventional marriages. A friend told me how he had once been propositioned by a couple he met on a train. The woman said that she was attracted to him and that if he was equally attracted to her, they could go to bed on the condition that her husband be provided with a female partner for the night. I thought this was fair and decent, though I wondered how often it happened that four people could be found who were all mutually and equally attracted to one another. My friend said he mumbled something about having to get off at the next station.

I didn't think it was morally wrong to be attracted to several people at once. Life is short and who can say when and why a person might find delight in someone else's arms? It seemed ridiculous to think that any person could know in advance who would be an ideal companion. But, for myself, since I was not planning to live very long, multiple desires and their attendant problems seemed like a tedious waste of energy.

Therefore my personal contract was headed by the item 'No Marriage' followed immediately by 'Sexual Fidelity'. I would only ever have one partner at a time. In case he or I became interested in someone else, we were each free to terminate our relationship by making a straightforward statement of intent. If it could be signed and sealed by a witness, that would be good and if a month's notice was given that would be ideal. In my opinion, the major source of anguish in human relationships lay in the breaches of contract that occurred, which was why I disapproved of them. I felt that there was no place for anguish in human lives and that we should all live with the aim of reducing to the minimum the need for experiencing or causing anguish.

For this reason, I had defined my idea of fidelity in careful terms. It included the upholding of beliefs shared in common. If I and Prashant had decided to become vegetarians, for instance, then I would consider it disloyal on my part to sneak off and eat steak. If I ate that steak in the company of another person, especially another man, it would compound the crime. If the person in whose company I ate the steak was someone whom Prashant disliked or disapproved of, so much the worse. And all of this, I explicitly stated, was true in reverse for me.

Like so many people before me who had tried to set up an orderly theoretical system into which the disorderly real world refused to fit, I had not easily found boyfriends who fell in with my ideas. Either they considered the notion of a contract too fussy to be worth a moment's attention or else the contracts they proposed were cramping and unappealing to me. Prashant was the only one who took an amused but tolerant view and said that whatever was good for me was good for him. We didn't actually have anything written down, but it had all been discussed.

Why then, I asked myself on the flight from Dubai to London, holding my skull together with my bare hands, why, why, why had I chosen to break my own so sincerely held beliefs? What did it all mean? How could I face Prashant now? I couldn't tell him the truth. I was sure of that. I could not stomach the idea of telling him that I had waged a cool-headed and precisely calculated campaign to go to bed with Piet, including taking the room in Zero's flat for that purpose, including taking one month longer to fly to the US and including finding reasonable arguments to account for all my actions.

Even if I could convince Prashant that what I felt for Piet was not romantic desire at all, but a fascination related to the search for cosmic truth and even if he found some satisfaction from such a thought, which he needn't after all, I knew that the more damaging kind of betrayal had been in my willingness to make him waste one month of his precious leave by going ahead of me. That was the kind of callousness that made parallel relationships so difficult to sustain. There would always be some system of priorities and there would always be someone who lost in relation to the one who gained. In this case, it had been Prashant, my companion of almost three years, who had lost in relation to Piet, an acquaintance of a mere two months.

There were no comforting answers to be found anywhere on that flight.

We began the descent to London and my head began to split again. There was a halt of three hours and then we boarded a fresh plane. I hoped that it was better pressurized, but I wouldn't know until we began the approach to J.F. Kennedy Airport. The movie for the transatlantic flight was *On Golden Pond* but when I plugged my earphones into my armrest, the audio I got was out of phase with the video on screen. I was feeling too exhausted to complain about it, not realizing that I only needed to change the channel to suit the section of the cabin in which I had been seated. So I saw the whole film listening to the dialogue two seconds ahead of the action, giving me a clairvoyant's view of events. When it was over, and the air hostess came around to ask 'Veg? Non-veg?' for the final pre-landing snack, I found myself pausing two seconds before answering, 'Non-veg, please – '

The plane circled in the air for an hour before landing. I could practically see the seams of my skull pulsing like neon lights. By the time we disembarked from the plane I was quite deaf. Aero-bridges were new to me, but I noticed the novelty with detachment, as if being unable to hear had muffled my thoughts. Even written words seemed to be unintelligible. The outside temperature was 6° Fahrenheit, but the interior of the airport was heated like a sauna. We were herded through corridors like hospital chutes, rectangular in cross-section, with no windows or artwork to relieve their bland, pastel-coloured monotony. I thought the signage was unusually terse: IMMIGRATION> US NATIONALS>ALIENS>. I had never been referred to as an 'alien' before. But in my hearing-impaired state, it seemed quite fitting. I felt entirely non-human.

At the immigration desk, the queues moved briskly, except when the arriving passenger was someone with a language disability. The old lady ahead of me, for instance, was an Indian, who spoke in a gobble-tongued dialect unrecognizable to me. Her cheeks were fallen-in with age and her head wobbled on its neck. She wore a shiny blue son-in-the-US windcheater over a widow's white cotton sari. The immigration officer was bullying her, though he called her 'madam', wanting her to explain where she had boarded the flight. She kept repeating a formula of words and then, after a point, began to say '*Hanh?*' meaning 'What?' until he got exasperated and waved her through.

When I got to him, the officer held out his hand wordlessly for my passport, ticket and the immigration slip. Then, to my surprise, he asked to see my handbag. I gave it to him, but added, in a voice which I hoped sounded like that of a deaf alien in a bad mood, 'Why? Why d'you want to see my handbag?'

He was a middle-aged man, with a shining bald head and rimless glasses. He looked up now with an expression of mild amusement and said, 'To see if you . . . ah . . . have anything hidden in here . . . ah . . . which tells me something different to . . . ah . . . what you've told me in your . . . ah . . . immigration form.' My handbag was the kind that had everything in it short of a minibar. He peered into it, then fished out a packet of letters and the bulging wallet that occupied more than half the available space. He slid the letters out gently, like someone handling containers of nitro-glycerine. As he riffled slowly through them, he asked, in a soft, careful voice, 'So. This izhyour . . . ah . . . first visit? To the US?'

I said, 'Yes.'

'And . . . ah . . . the purpose of your visit?'

I said, knowing that he expected me to say that it was tourism, 'To see my sister.'

He looked up and said, 'You've come all this way here just to be with your sister?'

'Yes,' I said.

'Not planning on doing any tourism?' he asked.

'No,' I said.

'Not even a little?' he asked.

'No,' I said.

'Florida's kinda nice,' he said, 'at this time of year. You should consider it.'

I said, 'I hate being a tourist.'

'How long do you plan to stay?'

'Three months,' I said.

'Are you married?'

'No,' I said.

'Do you have any . . . ah . . . boyfriends?'

'Yes,' I said. 'Two. An Indian one in the US now, visiting with my sister. And a Dutch one who's in Bombay just now, though he normally lives in Holland.'

The officer grinned and said, 'You're telling me too much!'

I said, 'Yes, I know. But I need to confess about this to someone. No one else knows.'

'Are you a Catholic?' he asked.

'No,' I replied. 'I always envied the Catholics being able to confess their sins. I have lots of things I'd like to confess.'

'Anything you wanna confess about immigration?' he asked, looking hopeful. 'Plans to become an illegal immigrant, maybe? Marry a citizen just to get a green card?'

'Oh no,' I said. 'I don't want to live here. I don't even want to live in Holland. It's a visit, that's all.'

While he'd been speaking to me, he had been scrolling through my letters. Two American airmail forms from Radzie caught his attention, but they immediately confirmed what I had told him. He turned to my wallet. It was a gift from Radzie, a sturdy American bill-fold-cum-coin-purse and credit-card holder. I had used the see-thru plastic of the card-sleeves to store a few favourite photographs. The first one showed Radzie holding her daughter up for the camera. The second one showed my brother-in-law, Radzie's husband Tim, also holding up their daughter. The third showed Prashant looking spaced out and the fourth one was of me, as a three-year-old child.

It was an old black and white picture, taken with my father's Leica, and featured me at my pudgy worst, wearing a satiny party skirt, of the traditional Kerala pavada variety, which I was apparently unhappy to be wearing because I was holding it away from myself as if it had been made from stinging nettles. My forehead was puckered, my eyes were full of tears and my mouth was drawn back in the position preliminary to a wail.

The officer asked me to explain who each person in the photographs were. When he came to my picture and I explained who it was, he grinned again and said, 'Hhh! See those dimples?' I started to protest that I didn't have dimples and that I was not smiling in that picture. But he stopped me and said, 'That's what I'd like to see now – those dimples!' Then, feeling pleased to have scored a point by making me look up in surprise, he stamped my passport and sent me on my way.

SIGHTSEEING

PRASHANT HAD COME TO the airport to collect me. With him was a burly man whose skin was the texture and colour of a dried tobacco leaf. 'Hi!' he boomed, holding his hand out to me, as Prashant made introductions. 'I'm Moody!' Prashant had already told me about the friends with whom he was staying in New York. They were Indians whose name had been Mody at the time they left Bombay but in their new incarnation, they had added an additional 'o' to make themselves accessible to the natives. 'But you can call me Bob,' he bawled into my ear, as if guessing that I had been deafened by the flight. 'Short for Bharat – you know? It means India, back in India – sorry! I get so used to saying that, you know?' I nodded dumbly, wishing that I were a little more deaf.

It was 11 at night. All the way to the car, Prashant walked with his arm awkwardly around me as if to ensure that I would not drift away in the faint powder of snow materializing silently out of the low clouds overhead. We were both wearing winter clothes to which we were not accustomed so we could only progress slowly, like participants in a three-legged race. Bob had commandeered my luggage trolley and was sprinting away with it towards the car park. I was too dazed to take any decisions.

Bob insisted that we must 'See the sights!' on our way to his Manhattan apartment, so he took us racing along interminable tunnels and streets till I was dizzy with the speed and the flashing lights. Prashant was sitting in the rear, leaning forward so that his face was close to mine between the two front seats. I was not used to seat belts in cars and felt as if someone had strapped me into the seat of a Cinerama theatre, with images of a Martian landscape careening along on either side of me. Traces of motion sickness flickered at the edge of consciousness. Bob kept calling out the names of famous landmarks, 'There's the Tiddley-Poo!' he would say, or 'Look at the Fiddley-om-Pom!' but none of it was registering.

I knew that I was being expected to crane my neck around to look at the buildings on either side of the avenue we were on so that I could feel blinded with awe at this display of raw wealth and power expressed in gargantuan statements of concrete, glass and steel. But I didn't want to be blinded. I didn't like being struck over the head with a cultural sledgehammer. I wanted to feel at home.

The America I knew was a cosy place where moms baked cookies all day long and left them out on kitchen window sills to cool so that little boys called Beaver could come by and steal them. Dads came in from unseen offices, tiptoed gingerly on newly waxed floors and went up the stairs to a bedroom in which there would inevitably be twin beds with a chaste little round-bellied reading lamp on the bedside table in between. It was a place where dolphins called Flipper talked in chirruping squeaks and dogs called Rin-Tin-Tin, 'Rinny' for short, had thrilling adventures every week. One's next-door neighbour might have a talking horse called Mr Ed or else might be a cute suburban witch who could work magic with a sideways twiddle of her upturned nose. A place where a pregnancy was confirmed from the moment that the heroine, with a wondering look on her face would say, 'Honey? I – I feel like eating some pickles and ice cream!'

I could sing the theme song from *Gilligan's Island* and perform *The Addams Family* signature tune complete with finger-clicks and weird groans. I could narrate the histories and relationships of *Bonanza, Lost in Space, The Donna Reed Show, The Lucy Show, Gunsmoke, The Legend of Jesse James, The Patty Duke Show, My Favourite Martian*, on and on. But that place to which those stories belonged was nowhere visible. Instead, we were looping in and out of streets between the gigantic buildings as if we were riding in a mechanical dust-mite, dodging between the fibres of a cosmic carpet. Around us hurtled other dustmites just like the one we were in, with their windows tight-sealed against the weather.

Then we came to an open area and Bob announced, 'Rockerfellah Plazzah! Site of the world's biggest Christmas tree!' and stopped. He wanted me to get down from the car and worship at this shrine of shrines. I opened the door on my side of the car, leaned out and threw up. Without even undoing my seat belt.

Bob drove straight home after that, convinced that the police would arrest me, us, the entire Indian 'communidy' for this shameful third-worldly use of public spaces. 'Mind you,' he added as an afterthought, 'mind you . . . they'd behave differently if you were white, you know? Oh ya. Racist? You wouldn't believe.'

I said, 'Really?'

Bob said, 'Oh ya. They say it's a free sociedy but . . . I can tell ya – it's naad!'

'Would you say it's better or worse than in India, where we have a friendly neighbourhood system called caste?' I asked. Prashant, who recognized the tone in my voice, lightly tapped my head. He wanted me to shut up.

Bob said, 'Oh ya. Ya. I mean, sure, there's no, like, *caste* here, so it's not like you can't go up and touch some guy who's cleaning the streets, buuuuut . . . y'know – the small things. I can't, y'know, f'r instance, jus' build a temple in the middle of the street, if I wanned. A church, maybe. But naad a temple.'

'A temple is hardly a small thing,' I said.

'You're not feeling very well, are you, Manj?' said Prashant.

To Bob he said, 'She's not feeling well. Jet lag.'

'It's not jet lag,' I said. 'It's brain damage. The aircraft wasn't pressurized. Because we have such a free society back home, you know? The maintenance crew were free to be incompetent. Now my skull has cracked into bits and my brain has leaked out.'

To this, Bob gave a startled snort and said, 'Oh ya?' and Prashant said, 'We're almost home.'

They lived in a structure that I never managed to see the top of. Bob drove into a parking garage and we walked up a ramp from there to the lobby of the building and then took a lift to the tenth floor. Every surface was carpeted. Bob and Prashant lugged my two heavy suitcases, while I carried an equally heavy sling bag and handbag.

In their apartment, the lights were blazing and the heating was turned up high enough to singe my eyebrows as we entered. Bob's wife Lolita ('Call me Lolly!') opened the door. She was wearing an orange silk caftan and was brightly made up, gold winking from her ears and neck and wrists. 'What took you so laaang?' she wanted to know.

Bob explained that he had tried to show me the big city, but alas I 'barfed up' on Rockefeller Plaza so they had to cut short the tour. 'Piddy,' he said, sympathetically. 'It's the best time of day to see the ciddy. At night.'

'Aww! Poor baby!' said Lolly. 'C'mon in and eat something!' The apartment was spacious, with a split-level drawing room. Bob was earning well. He was a senior executive in the American parent company of Prashant's ad agency. My battered old-fashioned suitcases sank into the white pile of the carpet on the floor looking like ancient relics. The wallpaper had a pattern of white-on-white velvet swirls alternating with silvery hearts. The sofa 'set' was covered in white leather with sheepskins draped over it. Brass accents peopled the room with Ganeshas and dancing Shivas. There was the inevitable tiger skin on the floor, snarling at the television set. I myself felt like a relic dredged up from the bottom of the Olde Worlde in my jeans and hand-knitted grey sweater, my thin-soled Bata sneakers and thick socks.

Lolly was inviting us to leave my things where they were and follow her into the dining room. But Prashant was pulling on my arm, insisting that I follow him into the room that had been assigned to us. I said I needed to wash. 'Ya, but come soon!' called Lolly to us. 'Food's getting cold awready!'

Inside the room, Prashant said, in a hissing whisper, 'What's the matter with you?'

'I told you,' I said. 'I'm brain damaged. And also, I'm deaf. It's just like the lady said at the lecture I went to at the Institute for the Deaf in Bombay – being unable to hear is a greater disability than being unable to see – I can't understand anything happening around me because I can't *hear* the world . . .' I started to tear off my clothes. 'Also I'm feeling so hot I'm going to explode if I don't take all my clothes off . . .' I had a caftan in my sling bag and I put it on. 'Also, every surface of this apartment has been covered in fuzz. Did you notice? It's like that fur-lined teacup in the MOMA catalogue. The walls, the ceiling – '

'Shut up,' said Prashant, shaking me lightly by the shoulders. 'It's their house and we're their guests. You can't be rude like this – '

'I can't help it. I'm feeling sick. I'm feeling choked – ' But Lolly was knocking on the door, 'C'mon, you guys – can't wait forever!'

So we went out.

The dining table was groaning under the load of the food set out on it. Lolly handed us dinner plates the size of cartwheels. Lolly said, 'I don't usually cook Indian, but I know how much you guys miss home-food when you come out . . .'

I wanted to cry. I hate eating Indian food away from India. It seems to entirely neuter the purpose of travelling. There were three kinds of curry, rice enough for a small army, dal enough to swim in. In addition there was spaghetti with meatballs in tomato sauce, a deep bowl of Russian salad, dahi raita and a glass dish with parathas in it. And there was lasagne. And Pringles chips. And an avocado dip. 'Just something simple,' said Lolly, 'to settle your tummy – come on! You go first, Manjoo! You'll feel better with something inside you!'

The calories on that table would have been enough to heat a small township in Siberia. I felt I was putting on weight just by breathing in the smell of the food, as if the fat was evaporating off it and into the air. Even my free-sized caftan was feeling tight. I gripped the cartwheel given to me by Lolly, trying to firm up my resolve to announce that I was on a diet and therefore could not afford to remain in the presence of such food for even five minutes, but my will failed me. Enfeebled by my journey, my self-doubts and the deafness, I succumbed to the beams of high-energy hospitality being aimed in my direction. *Just this once*, I told myself and dug into the rice.

When we had piled our plates high, Lolly took us to sit in front of the TV. 'This condo has its own in-house cable operator – he's Indian! So we see all the latest films from home. You name it, we've seen it,' she said with pride. 'And we've got them taped . . .' She patted the belly of the brass chest on which the TV stood.

That night's film had already started. There were two rival gangs of bandits. There were hideously evil police inspectors. There was a hero who was too fat to move fast in his white jeans so he got captured. There was his dog, who was a witness to everything. The dog ran off to befriend the chubby young heroine, whose school-going age was symbolized by the length and thickness of her plaits, at odd variance with the matronly bosom burgeoning out of her uniform. The dog stared deep into the girl's eyes to communicate that the hero was in trouble. Homework forgotten, she dashed off to save the Beloved Behemoth.

The pace of the film grew ever more frantic. I found I had eaten two more cartwheels of food before the climax, which occurred during a festival at a temple in which the idols came to life and slew the villains whenever the opportunity arose. At the end, of course, the heroine was restored to the hero. The dog, who had almost drowned while saving the heroine's father from a tidal wave, had been given the kiss of life by another dog. And the corrupt police inspectors had been turned into temple gargoyles, doomed to stand forever in the blazing sun with their tongues hanging down to their feet in thirst.

'Ice cream?' said Lolly as the final credits rolled. I was stupid with food. I nodded. I had a mental image of the stern custodian of my diet, wearing a trim red jacket and white jodhpurs, standing in the pit of my stomach, screaming instructions to my mouth to stop stuffing itself – but in vain. The tide of food entering my stomach slowly silenced that shrieking voice until I could no longer hear it. In the silence that ensued, there was only the familiar glug-glug-glug of food in transit. I ate until the silence within and the deafness without were in perfect balance. Feeling like a blimp with a thin film of consciousness printed on its outer surface, I waddled over to the bed in the guest room, threw back the comforter with its design of prancing lambs and fell into a bloated sleep.

A MUGGING

AT 7 O'CLOCK IN the morning, Prashant wanted to wake me up so that we could leave the house with Bob, who had a meeting across town and had offered to give us a lift along the way to 'wherever'. But I mumbled that I had to catch up on my sleep or risk being a zombie for the rest of my life. I could hear Bob and Lolly in the background, moving about their flat in preparation for an extended expedition. Prashant warned that if I didn't come I'd be alone in the house till late in the evening because it wouldn't make sense for him to be zigzagging back and forth across the city. I buried my head deep in the pillow and said that I didn't care. He said, 'What'll you do for food?' I said I didn't want to eat. Lolly yelled from the open door of the room that there were 'laaads of leftovers!' and that I was to help myself from the fridge.

Then they all went out and there was a blissful silence in the house.

I slept.

My normal cycle was six hours of deep, unbroken sleep and then another two in which I had dreams. I regarded my dreams as a bonus from my psyche, because they were invariably smooth, pleasing and stress-free. Even if they were about dragons and nuclear war, I could usually manipulate them so that they ended on a positive note and I could wake up feeling refreshed. But in New York my dreams had a purpose. I was desperate to smooth away the unnatural suddenness with which reality was shifting around me. I dreamt in order to blot out the uncertainties and doubts, sinking into a moist, sweet-scented well of soothing images and associations in which the only events that occurred were enjoyable ones.

These dreams were like films in which the main characters were Piet and myself. First I dreamt of all the many moments of contact and conversation that I had already shared with him. Then I dreamt of all the stages by which I would meet him again, in Holland. I imagined the conversations we'd have. The places we might visit, the things we might do. I imagined the moment when we'd meet again, what his face would look like, what words we would use to greet each other. I was not actually unconscious but I lay in bed with my eyes shut, and, like a film editor at a Movieola machine, I could cut and splice the existing footage of my memories, sometimes to make new scenes, other times to prune and refine scenes that had already occurred.

Of course, until I had actually left Bombay, I could always top up my stock of live-action shots by going across to meet Piet in Palm View. But in New York, there were only the beguiling pictures in my head. In many ways they were better than reality, because I could restrict what I saw to what I wanted to see. So long as my eyes were shut, I could see and hear Piet, I could smell him and feel him, to the exclusion of anything else. Then I would open my eyes, look around and tell myself that I was mad to imagine that I could ever escape the furry, heated, padded-cell triteness of rooms such as this one to the limitless freedoms suggested by Piet's world.

If I tried, for instance, to project the mental image of my Dutch friend within the room I was in, I couldn't manage it. He simply shimmered and faded out amongst these soft, nursery-room colours, the prancing lambs and baby-pink lampshades. I could see a faint, tolerant smile on his face, but he could not speak or act within these walls, not even in fantasy. It was difficult to convince myself of the need ever to keep my eyes open.

It was 2 in the afternoon before I was forced awake by the sound of the telephone. Prashant was calling to say that he'd be home at 4 o'clock and would I please meet him downstairs in the lobby. I got up then, to have a shower. I had not yet been alerted to the fact that there is some law of plumbing which guarantees that in no two bathrooms will there ever be a water-deployment system which is either self-explanatory or the same as any other. Just as soon as I had got used to one system, I would move to another house and have to endure the whole cycle of being scalded, then frozen, then scalded again until I learnt to get the perfect mix of water temperature and pressure. In New York, I stepped into the tub and turned on the bathwater tap by mistake, thinking it was the hand-held shower. I had also misjudged the hot–cold graphic. Consequently, the water that poured out of the tap was like molten lava, cooking my feet instantly.

I leapt up with a yell and dropped the hand-held shower. It didn't break, but it knocked its release valve in such a way as to turn itself on, becoming a snorting, hissing water-canon, with its nozzle set on needle-spray. It slithered in wild, unpredictable trajectories, while I hopped and slid about trying to turn the water off without getting myself entirely sautéed.

I felt I had narrowly escaped with my life by the time I completed my shower. I got dressed and went out of the bedroom. The apartment looked almost the same during the day as it did at night, because Bob and Lolly had heavy shutters on all the windows. Apparently they both suffered from vertigo and couldn't bear to look out. There was spotlight illumination over the plants. The TV had been left on, whispering detergent messages to itself, like the resident genie of the house.

There was a mirror covering the entire back wall of the living room. I hadn't noticed it the night before. Now, catching a glimpse of an unexpected movement from the corner of my eye, I almost had a heart attack, mistaking myself for a burglar.

I turned to look at myself and experienced a powerful moment of déjà vu.

It reminded me of the time that I had first seen myself in the nude.

It happened in the home of a friend from my school days, a princess who lived in her family's city palace in Bombay. I and other classmates had gone to her home to swim in her private pool. In the bathroom, changing out of my clothes, I turned to pick up my suit from where I had put it down and my first reflex was to turn my head away again, in embarrassment. I hadn't seen the wall-sized mirror when entering the room, and for that first second before recognition dawned I had assumed that I had walked in on someone else. I was seventeen at the time and had never yet seen any grown person completely nude, male or female, in the flesh.

I was overwhelmed by complex emotions. I was almost as acutely embarrassed as I would have been if it had actually been one of the other girls. I had seen countless pictures of naked women but it had never occurred to me to look at myself as if I were one of them. This was a very peculiar thought and I didn't know what to make of it.

On the one hand it could mean that I didn't see myself objectified in the way of nude models in photographs. On the other hand it could mean that I had been wandering around for years in a body that I inhabited as if it were a fancy dress belonging to someone else. I lived in it, I bathed it, I dressed it every day and undressed it every night and yet – I had never actually looked at it, neither in mirrors nor just with my own eyes. It was a genuine surprise to find that I looked remarkably similar to those other bodies I had seen in photographs, even though I didn't have the ideal statistics.

At that moment I had stared at myself, feeling a shy sense of recognition and acceptance.

This time, in the Moody apartment, I looked at myself and felt abject hate. The shapeless cold-weather clothes were whatever I had managed to scrape together from Gai's trunk of family woollens. There was never any need for them in Bombay, so they smelt of mothballs and looked as if they had been made by Billy Bunter's couturiers. I had had my hair trimmed just before leaving Bombay and it was plastered down to my forehead in damp strands. Despite all the sleep,

I looked tired and bedraggled. I was wearing an ancient anorak dating from my school days, khaki green and lined with nylon-fur. My jeans bagged at the knee and the cuffs were frayed from being too long. I was wearing long johns underneath them and in the stifling heat of the apartment I could feel my skin already growing scaly and itchy in reaction to the synthetic material.

It shouldn't be like this, I thought. Other people looked at themselves and felt delighted to confirm their existence. Why did I only ever feel disappointed? Quick as thought came the reply in my head, in Piet's voice: if I felt disappointed, it was because I did not take adequate steps to see that I did not feel disappointed. Meaning that I, in some way, willed myself to look disappointing to myself.

I would have liked to whirl around and yell at him, *NO! That can't be true – I'm not willing myself to be unhappy – there are some kinds of unhappiness that are NOT self-created –*

But his voice in my head was not equipped for debate.

Then the doorbell rang and the voice over the intercom told me that Prashant was waiting downstairs in the lobby.

'I've walked all over this part of town,' he said to me when I had left the flat and found my way down to where he was waiting. 'I couldn't get lost if I tried.' It was still fairly warm in the lobby, though cold compared to the interior of the Moody flat.

Holding the street door open for me, Prashant said, 'Watch out for the wind, it's a bit strong today . . .' I stepped out and the air slapped the breath out of my mouth.

I might as well have been wearing sheer muslin, for all the protection I got from the clothes I had on. Prashant said, 'It's not really that cold, but there's a breeze, you know?' The air being channelled between the tall buildings was like a razor, shaving whole layers of skin from my face. I shrank back immediately, drawing the hood of my anorak around me as tight as it would go, saying, 'I – can't! I'm not dressed warm enough!' But it was too late. Prashant had already shut the street door. 'I said we'd wander about till Bob or Lolly gets back,' he said, 'so I don't have a key. Anyway, it'll be good for you! I'll show you what people do here to protect themselves from frostbite . . .'

The grid layout of the streets allowed a measure of protection from the wind whenever we walked in a direction perpendicular to the blast. Even so, I needed to duck into shops every five or six minutes. According to Prashant, the wind-chill factor had dropped the temperature to minus 14 degrees and I should be careful about my ears. He had seen something on TV about it, aimed at unwary tourists. 'Keep touching your ears – when you find there's no sensation, duck into a shop and get the circulation going again. Otherwise – frostbite! From the wind!' According to him, a common complaint amongst new arrivals was the sudden loss of ears, noses and digits to New York's icy gale. I was too cold to ask if he was joking.

I had to keep my eyes almost closed in order to save my lenses from being blown off. And there was another problem. The lens solution I used was not formulated for cold weather. A dry patch kept forming in the central area of each lens. It cleared for a few seconds when I blinked, then gradually reformed, causing a fog to appear right across the primary field of my vision. Prashant had my right arm in his grip and he steered me about while I kept my left hand free for touching my ears. Whenever one of them went blank, we found some establishment to step into. Then I would relax and look around me. In effect, it was like blinking my eyes to find that each time they were open again, we were in a new location. A curious, hallucinatory experience. Finally we stepped into a Barnes & Noble bookshop. According to Prashant, this was where he had been heading all along. 'Isn't it a great shop?' he wanted to know. I was grateful just to be out of the wind.

Everyone had warned us about casual crime in New York. Prashant's response had been to dress in a black leather jacket with matching boots and gloves, with the result that other citizens, mistaking him for an Arab terrorist, edged away if they happened to find themselves beside us on traffic islands. Prashant had told me to bundle my handbag out of sight under my anorak, adding to the multiple lumps of my profile, and warned me against making eye contact with strangers anywhere. In his view I was disastrously trusting and naïve.

But in the shop he left me alone while he sped off to check the shelves for Graphis annuals to take back with him to Bombay. He had not been gone more than one minute before a young black guy standing close to where I was, in the fantasy and science fiction section, suddenly leaned towards me and said, 'Don' be afraid . . .'

My thoughts scattered like pigeons at the approach of a cat. I stared at the boy slack-mouthed with astonishment. How had he managed to pick me out from amongst the crowd of shoppers in that store as being the most likely bet for a mugging? I wanted to congratulate him. I tried to recall any films in which a gory shoot-out takes place amongst stacks of cascading books.

The boy was wearing a dark blue beret and an attractive fawn raincoat with the lapels drawn up high around his ears. He had an earnest expression and big beseeching eyes. He whispered, 'Don' be frightened. Ah'm not gonna hurt you. Ah'm a poor student, ma'am. Ah'm working my way through a college education. But Ah'd appreciate anything you can give me. Anything at all.'

My heart wanted to melt. I was ready to reach into my handbag to peel a precious 10-dollar bill off the thin wad I had brought with me from Bombay. But I was stopped in my tracks by one of those tiny flying demons who feature in Donald Duck cartoons. 'Halt!' said the little demon. 'Are you, titanium-hearted citizen of the Third World, spurner of a thousand lepers, cripples, blind-beggars and starving mothers, actually contemplating giving away 10 dollars of your hard-earned foreign exchange to this – this – scion of capitalism? This young person of unknown merit or conscience, who may or may not knife you in the next five minutes in case you are unable . . .' Etcetera, etcetera.

In order to buy time, I said, 'Urm . . . no! I'm a – a tourist? No foreign exchange?'

The boy blinked rapidly as if unsure whether to shoot me right away or to wait a few seconds in case I changed my mind. I said, 'No cash, really. Sorry.' I felt that he had perhaps made the mistake of thinking that, being coloured, I might be more inclined to be helpful than a white. I felt pleased to think it and briefly considered sharing the information that on the US immigration form I had filled up at the time of disembarking at Kennedy, I had ticked 'black' under the column headed 'Race'. I had always wanted to do this, ever since I had read about US immigration forms, even though I knew that other Indians ticked 'White' or 'Other'. I believed that all people of colour should be willing to show solidarity towards oppressed American blacks by claiming to be black too. I recognized that it was absurd to feel this surge of sympathy for a cause that was just one amongst the many in the world, certainly no better or worse than the wide selection I had to choose from in India. But I had not yet got around to considering the idea that it is easier to sympathize with minorities who live far away than with those who crowd one's doorstep.

The young man backed away slowly, not showing whether or not he recognized that I might have a legitimate reason for refusing his request. He did not take his eyes off me till he could duck out of my sight. I immediately looked around to locate Prashant before someone else tried to accost me. I told him what had happened but when he wanted to report the matter to the shop personnel, I hustled him out. 'Who knows,' I said, 'maybe the boy really was a student.' I wanted to give him the benefit of the doubt.

'He could be a hardened criminal!' complained Prashant. 'You're not doing him or anyone else any favours by letting him go!'

But we were already out of the shop by then. Just as we went out the revolving doors, I caught sight of the blue beret bobbing up close to another customer. A friendlier one, I hoped.

THE MORGUE

BOB AND LOLLY WERE shocked that I was unwilling to see the Statue of Liberty. 'You can't leave New York without visiting the lady!' they insisted. 'It's like going to India without seeing the Taj Mahal!'

'Lots of Indians have never seen the Taj,' I said. 'And besides, I'm still feeling sleepy.'

They thought it was bizarre that I had travelled halfway across the world just to sleep. They wanted me to be up and about, going window-shopping, museum-hopping and getting my money's worth out of my ticket.

I said that I was getting my money's worth from watching TV. 'You don't understand,' I said. 'I spent three years in Bangkok as a kid. I went to an American school. I drank five bottles of Coke a day. I ate Fizzies for lunch. I finished three half-gallon packs of Foremost ice cream a week. And in the evenings I watched American programmes on TV. For me, watching TV is the same as going to see the Taj in India!' In my American school we received regular doses of pro-war propaganda in support of the action in Vietnam. I learnt that communists were blood brothers of the Devil. Unfortunate little countries like Vietnam, I was told, were better off being blasted to Hell than becoming communist devils themselves.

My classmates were the children of American army personnel. From them I picked up an accent that made Donald Duck sound like Masterpiece Theatre. When I was back in India, the girls at my convent boarding school made me feel as if I had a speech defect. In college, my pro-American views were treated with contempt and derision.

The Hollywood movies I liked were regarded as escapist fantasies. Feminist literature showed me the many ways in which American society was riven with paradoxes. My leftist friends showed me how American interventions had caused bloodshed and regional instability in many parts of the world. The newspapers showed me how often the American government sided against India and in favour of Pakistan. And the American media itself was so obsessively self-critical that it was hard to recover the comfortable mythologies with which I had once associated the US.

Bob said, 'I geddit. You don't wanna be a regular tourist. You don't wanna see the regular things.' He said he knew just what would suit my taste. 'Stay right there!' he said to me, leaping up from the dining table where we sat ploughing through the mounds of food left over from the night before. I had eaten three helpings of lasagne and was starting on the biryani, the egg curry and the chicken tandoori. The internal voices which warned that I must either stop gorging or risk regaining all my weight were growing fainter with every passing morsel. There is a certain pleasure in drowning such voices out. My tummy felt warm and round, like a satisfied cat. It was a relief to relax and to allow myself to be carried along on the tide of consumption lapping the room. Then Bob came back, grinning broadly. 'I've fixed it all up!' he said. 'Tomorrow morning – a visit you'll never forget!'

He took us there himself, on his way to work. 'Pick ya up in one and one-half hour!' he said and sped off. The place he had dropped us at was the New York City Morgue. A friend of his was one of the four coroners. Prashant had met him two evenings before my arrival, at a party in Bob and Lolly's house. His name was Dr Pramod Bhatt, a beaming moon-faced person who greeted us, when we were ushered into his office, with the words, 'So? Ready for the morgue?'

He laughed, as he led the way, saying that he had accepted the job just so that he could enjoy the expression on his friends' faces when he delivered that line. 'It's the world's largest facilidy,' he told us, showing us through double swing doors painted a sober green. 'Capacidy for fifty . . . ahhh . . . residents. Air-conditioned rooms, guaranteed peace and quiet! In fact,' he said, hamming like the doorkeeper at the Waldorf Astoria as he opened the next pair of doors, 'none of our guests has every complained!'

We entered a brightly lit space, a bit like a hospital after visiting hours, very still and very cold. The colours were autumnal. All the surfaces, the floor, the ceiling, the metal-fronted locker cabinets which formed the walls around us, gleamed as if they had been recently polished. A block of cabinets filled the middle of the room. There was a tall, silent attendant wielding a long-handled floor-mop like a reaper with a scythe, swiping the floor in slow, meditative arcs. He looked up, smiled a greeting at Dr Bhatt and continued his swabbing.

I had not formed any clear impression of what we were about to see. A notion lingered from something in an encyclopaedia, of a cavernous room in which bodies were laid out like Roman emperors on slabs of marble, covered in drapery. I had never seen a dead body before and wondered whether I would find it unpleasant. I wondered where the marble slabs were and how long it would take to reach the place. A second attendant materialized from around the corner, holding a walkie-talkie out to Dr Bhatt, who acknowledged him and took the handset, while motioning him to show us around.

The attendant smiled and nodded, whispering, 'Hi, I'm Stacey.' Prashant and I whispered, 'Hi,' back in response. Stacey whispered, 'First-time visit?' Then he laughed self-consciously, under his breath, 'Better the first than the last, eh?' He turned, not waiting for our reaction.

There was no preamble. Reaching for the door of one of the locker cabinets, Stacey opened it and pulled out a corpse.

I don't know if I gasped.

The body belonged to a young black man, naked and beautiful as a sculpture in mocha velvet. His face was serene and pure. His eyes were shut and his skin seemed supple, faintly oiled. He may have been asleep and yet the circumstances of our sight of him made that impossible. Only in the presence of death may we stare with such clinical attention at a body. His deadness was so absolute. Stacey had not pulled him out completely, so his modesty had been preserved. His arms were neatly folded and his hands rested just above the navel.

Stacey said, in his low voice, 'A new one. Gunshot wound, left temple.' I saw the wound. Stacey's words echoed strangely in my head. *A new one.* Never to be an old one. No longer someone. An empty casing that had once been known by a name and a family. That had once had friends, lovers, thoughts, dreams and ambitions. 'Nineteen, eighteen, I don' know,' said Stacey, 'a young 'un all right.'

It embarrassed me to be staring so greedily. I felt ghoulish and yet I could not turn my attention off. Wasn't staring the reason that we had been brought there? To look at what is not given to everyone to see, the bodies of strangers to whom we bore no relation?

I wondered if the attendants whispered when they were amongst themselves. I would have liked to have asked them whether they got used to being around these bodies but I felt literally speechless. It seemed indecent to be where we were, looking at dead beings. I wondered if there weren't regulations prohibiting such visits. And, if not, then I marvelled at a country that could afford to showcase even its anonymous dead.

We saw another body – that of an older man, maybe in his fifties. He was white. I noticed something I had never consciously thought of before, that the colour of his skin rendered him more visibly dead than the other man. There was no mistaking the waxy pallor of his nose, eyelids and lips, for anything but what it was, a lack of life. He lay on his back but we could see the empurpled colour of the skin on the underside of his body, where the blood had evidently collected, a sharp demarcation along the whole length of the sides of his arm and chest. Just to see that line was to be reminded that for all the near-supernatural qualities we attribute to the body, in death it is reduced to an intricately wrought container, filled with varying densities of gas and fluid.

The attendant pushed the body back into its locker and, as he did so, the man's left arm twitched. Adrenalin jolted through my system even as, in the same instant, I rationalized the movement as the arm being snagged on the edge of the locker. But it unnerved me. I felt I had seen enough. I wanted to leave. The attendant, who had not noticed my reaction, straightened the arm out with an impatient click of his tongue and pushed the drawer smoothly back into place.

Dr Bhatt had returned to our side. He said, 'Too bad there's no autopsy going on just now, or we could have shown you one – but there's the gas-gangrene room! Wanna step in for a moment?' I said I didn't, hoping that I didn't sound as anaemic as I felt.

The walkie-talkie beeped again. Dr Bhatt listened a moment, then glanced around to locate the wall-mounted intercom. Walking towards it, he mimed to us to look around while he attended to the call.

Stacey steered us towards a room where, he said, autopsies were usually done, though it was empty now. Then he turned, distracted by Dr Bhatt calling to him.

So Prashant and I stood just outside the room, undecided about whether to go in or remain where we were. There was a green-tunicked orderly inside, standing beside an autopsy platform. He looked up briefly from what he was doing and nodded an absent-minded smile in our direction. He was fidgeting with a small bundle of cloth. Turning my head in the other direction I saw a gurney which I hadn't noticed earlier, on the far side of the locker room. There was a mound of white dough lying on the trolley, like pastry awaiting the attention of a chef to pat into shape. Then I blinked and saw that it wasn't dough but the body of a woman, perhaps in her late sixties. Instinctively, I averted my eyes, as I would have had she been alive. But I reminded myself that she wasn't, after all. So I looked again, feeling guilty. Feeling that all curiosity has a measure of the obscene in it.

Dr Bhatt was still talking on the intercom. Prashant had noticed that his shoelace was untied. He bent to tie it. I turned my gaze back into the autopsy room where the orderly continued to stand where he was, fidgeting with a bundle of pinkish cloth. It must have been the quality of his concentration that caused me to stare then, from where I stood, trying to understand what he was doing.

Between his hands the orderly had been gently manipulating a cup-shaped object. It looked as if it was made of plastic. The cup appeared to be in two or three sections which he was trying to fit together smoothly. As I watched, a moment later, it was done and he completed his task. As smoothly as drawing a stocking over a foot, he drew the scalp of a very tiny but deceased baby up over the pliable, empty shell of its cranium. He smoothed the pelt of fine, dark hair down as he drew it taut to the nape of the neck where the skin had been incised.

Without warning, the minute features of a little human face popped up in three dimensions, giving me no time to anticipate it, to defend myself against the shock of seeing it happen.

Bob was right. This was one visit I was never going to forget.

THE PATRIOT

FOOD WAS THE UNIVERSAL punctuator of our days in New York. Breakfast was an exclamation mark. I had two bowls of Cocoa Puffs with full-cream milk and honey, followed up with three fried eggs made by Lolly and six slices of toast each the size of a paperback book, smothered under Skippy's Extra Smooth Peanut Butter and Smucker's Grape Jelly. I finished with melons, strawberries and thick lashings of double cream. And coffee.

For commas, all through the day, there were Cokes, chips and chocolates. Burgers and ice creams were semi-colons. Lunch was a full-colon: if Prashant and I were in, we got Pizza Hut pepperonis or Chinese takeaways to eat while sitting in front of the TV soaking up the local soaps. And at night there was always another exclamation mark in the form of dinner. One time we went to a place called The Blue Lobster, where the beer was served in small kegs with spouts on the side and the steaks were like foam mattresses. Another time we went to Wings of Heaven where every dish had a chicken theme. There was even a chicken-flavoured dessert called Sweet Chick-a-lets in which diced cubes of chicken were soaked in honey and flamed in brandy.

So long as my mind was stopped up with food, I couldn't think. I ate continuously.

Prashant tried to talk to me, but I deflected all attempts at conversation. He might start with, 'Manj? There's something I don't understand . . .' And I would respond with, 'Just hand me a Coke, please?' I wasn't ready to face any discussions. I slept whenever I could and when I wasn't sleeping I watched TV. Prashant laughed uneasily at me, saying that he had never seen this side of my character and I replied that it was because we had never been to America together before. We watched *Star Wars, Close Encounters of the Third Kind, Saturday Night Fever* and *Looking for Mr Goodbar.* Prashant bought seven bottles of different aftershave lotions, saying that it was his way of supporting the consumer industry since he couldn't afford a car or a yacht.

I decided that I hated going shopping because there was always more to buy than my mind could cope with. Going into an art supply store was a nightmare. It was like being a heathen at the gates of Heaven. Looking at the stacks upon stacks of colours, brushes, erasers, pencils, drawing boards, canvas frames, palettes and paper all I could feel was the intensity of my deprivation.

Then it was the weekend and Bob invited 'a few folks' over for dinner. Lolly had someone come in to cater for the evening. The guests were all ex-pat Indians except for one woman, a neighbour, who lived two floors down. She was the same height as me, but widthwise, she dwarfed me. I had already seen a couple of people like this, walking about the streets, people so big sideways that they looked like optical illusions.

Nevertheless, I gravitated towards her like a pigeon in sight of its home-roost. Though I had been in the US over a week, I had not yet had any conversations with real Americans. Her name was Ruth and when she smiled her pale blue eyes almost disappeared from sight. She had blonde hair worn loose over her shoulders.

I wanted to ask her how she came to be her size, wondering whether she had a glandular problem or whether it was the result of food. And, if food, then what kind of food, and did she really eat obsessively and did she enjoy it and did she feel, at the end of the day, that it was worth it and wonderful not to worry about dieting and appearance? But I found that the questions would not form in my mouth. She said, 'Is this your first visit to the US?' I said it was.

'Uh-huh,' she said. 'So . . . how do you like it?'

'I haven't seen very much,' I said. 'It's a big country.' I wondered, as I said it, if the word 'big' was inappropriate in her presence.

'Oh yeah,' she said. 'It's big all right. I hear that India's pretty big too?' I was glad to hear that she was willing to say the word.

'Ermm,' I said, 'of course size isn't everything.' But maybe she thought it was? It was so hard to know what she might think, what might upset her or make her feel she was being ridiculed! Was it possible that she was unconscious of her proportions? Was there any chance that she had grown up magically unaware that her shape was considered unlovely? Was it possible that she, when she saw herself in mirrors, preened and smiled as if the vision gave her pleasure?

I couldn't contain my thoughts about her physical size within a polite and friendly corral. My mind seethed with unkind epithets, such as 'human beach ball' and 'Michelin Woman'. It embarrassed me acutely to acknowledge my intolerance. It made me feel that there was no hope for the human race if I, who actively supported liberal causes and who considered myself unpleasantly fat, could be distracted to the point of incoherence merely because the person I was speaking to was larger than usual. I felt relieved that I only had another five and half years left to live.

'So . . . ahhh . . . are you related to Bob and Lolly?' she asked.

I said, 'No, I'm with a friend of theirs.' I pointed across the room. 'That's Prashant. We both live in Bombay. He works in a company which is associated with Bob's company.'

'Ohh,' she said, 'he's your husband – '

'No!' I countered. 'We're not married.'

'That's sweet!' said the lady. 'You know – I went touring with my fiancé too, and it was the *best time we ever had*!' She said the last words in a whisper, leaning close to me, conspiratorially. I saw the pupils of her eyes suddenly widen out and was reminded of what Piet had said about pleasure and increased pupil width. I could feel myself blushing with the intimacy revealed by her remark.

I was dying to ask if she had been as large then as she was now.

And, if so, what kinds of beds would accommodate persons of astonishing girth? Was her partner the same size or less? And was it more or less difficult, depending on which? Instead I said, 'Oh – he's not my fiancé!'

A faint crease appeared on her brow. 'Oh?' she said. 'Then . . . what . . . ?'

I said, 'I don't believe in marriage.'

'Awwww,' said Ruth. 'Isn't that so sweet? I was like that too, once. You'll git over it though. It's a passing phase – '

A voice said, 'What's a phase?' It was one of the other guests. I had already been introduced to her, a short pugnacious-looking woman called Kamala. Her skin was the colour of bleached almonds. I would have called her plain verging on ugly. She had a great beak of a nose and a bony forehead. A downward tending mouth and a weak chin. Nevertheless, she carried herself with confidence, and clearly took pains over her toilette. She had her hair drawn tight over her skull, oiled so that there were comb-tracks in its enamelled blackness, leading towards the point where it was gathered up into a rigid three-tier bolus. Her *tikka* glowed on her forehead like a lighthouse beacon proclaiming her married status. The lower lids of her eyes were stained with *kajal*.

I said, 'We were talking about Prashant,' and pointed him out, across the room, where he stood, chatting with two men from Bob's office.

'Ah – your husband,' said Kamala.

Ruth smiled and bent her head to the side, looking conspiratorially at me. Since she had no discernible neck, the effect was that of the flesh being made to bulge out on one side of the triangular area at the apex of which was her face. I said, 'We're not married.'

Kamala raised her eyebrows and said, 'Oh? Lolly told me the two of you were travelling together?' I nodded and said we were. Kamala's expression didn't change, but I saw her pupils, like camera shutters, narrowing to pinpoints, cutting out the light entering her eyes. 'Oh,' she said. 'A modern girl. From Bombay, are you?' She nodded quickly when I confirmed her guess. 'Such a shame! I thought that at least we in India would be free of such –' she glanced up, saw Ruth staring at her in frank surprise and completed her remark – 'behaviour!' Then she said to Ruth, 'You see, in our society, it is unknown – young people allow their parents to find a life-partner for them and they are happy with the match – '

'Even if they are completely unsuited – ?' I said.

'Never mind, never mind!' said Kamala, her voice rising. 'Even if they hate each other – the point is, they remain married forever. Divorce is unknown, in India, unknown! Unlike here – where every third marriage ends in chaos.' She turned back to me and said, 'I'm sorry, my dear, but you have to face some facts! They might be unpleasant! What is your full name? Are you Maharashtrian?'

I could feel heat rising within me like magma inside a volcano. 'No,' I said. 'Prashant is Maharashtrian. I'm from Kerala – though,' I added as an afterthought, 'I've never actually lived there.' I turned to Ruth, who was clearly floundering, out of her depth in this conversation which had suddenly changed from paddling-pool party banter into a deep-sea convulsion. 'She's talking about the different states to which we belong – '

'You're not Indian?' said Ruth, helpfully.

'Not really,' said Kamala, stepping in. 'No Indian woman would do what you are doing. It's wrong, it's un-Indian, my dear, I'm sorry to say this! You're a disgrace to our great nation – excuse me for saying this – no, no! It's a shame! Is it for this that my grandfather fought for independence? Is this the reward you give your country for five thousand years of culture? Huh! The government should horsewhip young people like you! Yes – and take away your passports! Ruining the reputation of the country! Travelling abroad like a – a – a Scarlet Woman! Yes! Have you no pride? No respect? We Indians living in the West, we try to hold our heads up high, we try to show the people here that their culture is nothing compared to ours, that we can show them the tallest mountain and the highest arched gateway and who has seen anything to compare with our temples in the South? But then you people come here from home and destroy every impression that we try to create – yes! You drag the name of all Indians in the mud – with your short hair and your shapeless clothes! I'm sorry if you don't like to hear a few truths – I'm sorry, I'm sorry – ' And with this she abruptly drew away and began to snort into a tiny lace handkerchief that she whipped out from where it had been tucked under the neckline of her sari-blouse.

The whole room had come to a standstill. Lolly had been making her way through the party towards Kamala and had reached her now. 'Now, now, Auntie,' she was saying, while Kamala's husband, a tall, graceful-looking man, came up too and between them they led her away towards Lolly and Bob's bedroom.

My face felt as if it must be throwing light, it was so hot with a mixture of embarrassment and pain. But Ruth reached for my hand and patted it, saying, 'It doesn't madder, you know?' I looked at her, unable to get my teeth far enough apart to make an intelligible response. 'People say things. That's all. It's just words.'

I felt as if I was seeing her for the first time. Not as someone abnormally fat but as a warm, kindly person who was responding to what she knew must be my distress. 'Look at me,' she said. 'People laugh at me. All the time. I know it. I know whut they're thinking. Whut they're saying. But I don't give it no mind. I just go on ahead and do my thing.'

I noticed tiny gold and red curls glistening in her hair as it flowed over her shoulders. Her skin was warm and glossy. I found myself thinking that she was actually quite beautiful. An image of loving givingness, enveloping softness and security. I gripped her hand back in response and said, 'Thank you for saying that. You're very kind.' It seemed to me that she represented the uncomplicated goodness that I had once, as a child, associated with this country.

THE TEMPLE

ON THE EVENING JUST before we caught the Greyhound bus that would take us to where Radzie lived in Pennsylvania, Bob insisted that Prashant and I should pay a visit to the local temple. I started to refuse, but Prashant looked daggers at me. So I ate half a pizza and agreed.

My suitcases were taken down to the car and we checked the room carefully to ensure that nothing got left behind in the apartment because, said Lolly, 'We won't have time to come aaaaall the way back to geddit before you ketch your bus.' Fortunately, we didn't have to get to the bus terminal until much later, so there was no panic.

We talked about Kamala's outburst of the previous evening. According to Lolly, Kamala was a borderline hysteric. 'Her parents were involved in the Freedom Movement. She grew up with all this patriotic stuff going on – demonstrations and arrests and secret plots. I guess she never gaat used to being an ordinary citizen any more.'

I knew a lot about patriotic stuff.

Though I was born in India, my parents left almost immediately for Sweden, two years later for Switzerland, three years later for Pakistan. I was seven and a half by the time we left Karachi to return to India. I was looking forward with intense anticipation to being in My Country. I had been told that whatever Pakistan was like, India was a thousand times better. This suggested to me that the few small things I hadn't liked in Pakistan would be utterly absent in that place of myth and culture across the border, that fabled land where five thousand years of history wafted like perfume in the daily air and the people were beautiful, clever and kind.

It wasn't surprising that I had this impression. I had grown up within the walls of an embassy. And what is an embassy if not a propaganda machine for the country it represents? The mere presence of its offices and officers is an indication that there on the map, bounded by double lines, is a patch of colour which is mysteriously more special than every other patch of colour sharing the map with it. Whole generations of children grow up into adulthood, reproduce and die, sincerely believing that there are factors which pick out this one spot to which they belong as being so vastly, so famously more special than any other place, that they themselves are automatically dignified by the fact of being born within the boundaries which have contained these histories, these artefacts.

I believed this myself, without question, until the fateful train ride from Lahore to Delhi. All the way, I had been anticipating that precious moment when the flat, dust-grey plains of Pakistan would give way to the golden, honey-scented magnificence of India. And yet outside the window, the miles flew by, unchanging, unbroken, giving no sign of the transformation that was about to take place.

I wondered from what distance the change would be visible. Whether the land would gradually firm up and become splendrous or whether there would be an abrupt transition: one moment the featureless plains and the next – a glittering barrier, a gateway made of diamonds and – we would be There. I asked my parents about it from time to time but they gave the kinds of answers that adults give when they are too busy talking about their own affairs to pay attention to their children.

It was only very gradually that the truth became apparent, to the tune of the train's hypnotic clickety-clack. There was going to be no visible difference. We had crossed the border into India while I slept and no one had told me. What I saw outside the window now was India and . . . *it was just like Pakistan*! There were no jewels winking from every tree, no healthy and handsome citizens, nodding from tall stately homes along the way. Here, just as there, the people were poor, wretched and hungry. There would be rabid dogs and hot weather. And madness.

A few weeks before leaving, a young girl of around fourteen stood, wild-haired and fierce-eyed, just near to where we sat. She seemed impervious to our need for privacy. I kept looking at her, wondering why she didn't move off. Her staring made me uncomfortable. I couldn't understand why she was invisible to the rest of my family. I whispered to my mother, who told me not to look at her. 'She's probably mad,' said my mother dismissively, 'any moment now, she might come running this way or do any which thing.'

It is astonishing what power a casual remark can have. For years afterward, that young girl represented for me a vision of horror made flesh. I could not bear to accept that a person who seemed outwardly human could yet be so disordered internally that she ceased to observe ordinary human conventions. I had felt, at the picnic, as if one layer of my skin had been peeled away and that if I remained in full view of the girl, I might get scorched, perhaps to death. I couldn't believe that the adults were so foolhardy as to remain calmly seated in that place. I couldn't understand why such a ferocious being had not been confined to some distant asylum where she could not be a threat to picnickers.

I had assumed that madness could exist only in places of lower consequence, which is what I thought Pakistan was until I realized that India was the same. I felt betrayed then, by all the adults who had filled my mind with illusions. Either their judgement was severely flawed or they were telling shocking lies. But worse than this was to realize, once I had spent a short while in India, that these deceits or delusions were maintained by everyone, including my teachers at school, the friends I made, the textbooks we read. It was everywhere, this idea that the country which surrounded us was a delightful place, the equal of any other.

This form of patriotism which blinkered its citizens, so that they could not see poverty and squalor and could not rectify defects, was something that terrified me as a child. Even the art and culture of India frightened me because its stylized forms suggested to me ways of seeing that were restricted to the initiated, to those who could understand the symbols. European art, by contrast, appealed to me because it was obvious, it did not require specialized knowledge to be appreciated. What you saw was what you got. Realism in art was a method of telling the truth on the visual plane just as science was a method of telling the truth on the physical plane.

Meanwhile, in New York, we reached the temple when it was too late in the day to see it clearly except in outline. Its curves and bulges rose exotically amongst the severely linear buildings around it like a platter of grey stone fruit surrounded by soaring decanters of steel and glass. There was a modest crowd of jeans-clad and winter-enwrapped Indians at the entrance, all struggling to remove their heavy footwear before entering the glass doors to the central chamber. We, too, took off our jackets and shoes.

As a child I had never liked temples because of the darkness and the crush of bodies and the air thick with the reek of oil and decaying flowers. I dreaded losing sight of my mother, of falling and being ground into paste on the black stone floors by the feet of the devotees streaming like ants past the place where the deity was visible. Around the temple walls there would always be at least one horrific sight. A queue of limbless lepers on their miserable little carts perhaps, waving their tattered digit-stumps like a row of human sea anemones, waiting to receive alms. Or a dog with its skin flayed and sore, surreptitiously licking at a splash of milk on the floor. I hated having to remove my slippers, to walk around barefoot on floors that might be muddy or squishy with unknown, invisible deposits in the unlit corridors leading to the deity's inner chambers.

In that sense the temple in New York was a tremendous improvement. Only its outer skin was a temple. Inside, it was a museum with interactive deities, in front of whom puja could be offered. Around the walls were friezes. A few deities were confined behind glass, like regular art objects. Some of the visitors were in Indian dress, but the majority was clothed as Westerners. The floor was carpeted. The room was well lit, with spotlights trained on each exhibit.

Lolly had brought items for use in the puja. She handed these over to a middle-aged man who had still not changed into his priestly gear when we met him. He looked like a bank clerk. When he was ready, his top half still looked like a bank clerk, but from the waist down he looked like a priest, in his dhoti and his bare feet. He spoke in a nasal quack.

Lolly knelt in front of the deity while Prashant and I stood. Bob had decided against coming in, he said, because it was such a hassle to find a parking space. The priest explained, with his eye darting about the room, falling in particular upon the young children in their pint-sized designer-label jeans, 'A'right. For the benefid of those of you in this room who would like to unnerstand our ancient customs, Ah'm gonna take a little time to explain. Whut Ah'm doin' here is aaafferin' these idems, you know, to the gaad and while Ah aaaffer them, Ah say his name, you know, so that he knows that Ah'm callin' im. The aaafferin' represense the diffren' elemen's – thad is . . . urth, waaader, fire, ayer . . . an' Ah ask him to accept these aaafferings and to grant me the indulgence of his audience. The gaad is represenned by the carved idol behind me. He wears his gorejuss robes and becuz he doesn' like to take' em off every day, he allows us to make our aaaffering to this smaller idol in fron' of us, right here –' he indicated a diminutive image raised up in front of him on a platform with a groove running around it – 'he allows us to make our aaafferin' to this smaller image of his holy self, here. So that's whut I'm gonna do.'

He took in a deep breath and then, like pouring water out of a spouted vessel, loosed a rippling stream of Sanskrit words out upon the air. He had in his hands half a conch shell, made into a receptacle for liquids, with one end tipped in silver so that it would pour efficiently. He had a brass container of water, from which he poured a portion into the conch shell container. Then he poured that water over the small idol in front of him. He turned to where he had kept Lolly's ingredients, a half-gallon carton of Crowley's Full Cream Milk and a new bottle of Aunt Jemima's Golden Syrup. He got the carton open with no difficulty, poured a little from it into the shell and emptied that too upon the small image. But the bottle of syrup did not yield to his efforts at twisting off the lid.

Still chanting, he glanced up and around. Prashant leaned forward, took the bottle from him and strangled it for a few moments but the lid would not be shifted. The priest waited a couple of seconds, and then, fitting the words in at the end of his chant cycle said, 'Aww, it's okay – we'll use the house bottle.' Reaching around himself, he brought out an identical jar, half full, from which he poured a small quantity into the conch shell and then on to the idol. He sprinkled a handful of rose petals from a nearby basket upon the small figurine. Finally, he held a brass plate with a tiny flaming oil-lamp in it in front of the idol, rotating the plate slowly. The flame of the lamp described a glowing circle in the air. He had timed himself perfectly so that the chanting came to an end.

He held the plate forward to Lolly. She made a soft waving gesture with both hands open around the flame, as if encouraging its consecrated heat to be wafted towards herself. Within the brass plate were flower petals and a small mound of ash. Lolly leaned forward and the priest, taking a pinch of the ash between his thumb and forefinger, placed a smudge of it on her forehead. Lolly sat back and started to get to her feet. The priest looked up towards Prashant and me. Prashant leaned forward and automatically did what he had to do, just as Lolly had. But I shook my head and took a step back. The priest smiled slightly and shrugged, while immediately some of the other people in the room came forward to take the benefit of the blessing.

When we were once more in our shoes and jackets and stepping out of the temple, Lolly said to me, 'I'm saarry, I thought you were Hindoo?'

'I don't call myself that,' I said. 'On forms I write "AGNOSTIC".'

She laughed and said, 'Ag-*whut*?! Is that a religion?'

Bob had been circling the block and by some miracle caught us at the very moment that we reached the kerb. We bundled ourselves into the car and set off.

'So you're not religious, huh?' said Lolly.

I said, 'All through school I wanted to convert to Christianity. But then I didn't and after that it seemed too much of a bother.'

'But what do you *believe*?' Lolly wanted to know. I said I didn't know.

Lolly told us that she was doing a series of pujas because she was very keen to have a child. 'I don't know if I really believe or naat,' said Lolly. 'But I get something from coming here. I kin remember going to the temple with my mom when I was a kid so when I go here and I smell the, you know, incense, it's like being a kid again and waiting to get just that little bit of sweet prasad at the end, which sometimes they give and sometimes they don't. It's like being safe again, with my mother. I know it looks a bit corny here, and there's the priest and his phony accent and all, but in the end we do the things that make us feel safe and comfortable, you know? And if I've asked for something and if that thing comes to me I don't care if it's Gaad who gives it to me or – or whut. I just feel happy and because I feel I happy, I come here and say, 'Thank you.' Or 'Please help me again.' Or – whatever. It's a way of feeling that I have some control over my life even though my rational mind tells me that it's really all just fate and chance.'

Hearing her talk about fate and chance reminded me of the chances I was planning to take with my fate. Wanting to reassure myself by looking at my few remaining traveller's cheques, I reached for my handbag, which was when I discovered that I had left it behind in the temple.

A tense half hour passed as Bob drove heroically all the way back to the temple, with Lolly assuring me that no one would steal the handbag from there. I smiled weakly, trying not to show that the strings holding my lungs together were coming undone so that I was starting to breathe in wheezing gasps.

Prashant said, 'What's the worst that can happen? We'll have to apply for a passport from the Indian Embassy – that's all. The tickets and TCs can be reissued – though it's a pain in the neck . . .' No one talked about the expense and nuisance that it would cause all of us and the fact that Prashant and I would have to find another home in which to stay on in New York for the next few days because Bob and Lolly were about to receive another contingent of guests.

I could not explain, of course, that my anxiety was on a different plane. My address book was in that handbag. Even assuming that we recovered the traveller's cheques and ticket, even allowing for the time it would take to get a new passport issued, if I lost Piet's telephone number and address, then my plans for a European detour were in ruins forever because I had not copied it down anywhere else. I was gasping because I could see the immediate future collapsing like a pricked balloon in front of me, with nothing to take its place.

We got to the temple and Prashant ran up the steps with me to look in the place that I last remembered seeing the bag. And there it was, just as Lolly said it would be, with all its contents intact.

FROZEN WASTES

RADZIE COLLECTED US FROM where the Greyhound dropped us off, in Elmira, on the border of New York State and Pennsylvania. In twenty minutes we were in her house, the last of eight homes along a short stretch of road. There were neighbours to her left and directly in front but on the right was a stand of dark green conifers, a pocket of local wilderness.

I was not looking forward to a month in Prashant's company with nothing to do aside from watch TV in cosy togetherness. Radzie left for work at 7 a.m., driving 40 miles to the hospital in Corning where she was a pathologist. Tim was a paediatrician in a local clinic but he was often on call and was usually up and out by 8.30. He took my niece to school and later in the day she was brought back by Mrs Meadows, the housekeeper-cum-babysitter.

There was nothing I could find to say to Prashant. We played non-stop games of Scrabble, watched TV and went for walks. The roads were not constructed for pedestrians. There was no discernible footpath and it quickly became apparent that we were a traffic hazard. We may even have been breaking some law. Whenever a car caught sight of us, it reared and snorted, skidding sideways as if we were a danger to it in some way. And no doubt we were, standing on the wrong side and leaning into the road like two-legged elk with our heads turned to the right. After the first couple of attempts, we had to give up anyway because it began to snow. Whereas in New York there had been flurries, this was now serious precipitation. In the course of one evening, a magical whiteness blanketed the world around us.

I felt the snow falling within me too, a white stillness which made conversation feel like an irreverence. By the second evening, the driveway was obscured and needed shovelling.

The local snow plough had chuffed industriously up and down the road in front of the house. There remained only the strip of about 20 feet wide and 40 feet long to clear from the double-door garage to the road. I had seen countless cartoon and TV heroes shovelling snow and thought it would be fun.

Radzie said, 'Wait! You're not used to the cold!' But I paid no attention. What harm could possibly come from doing something that Dennis the Menace did with his little red toy shovel? I put on all the warm clothes I had and grabbed the spare shovel that Tim handed to me. He smiled in the tolerant way of men who know that women cannot match a man's ability to perform certain physical tasks. He showed me how I could avoid back sprain by bending my knees, pushing the blade under a comfortable mound of snow, heaving up by straightening my legs and tossing the load of snow over to the side. A cinch, I thought. Why did all those cartoon heroes complain so much?

Tim had already cleared a space about 5 feet wide in front of his carport, and he went back to his job. I raised the door on the side of Radzie's carport and began to attack the white mass, about 3 feet deep, lying outside on the ground. It was 8 o'clock in the evening and the sky overhead was glassy black, prickling with stars.

I hadn't been out more than three or four minutes when I began to understand that this cold was altogether different to what I had encountered in New York. Here it wasn't the air or the wind. It was a presence, all on its own, a dark animal with a million metaphysical teeth, gnawing patiently at my extremities with the confidence of a predator.

My breath parted company with me reluctantly, in white wads of cottony warmth, while each replacement felt like a hail of needles entering the heated cavern of my throat. My hands and feet were transformed into unfeeling blocks of wood. I couldn't believe that mere weather could do this to me. In the tropics, though we have rain and sun and heat strong enough to stun buffaloes in their wallow, the elements do not have the sheer mass of ice and snow. Still, I could not convince myself that there was anything actually to fear here, so close to my sister's warm house, within 3 yards of her front door. Reminding myself of Scott, the South Pole and frostbite, I went on.

The muscles of my arms were beginning to shriek with the unaccustomed activity. My legs were refusing to straighten up on schedule. I couldn't understand any of it. Was it possible to be so weak? I had not managed to clear more than a few feet in front of me! I told myself that I must be made of Jell-O, to be so ineffectual, so effete. I went on. My lungs were hurting. My back was breaking. My ears were dimming out. But I was making almost no progress. When I looked up and around to where Tim was, I saw him ploughing away, just like in the movies, big clumps of snow flying up through the air and on to the deposit pile, in rhythmic bursts. I felt completely humbled and even a little sick. I felt like crying.

And then, just as I was about to collapse with frustration and defeat, a most unexpected sensation began to steal over me. A cuddly warmth that spread all across me, like a fine golden sheath. Sounds slowed down and my sight began to waver. Sleep. I wanted to sleep! The desire was sudden and violent, like being struck over the head, so much so that I felt it must already have happened. I could no longer tell whether my eyes were open or shut. I may even have stopped with my shovel raised up in the air, frozen in mid-movement like the Siberian woolly mammoth preserved in its icy tomb with its trunk upraised. I had always wondered how it was possible to die of hypothermia when the option of going indoors existed and now I knew: because it felt so wonderfully warm and cosy to remain just where I was. My last thought before Radzie dashed out and caught me was that this would make a nice addition to the personal despatch methods I was collecting for myself. It might mean being dug out of the permafrost centuries later, to enjoy an afterlife as a museum exhibit, but so what? I wouldn't be alive to care about it any more than the woolly mammoths were.

I slept for two days like the dead, waking slowly to dreams of polar bears, aurorae and afterlives.

The reason I had nothing to say to Prashant was that I could not tell him about Piet. I'd had plenty of time to consider my options but there was still no formula of words I could use which would not sound as if I had deliberately set out to hurt him – which I hadn't, except in the sense that I had placed my desires ahead of his.

In some ways, it may have been easier if I could have claimed raw passion as the reason for my actions. But that was not what I was claiming. I believed that everything I did arose from a feeling of being trapped by the circumstances of my life. I believed that Prashant was part of the trap and if I were to tell him about it, and even if he were, by some extraordinary chance, to be sympathetic, there was no way that he could approve of the further plans I had. It wasn't just that he or anyone else could be made to approve if I spent long enough explaining my actions to them. It was that I wanted to rid myself of the need to explain. I wanted to act without reference to the approval of anyone I knew. Regardless of whether it was considered irregular, foolhardy and different to what was considered respectable in the society to which I belonged, I wanted to follow through my plan because I saw it as a means of breaking out of the shackles and constraints of that society.

Being unable to discuss Piet or any of the changes taking place in my way of thought made every other exchange I had with Prashant seem like shopping with counterfeit notes. Nothing I said was backed with conviction because there were too many experiences to which I could not refer without having to explain their whole context. So I preferred to say nothing.

I knew that Prashant was feeling puzzled and left out. We did not normally chatter a great deal. We had been together long enough that the silences between us were comfortable. But these silences now were different, because I knew that he did not know what was on my mind. He sensed the difference in me, but, like a suitor who will not visit a house where he fears he will find a rival, he preferred not to ask me what I was thinking about.

The US is not a country for non-drivers. Without a means for getting out and around, without even roads that were comfortable to walk on, the only option we had aside from staying indoors in Radzie's house was to go into Corning with her.

Her hospital provided her and other doctors like herself, who had long commutes, with a one-bedroom service apartment which they used in rotation. We had to leave the house with her, which meant waking up at 7 a. m. and struggling into three layers of clothing in preparation for facing the elements. The drive took forty minutes in pre-dawn darkness, when there was nothing to see out of the windows but the lonely beam of the headlights on the freeway, the winking of the cats-eyes embedded in the surface and the intriguing signs that appeared now and then. It took me forever to figure out that the graphic of a prancing stag with the letters 'XING' beneath was to be interpreted as 'deer crossing'. In my mind I pronounced it as 'deer ecksing' and reasoned, in my sleep-befuddled way, that it must be hunters' arcana meaning 'here be deer to kill'.

Radzie would deposit Prashant and myself in the apartment en route to work and there we would stay until she was free at lunch or at the end of her working day, to grab a bite, visit the local shopping mall or catch a movie.

It was a pristinely antiseptic place, that apartment, with its bare white walls and the studied anonymity of its décor. We never actually saw any of the other itinerants who had the use of the space, but their phantom presence lingered in the form of the unfamiliar brand of biscuits filling the communal Mason jar or the freshly opened roll of lavender-scented toilet paper rather than the tangy lemon which was Radzie's household staple. Once I saw what I thought looked like the corner torn off a condom foil wrapper, but it may just as well have been from a packet of wafers.

If the silence between Prashant and myself in Radzie's home was oppressive, then there in that impersonal little apartment, the individual words which remained unspoken and unspeakable became like solid bricks and permanent walls between us. I usually spent the first two hours after we got there lying in a heap on the sofa in the living room, asleep. Prashant sat in front of the black and white TV set pretending to watch it even though it was stubbornly local and yielded nothing beyond fitness programmes and ABC news. When the stillness became too oppressive to bear, I would wake up and we would go out, preferring to wander the frozen streets outside than to endure the interior muteness.

We would go to the closer of the two malls, or to the library near Radzie's hospital, or to the park across from it. We might watch the traffic streaming past us or we might take in a bite of breakfast at the local McDonald's, where the fast-food culture was still enough of a novelty that it seemed miraculous and not nightmarishly boring, to go to different restaurants in the same chain, to find that the girls behind the counter all had identical ponytails and that the coffee tasted uniformly of scalded styrofoam.

Prashant would continue to be gamely enthusiastic, talking about his latest finds like an archaeologist at a dig. Did I know, he would ask, as we bit into our Egg McMuffins, that the explanation for the perfect uniformity of McDonald's fried eggs was that the whites and yolks of countless eggs were separated in advance so that they could be measured into moulds and fried into place perfectly proportioned for the waiting bun? Had I noticed that the ambulances here had their signs spelt backwards on the fronts of the vans so that the drivers of other vehicles could read the word correctly in their rear-view mirrors and move aside? Had I realized that the sugar in the dispensers in restaurants was actually less sweet than what we were used to in India because here it was beet-sugar, not cane?

I would react to his conversations with appropriate remarks, knowing that he was maintaining a brave front and that in some way it was for both of us. He preferred the fiction that nothing had changed between us, in the hope that I would return to my earlier self without our having to acknowledge that there had been a break in our closeness. But I knew that the thing that was wrong between us could not be corrected by conversations about McDonald's mass-production techniques or anything else. It was part of all that is cruel between two people whose friendship is coming unstrung that neither could I tell him to stop, nor could he stop.

It was only on the last such morning that Prashant finally lost patience. He was due to return to India on the Sunday after this final Friday that we had come with Radzie to Corning. Whereas he had already been to see the Glass Museum connected to the Corning Glass Factory once, having come on an earlier visit before I arrived in the US, for me it was the first time.

We had spent our regulation two hours in the apartment. It had been as quiet and expressionless as ever before. But then, just after we had stepped out, Prashant said with no preamble, 'So? Was it one or both of them?'

I said, 'What?'

He said, 'Your Dutch friends. One? Or both?'

The sky was a dizzy blue, with extravagant clouds and thin sparkling sunshine. Fresh snowfall from the night before still lay in brilliant heaps, making hillocks out of parked cars. The road glistened like a carpet of wet black diamonds beneath our feet. It was very cold.

I said, 'I don't know what you mean.'

Our breath emerged like speech bubbles in a cartoon, great white plumes, wanting only for someone to pencil in the text. I wished someone *would* do that, to save me the anguish of silence.

He said, 'You've always said that you believed in being truthful.'

I said, 'That's right, I do.' I would have liked to scream or to cry or to do anything other than have to answer questions of this nature. But where, in that emotionless street, would there have been an appropriate spot in which to do it? I could not imagine the reaction of the other citizens we could see around us, striding in their swift, purposeful way, if two persons coloured in shades of unfashionable brown began with no warning to bay and howl at each other.

It was easier by far to imagine two women declaiming loudly to one another about the virtues of Fabergé wheatgerm oil and honey shampoo while standing on a traffic island than to dream of creating a scene, in a public arena, centred on our own personal lives. We were, for all practical purposes, invisible. We were surrounded by a culture in which everything that is worth seeing is instantly sucked into the visual vocabulary of the advertising industry. But of our own selves we saw no echoes in our surroundings. It was like looking into a selective mirror and discovering that we were too dull to be reflected. We were drowned out by the sheer mass of local sounds around us.

'But you're not being truthful about this.'

'I'm being truthful,' I said. 'There's nothing to say.' My contact lenses rose off the surface of my eyes and wobbled dangerously. Tears could sometimes cause that to happen. I blinked a few times to clear them away before they spilt down my cheeks. 'I don't have anything to say.' I do not cry easily. I don't like to cry. When I was a child, my mother, who was a strict disciplinarian, had made it very clear to me that though she did not, in principle, believe in hitting me, if I cried when I was being scolded, she would hit me. Some children would break the will of their parents by crying more violently than any parent would care to hit them. I had chosen the path of not crying and it had stayed with me.

'You do,' said Prashant, softly and angrily. 'Or at least your conscience does. It said something for you in your sleep last night.'

Actually I had a memory of this, like a handprint appearing on a steamed mirror. 'Said what?' I asked. I remembered only that I had said Piet's name out loud and at that instant had emerged out of the cocoon of sleep. I registered that the name had escaped into the world outside my mind. Then I returned to sleep. I had sensed Prashant stirring beside me, to say, his own voice thick with sleep, 'Wha-a-a–?'

'His name. One of those Dutch fellows. Just the name . . .' We had reached the entrance to the museum.

I made a face and looked away. 'It's true that I said something last night. But it doesn't mean anything. Really.'

'You mean, it doesn't mean anything to you, or . . . nothing happened?'

'I mean,' I said, trying consciously to breathe shallowly, to avoid weighing my voice with the awareness of my own perfidy, 'that nothing happened.' I told myself that if he were really ready to hear the truth, he wouldn't have to ask me about it.

We entered the museum. Aside from showcasing the astounding range of objects and uses to which glass has been put, it also gave access to the Steuben Glass studio. Visitors could sit in a gallery watching a handful of men, standing about, talking softly, paying no attention to their audience. Four ovens like giant beehives were spaced around the area which had a high ceiling and the unadorned dignity of a quiet rural chapel. Rods stuck out of the ovens like giant skewers. Prashant and I took our places. As we watched, one of the men strolled up to the beehive closest to where we sat and casually drew out one of the rods.

A blob of bright blood-gold glass bloomed at the end of it. As easily as if he were blowing a balloon, the man breathed life into that incandescent mass, so that it writhed and grew, even as he shaped it and gave it a flowing, tender form. His actions were quick and assured as if there was no element of choice. What he did and what he produced seemed perfectly ordained. Within seconds, at the end of the tube was a graceful crystal vase, miraculously conjured from the void. Just as he severed it from the tube, another man wandered up, holding, at the end of another tube, another gleaming blob. The first man received the semi-fluid glass in a pair of giant tweezers and, pausing only to elongate it lightly so that it looked briefly like a glittering airborne wraith, placed it with seamless precision along the upper edge of the just-created vase. He repeated his action a moment later as a third man brought up a third twist of molten glass.

And it was done. A shallow, elegant bowl now existed where none had been before.

We visitors clapped in spontaneous exhilaration. It was a moment of great beauty, so that even the tension between Prashant and myself received a certain respite. I felt a yearning to be rendered down, to have my impurities burned away, my untruths vaporized, leaving only the transparent essence. But it was not to be.

GODS AND PHANTOMS

IT WAS A RELIEF for me when Prashant left and for him too, I think. Just before he left, we talked about the film *Looking for Mr Goodbar* which we had seen together in New York. I had loved it, while Prashant hated it. In particular I was very struck by Diane Keaton's character, an attractive and idealistic schoolteacher who preferred the wrong kind of men.

'It was just like *Saturday Night Fever,*' I said, 'in gender-reverse.'

'Bullshit,' said Prashant. '*Saturday Night Fever* was a musical and it was fun – '

'On the surface!' I said, 'But just *under* the surface, there's this story about a young guy who's really a loser – '

'He's not,' said Prashant. 'He wins the competition, he wins the girl – '

'No!' I said. 'That's what I'm trying to tell you – he wins the competition only after he understands that it's been rigged in his favour and against the Chicano couple – you can see it in his face – his girlfriend goes off and sleeps with one of his buddies on the back seat of the car, then the buddy dies on the bridge– and when Travolta's dancing with that other girl, he knows there's no spark – '

'You're reading too much into it, ya!' said Prashant, impatiently. 'It was just another musical – you snap your fingers to the music, you laugh a bit, then you come out and forget all about it – '

'You missed the whole point, in that case,' I said. 'It was about growing up poor in – whatever – on the wrong side of the Brooklyn Bridge. It was about looking across the bridge and fantasizing – didn't you see any of that? You know, that scene at the end when he's with the new girl? It's really a metaphor for all the longings of second-generation immigrants who've earned the right to sleep in American beds, but their dreams still haven't got across the bridge – '

'If you say so,' said Prashant, in the tone of someone saying 'no' to a door-to-door salesman.

'*Looking for Mr Goodbar* was also about looking for personal freedoms, but because the main character is a woman, she isn't allowed even a partial success at the end. I mean, if she'd been in a dance competition, she'd have lost it completely – both her legs in a car accident or something – d'you see what I mean?'

Prashant shrugged and repeated, 'If you say so – '

'She had to fail completely. She had to actually die. I mean, the film was a – a *warning* to adventurous women – I mean, in *SNF*, the hero has dreams, he has ambitions, even if they're only about winning a dance competition at a discothèque. But in Keaton's film, she's not allowed anything but the hope of finding the "right guy" – and, of course, she never finds him because she rejects the conventional kind of man – and oh, yes! It's because she doesn't want or can't have children! There's that scene where she explains that she has some hereditary back problem and doesn't want to pass it on – I mean, even in *this* film, the character had to justify her decision not to want children – even in an American film it's unthinkable for a woman who is the heroine of the film not to want children – and in the end, she's punished for it . . .'

Prashant and I were sitting at Radzie's dining table. 'Ask yourself,' I said. 'Aside from *Casablanca*, how many main-stream, box-office hits can you name in which the female lead has more than one lover without being a whore or a loser?' I didn't wait for a response. 'You can't! And even in *Casablanca*, it was only two men, one was a war hero, the other was Humphrey Bogart, and of course the woman was Ingrid Bergman . . .' My sister was a great *Casablanca* fan. We had all seen the film twice. We all wept on schedule during the 'Marseillaise' scene.

Prashant was silent. There was a 2-gallon keg of Coca-Cola open on the table and we both took swigs from it, not bothering to use a glass. I had a brick of Philadelphia cream cheese open in front of me, its foil wrapper peeled back. Beside it was an open packet of sesame-seed Danish crispbread. I sliced a section of the cheese down the whole end of the brick, placed it on the rye-bread so that it covered approximately half, then broke off the remaining half of the long rectangle of the crispbread to place it over the cheese, making a sandwich. Already my waist was bulging above and below my waistband. My cheeks had ballooned out like a squirrel's nut-filled pouches. Whenever I looked in the mirror I got depressed and to cure the depression I headed straight for the fridge.

'Well?' I said. 'What d'you think of that analysis?'

Prashant said, 'You identify with her, don't you? Diane Keaton, I mean. The schoolteacher.'

It was my turn to say nothing, though I pretended it was because I was engrossed in my snack.

'I wouldn't think twice about that movie,' he said. 'I found it depressing as hell. So it's about a loser, so what? Everyone makes mistakes, so what? She gets dumped by the college professor, she doesn't want children, she shouldn't have gone out with that second guy – the Richard Gere character – and then, I mean, anything can happen in a singles bar. But what's the point of making films like that? They don't have any message or any story – like art films. So okay, one or two art films are all right, but the rest, they're just made by weirdos who want everyone to go home and commit suicide! And okay, a few people see them and get something out of them, but most people just want to forget them as quickly as they can. And you're no different, normally. We've always liked the same kinds of films. But it's all different with you now, isn't it? Suddenly you're bothering with this dumb story about a loser woman and her asshole boyfriends, and the *only reason* you're bothering is that you've got yourself into . . . all kinds of . . .' He let his words trail off.

I tossed the Coke down, pretending to be a lumberjack drinking beer. Since I'm not a lumberjack, and the Coke wasn't beer, it came fizzing up the back alleys of my nasal passages, so that I choked and gulped, feeling like a helium balloon at bursting point. I said, 'Prashant . . .'

He continued, making an effort to moderate his voice. He didn't want to antagonize me on this last afternoon we had together before he returned to India. 'The fact is, you're *not* really like the Keaton character at all. Her problem was that she was alone. Her parents didn't care for her and she had no friends. But you – you've got lots of friends. And your sister. And parents. Even your brother, though you don't think so. And . . .' He paused. I knew what he was going to say. I wished he wouldn't, but he had to. I knew that. The moment was ripe for it. If we had been in a film, a single note on a bass viol would have vibrated suspensefully in the background. Studied and yet sincere, both at once, he said, 'You've got me, baby. Just remember that. Please.'

But we weren't in a film.

In place of the bass viol, I burped in embarrassment and guilt. When I had a voice, I said, 'I've been . . . distant. I know it. I don't know how to talk about this. But I can't say much. I can't even explain why I can't say much. I've got to go through with, with . . . something. It's something I'm trying out. A person I'm trying to be. It's like trying on new clothes, or a new costume – I don't know what I'll look like at the end of it. I don't know if I'll stay that way or come back to what I was. I just want you to know that I don't want to hurt you – but I know that I have. I can't say anything more friendly than this, but please understand that hurting you is *not* what it's about.'

He looked me straight in the eye and we nodded to one another. It was a good moment. He said, 'Will you call me when you need me?' I said I would.

He left the next day for New York, saying that he had had a wonderful time but that he was looking forward to getting back to work again. He laughed to hear himself voice such opinions. He seemed pleased to think that he was a hard-working professional after all, not the witless sot that many young men of his age affected to be.

Once Prashant left I was by myself until late afternoon. Mrs Meadows let herself into the house to vacuum, do the ironing and put away the dishes from the washer. She fetched my niece from school only at 3 o'clock.

I spent whole mornings entertaining fantasies about Piet. Then I got out of bed, brushed my teeth and spent whole afternoons with another kind of fantasy, on TV. Soap operas like *All My Children* and *General Hospital* were a revelation, commerce and monotheism in passionate embrace. The one true god was represented by the loyal, omniscient, omnipotent and dandruff-free husband. Heaven was a place of static-free carpets and gleaming glassware. Women represented morality in all its variety: the faithful, the ignorant, the temporarily confused and the hopelessly damned.

Those who strayed from the path of righteousness during the programmes were more than offset by the always-smiling wives, mothers, mothers-in-law and grandmothers in the commercials, priestesses in the church of good housekeeping. Between their brand-loyal, thrift-conscious and well-manicured hands, the indiscretions of the few were as insignificant as the carpet stains that could be exorcized by means of a spray-on prayer called Scotchguard.

These messages of domesticity profoundly disturbed me.

Where, in this dishwasher-friendly universe in which a woman's worth was assessed by the sparkle on her cutlery, did I fit? Nowhere. Only one programme offered me hope and that was *Star Trek*. Only in the multi-ethnic crew of the United Space Starship *Enterprise*, with its peak-eared half-Vulcan Mr Spock, its mini-skirted African-American communications officer Uhura, and its Japanese first officer Mr Sulu, could I see a society in which I would neither look alien nor be considered unnatural for being disinterested in housekeeping. There was no dust to clean. Food was dialled up from the replicator, complete with garnish and starched napkin. No one wondered out loud about the brand of mouthwash used by Klingons or whether the visiting Cardassian Ambassador favoured the scent of lemons as a room-freshener.

I thought enviously of the future. If I could travel back and forth by transporter beams, how easy my life would be! 'Steady on warp six, Mr Sulu,' I could say, 'there's a space-time anomaly on planet Holland that needs looking into.'

CALLS

CHRISTMAS AND NEW YEAR came and went. Then in the first week of January, there was a piece of bad news for me. Prashant called to say that Zero wanted his room back. 'I – I – I'm most *awfully* sorry,' he'd said on the phone to Prashant, 'but, oh dear – the fact is – I'm getting married! I'd like to have the room back, you see – before the end of the week! Right away, actually . . . if it's not a bother? If you could just clear all the stuff out, please? Or risk having it all thrown away?'

A bombshell. I had the same sense then as I'd had standing with Piet at the top of the Grant Road bridge, of having stepped on to a carousel that I wanted to get off, but couldn't because it was already in motion.

No one could understand why I was so upset. Radzie said, 'But it's no big deal, Gai's gone across and collected your stuff already – it's all safe with her . . .'

Prashant told me, over the phone, that he would make certain that Zero returned the money he had taken from me as advance payment.

I had grown complacent, living in Radzie's house. The cosy familiarity of my sister's company and the supreme indulgence of being cared for without having to take much responsibility for myself had lulled me into a low-energy state. I could still see Piet's phantom presence and I could still make myself believe that I would jump all the hoops required to get to Holland, but at the same time I hadn't taken any of the final steps to ensure that I would go. I was back to being 5 kilos overweight and I had lost the edge of determination that had animated the two months in Bombay before I left for the US.

Zero's news changed all that. I could just see, in my mind's eye, the scene of my return. Back in Gai's house, under my brother's thumb, nothing resolved, no new work in hand, all the same pressures with no fresh horizons in sight anywhere. No money. No independence. No avenues of escape. In one more month I was due to fly back and then . . . nothing. I could see nothing. A blank greyness awaited me. Prashant's friendly embrace. His friendly office parties. I could see the parties, the familiar faces, the familiar food, the familiar subjects of conversation. The only person I could not see was myself amongst them. I felt distraught. I had made no wish-films to cover this contingency. I could not see my own immediate future.

I dashed two letters off at once. One to Piet, asking him to call me on a particular day at a particular time, so that I could be sure to be the one to take his call. The other letter was to Micki, in Germany.

I knew that she was about to give birth to her first child, early in the year, perhaps in February or March. So I wrote to say that I wanted to visit her. Not immediately, but maybe a month after the birth. I told her that I would only be able to explain the whole situation once I had seen her. She had known me for a long time and would, I was sure, be understanding.

If the birth was in March, I needed to reach Germany in April. That meant I needed to spend another month in the US. It meant getting an extension on my American visa and buying a ticket for a flight via London. It meant making a trek to New York. It meant explanations and justifications. But I couldn't see any other route open to me. So I took it.

To Radzie I said that I wasn't ready. 'I can't go back just yet. I – can't! And besides, Micki's going to have a baby and – and I'd like to be with her!' There. It was out.

'What?' said Radzie, starting to laugh, 'You? Are going to be with someone who's going to have a baby?' She couldn't believe it.

My cheeks felt hot as I said, 'No, but . . . maybe I could do things around the house?'

Radzie started to sputter with laughter. 'Like opening the freezer door, you mean? Burn some toast? Flood the bathroom?'

Having the house to myself since Prashant's departure had meant a series of minor disasters. None of the domestic gadgets seemed to like me. The fridge, in particular, was a real stinker. The first time I opened its freezer compartment looking for some ice cream, it flung half the contents of its ice-tray out at me. I thought it had gone mad, like the computer in *Demon Seed*. I didn't know whether to speak to it calmly or just pull its plug. Then I saw that it didn't even really have a plug. Just a sort of tail vanishing into the wall. It was practically smirking at me. When I complained to Radzie she fell apart laughing, saying, 'Are you telling me that you *can't even open the fridge*?!'

The spectacle of my attempting to help someone with a newborn was difficult to contemplate. 'Poor thing!' said Radzie, rolling on the floor with laughter, while I tried to look sober and reliable. 'What's she done to deserve you as her helper?' She couldn't stop laughing.

But the idea was established. And the next time we talked about it, I was able to say that Micki had written back telling me that she would love to have someone with her because when she came back from the delivery. Kurtz her husband would be working all day and I would be of help even if I did nothing but boil nappies.

Piet called too, in response to my letter. The call came precisely on schedule, but because daylight saving time was on a different cycle in Europe it was one hour ahead of the time that suited me, which would have been after Tim had left the house. Instead, he was still there, looking at the newspaper over his morning muffin. As a paediatrician, he was always on call, so he picked the phone up instantly. But I had woken up early because I was anticipating the call. The buzzing ring of the phone was all I needed to know that it was from Holland. I was out of bed and in the hallway before my brother-in-law could say I was asleep. I took the receiver from him with my ears burning with embarrassment but he did not seem to notice anything unusual. It was two and a half months since I'd heard

Piet's voice in real life. He sounded like a distant stranger. I could barely recognize him.

'Thank you for calling!' I said. I had told him in my letter that I might not be able to speak openly, because there may be family around me. 'Uh . . . so what d'you feel? Will it be all right?'

He said, 'Oh yes. It's no problem. It's no problem at all . . .' But his voice was unconvincing. I could hear an echo. The cold dark waves of the Atlantic murmured between us.

I said, 'That's . . . great. Thanks for calling, I just needed to hear that. I'm going to Germany, by the way. In the first week of April.'

'That's nice,' he said, and seemed to laugh. But it may have been the echo. Or my brother-in-law, coughing discreetly while he listened on the other line? Not that he would. He was a scrupulously polite and solicitous person. I didn't think he liked me much, but he held his own counsel and didn't allow his opinions to alter his behaviour towards me. 'Do you have any idea of dates?' asked Piet.

'I'll call you from Germany,' I said. 'I'll know a little more by then.' Elsewhere in the house I heard my niece calling for her father to hurry up. 'I can't say much now.' The front door slammed. 'It's a bit difficult to talk.' It no longer was, but the mood had been damaged and I couldn't undo the strain of speaking elliptically.

He said, 'Yes. Anyway, I'm here most of the time. Maybe I'll go away in the summer, but that's later. So it's no problem. Stay as long as you like. I have a big house. Really.'

We hung up quickly after that and I went back to my still-warm bed. Electric currents trembled around me, crackling and throwing sparks. However substantial he was in my memory of him, the power of real speech on real airwaves had a consequence that no fantasy could match. I could use the memories I had of him from Bombay to create a composite model of him. And it could seem concrete and tangible. But the first syllables of sound penetrating across time and space instantly ruptured the dream pictures, making them seem shabby and wraithlike by contrast.

For several days after the phone call, I remained in a type of limbo. In my mind, the text of that telephonic conversation was rewound and played back repeatedly, as I searched for clues, for signals that would help me confirm the decisions I was taking about the months ahead. I didn't find many. Just a pause here, a word there. We said nothing to one another which would have sounded to anyone listening on either side of the conversation like intimacy, warmth or friendship.

Radzie was concerned for Prashant. 'He's waiting for you, you know,' she said. I had told her that Prashant didn't know about my plan for making a German stopover.

I said, 'I know that. But I – but I – need time. Away from him.'

Radzie said she wondered if I realized that it hurt Prashant when I made a point of saying that I wasn't interested in getting married. Apparently they had talked about it. He had told her about the party in Bob and Lolly's place and about Kamala's reaction.

I said, 'But that was the condition of our relationship! I gave him fair warning!'

She smiled and said, 'Yes – but – that was before he knew that he wanted you! And now he does. And he will be hurt – he *is* hurt.'

I felt the familiar knot forming around my neck. Like a leash, a noose. I said, 'I'm not right for him. Not in the long run. It's different, don't you see? We get on nicely, as friends. But in the long run . . .' To me it was so obvious. We were all right so long as we weren't married. We could structure the hours of our day as we wished. Work all night when we wanted to, or see two movies in one evening and eat steak three times a day.

Marriage would change all that. We would become that two-headed social monster, A Couple. We would go to parties thrown by Prashant's colleagues in the agency and we'd give some ourselves. It wasn't that I didn't have a good time when I went to a party. I could, if I wanted to, simper and say, *Long time, no see! My, but you've lost weight! Did you read about the Iran crisis? They say there's going to be a war. Great food!*

But I didn't want to. I tried to explain this to Radzie. 'It's not Prashant. It's the lifestyle. I must be able to find my own pace in life – I can't just dance to the same tune that everyone else dances to – '

Radzie had said, 'Yes, but – meanwhile, he's hurting. He's sweet, he's kind, he's affectionate and he . . . there's no other word for it . . . he loves you.'

'He thinks he does,' I said. 'But it's not what I call love.'

'Yes – but – *he does*! And as long as that's so, what is he supposed to do with his feelings?'

'I don't know,' I said.

'And you don't care?' said Radzie. 'It really doesn't matter?'

'It matters,' I said, struggling to be honest, knowing that everything I said sounded harsh, 'but unless it matters equally for me, it's not enough.' I tried to explain it materially. 'I want to live in a tent and he wants to live in a safe, comfortable prefabricated house – '

'And isn't that all right?' asked Radzie. 'Don't we all have some kind of favourite, impossible dreams? Is he *wrong* because he dreams of comfort and safety?'

'Of course he's not wrong,' I said, 'except for wanting me with him. I'm the one who's wrong. For him. He thinks my problem is just one of scale, and that if I would only *adjust* myself to his view, I could live in his concrete house. But he's wrong. I can't. I'm a nomad. A house would stifle me, choke my spirit, suffocate me . . .' I felt breathless just contemplating it. And, besides, I was going to die at thirty. That was also a factor. Maybe the main factor.

'Really? Are you really, really sure that you *are* a nomad?' Radzie had asked, looking unhappy.

'Yes,' I had said. 'Yes.'

FEBRUARY

AMONGST MY SISTER'S FRIENDS was a German lady called Ilse. Her husband was a surgeon in the same hospital as my brother-in-law. Ilse had grey eyes shot with brighter, clearer sparks. Her blonde-streaked hair was cropped short and her well-chiselled features seemed always on the verge of a lovely, ironic smile. We met because a local women graduates' club organized a morning when they invited Radzie, myself, Ilse and a young Swedish girl to talk about our experiences in education systems outside the US.

It was a surprise to understand that Americans seemed to feel a strong sense of their isolation from other parts of the planet. It was a theme that often came up in conversation when I met Americans. At the same time, the fact of belonging to such a self-contained world, so intensely self-aware that other worlds, paled in significance, made ordinary exchanges difficult. At the graduates' club discussion, I realized that even though we were all speaking in English, the precise meanings of quite ordinary words were altered by the context in which they were used. A house in Pennsylvania, for instance, was a very different type of building to the kind in which I lived in Bombay. And beyond that, when I tried to describe the system in the schools I'd been to, of grouping students into 'houses', each with their own names, colours and identities, I could see that there was no comprehension at all. It was a completely alien concept and the use of a common word like 'house' only made it that much more impossible to explain. The closest approximation I could make to the idea was a fraternity house in college, but it was not a good analogy and I gave up the effort very quickly.

Once, in a shop, when I had handed over my Thomas Cook traveller's cheque for encashment, the young woman assistant asked me where the cheque had been issued. When I told her, she exclaimed so loudly that other customers looked around at us, 'BOMBAY??!! Wow!'

It felt very strange to fulfil someone else's definition of exotic. Ilse was in this sense a comfort to speak to, because she understood the complexity of being a foreigner even though she was so much less of one than me. She had only a faint German accent and she looked indistinguishable from the majority of the people on the streets and in shops. We spent a couple of very pleasant afternoons eating her home-baked bread, talking about being outsiders in a culture of insiders who had themselves been outsiders not so long ago. Neither she nor Radzie had changed her citizenship though it was growing annually more absurd not to, considering that they knew that the US was their permanent home. Some final commitment remained yet to be made. I found it easier to talk to Ilse than to the few other Indians I met.

This should not be surprising. I often found myself thinking that instead of comparing India with any single country, if it were compared to the whole of Europe, it would be easier to understand why I found so little in common with people who came from vastly different regions of my home continent. As a South Indian I was the equivalent of, say, a Portuguese attempting to feel deep kinship with a Swede or a German. Back in India, it would have been unlikely for our paths ever to have crossed.

Most of these Indians came from backgrounds in which English was a second language. They were the brightest and smartest of their generation. They were hard-working, highly paid professionals who had every right to be proud of their achievements in their adopted homeland. Yet they routinely spoke of the 'old country' with nostalgia and yearning even though it was clear that they could never actually live there again. Their standard of living had been raised too high for them to be able to adjust back to the irregular power supply and waterborne diseases of their origins. I knew that they found my irreverent attitude to the sacred homeland an unpleasant example of cultural contamination.

One of Radzie's senior colleagues at the hospital was an officious busybody by the name of Dr Mrs Uma Parthasarathy – she was the sort of woman who insisted on using the title 'Mrs'. She considered herself a leading light in the Indian community, having migrated to the US ten years before most of her younger contemporaries. She lived five minutes down the road at the next turn-off from Radzie's home and whenever she came over for a visit, she and I had a disagreement about something.

One day, when she was visiting, she told us that she had successfully convinced an Indian colleague not to waste her money sending it to an Indian child-sponsorship group. 'Why take the risk?' she had said, meaningfully.

I said, 'What risk?'

'You can never be sure,' said she. 'Sometimes these agencies . . .' And she shook her head.

I didn't understand what she meant so I asked her to explain. Radzie was away at that moment, talking on the phone.

Dr Uma said, 'You never know – she may have ended up sending money to support a Muslim child by mistake. And then where would we be? At least our own hard-earned money should go to our own people – '

I felt a curtain of rage fall across my reason. So I spoke immoderately. I said, 'Funny you should say that. I have six adopted children back in India and they ARE all Muslim.'

She gaped at me for instant and said, 'Really! – I thought you said you weren't married?'

'I'm not,' I said. 'The adoption agency doesn't care about such niceties. It specializes in Muslim children. I assured them that I would do my utmost to ensure that these children – they are all boys – would grow up to be virile enough to seed a whole township with their progeny!'

Dr Uma was certainly no fool so she must have known that I couldn't be telling the truth. But she was so taken aback that she stammered, 'I – I don't understand . . .'

I said, 'I belong to a group which believes that our Muslim brothers might become an endangered species, with people like you around. And so, in the interests of maintaining our nation's ethnic diversity, I support any activity which makes it easier for them to multiply and be fruitful.'

She said, her eyes bulging, 'It is well known that they are traitors, all of them! They will betray us to Pakistan! They will overrun us with their – their – '

'Taj Mahals and mughlai cuisine, yes!' I said. 'The fact is, I've always preferred the culture of Islam and feel it was a great shame that the Mughals didn't rule India for long enough. Think what it would have done to modern tourism to have had a Taj in every state!'

She was practically snarling. She said, 'You are a very foolish and dangerous young woman! Just imagine what it would be like to wear a burkha! Covering your face in the heat of summer, saying prayers all day long and being married to a man who has four other wives!'

'Well, no, actually only three, since I would be one of them,' I said. 'And the prayers aren't all day long, but only five times every twenty-four hours. A burkha's okay, once you get used to it. And I think it might be fun to have co-wives. More company while doing the housework after all and – ' I was going to add *no need to service the stud every day* but Radzie returned just then and decorum was abruptly restored. I said nothing more. Dr Uma changed the topic immediately and left soon after.

When I told Radzie what I had said, she scolded me very severely, telling me that, rather like Kamala in New York, the lady had faced some sort of trauma during the partition riots because her father was posted in Delhi at the time. I was unrepentant. Traumas were part of the human landscape, I said, so what? 'It's bad enough to be bigoted back in India,' I said, 'but to export those far-off hates to this country and to prevent some poor Indian child from being sponsored because of it – well, I think that's really more vile than I can accept.'

I knew that Radzie agreed with me. Nevertheless, she reminded me, 'It's easy for you – you're a visitor, you'll have your say and then you'll go away again. I live here and I need to get along with the people around me!' But then she laughed, imagining what Dr Uma was thinking. 'Poor Uma! She'll never stop wondering whether or not you meant it . . .'

As my stay came to an end, we did several rounds of shopping to buy clothes and suitcases for the trip. Radzie paid for everything. The cumulative sum was so much more money than I was used to spending that I didn't try to imagine how I would pay it back. I told myself that I would just have to work very hard in Europe, when I got there, in order to be able to return the loan some day.

LONDON TO MÜNICH

I HAD FOUR FAMILIES of close relatives in London. They were all dear to me, uncles and aunts whom I had known since early childhood. Everyone wanted to know where I was going and what I was doing and to all I said, 'I'm going to Germany to see a friend who has just had a baby.'

When I was by myself, which was often, either on my way to a tube station or from it, I felt a melancholy satisfaction. The satisfaction was from knowing that I had succeeded in at least one part of my objective. I was on my way to Germany. In those years, Indians didn't need a visa for Germany, so there was nothing to worry about until I was ready to go to Holland. The melancholy was because I was discovering once again and in a more robust form that the difficulty with secrets is not that they are hard to keep, but too easy.

It is only when a person has something to hide that she realizes how much of an adult's life is already invisible, requiring no special effort to maintain it that way. There is no audience trained on the heroine's movements, keeping track of exits and entries on the stage of known events. I did not want a secret life– I wanted to be able to live as I wished, but without having to make explanations and justifications to anyone.

I was reduced to living with secrets because I didn't have any other option. I found my reality dwindling to the dot on the lower-case 'i' of my own private consciousness, as I walked around, alone with my thoughts. A moment's inattention could wipe me out forever.

The cheapest way to get to Münich from London was to take the ferry from Dover to Oostende in Belgium and then the Trans Europ Nacht Express overnight to Münich.

I packed as if I were going to another solar system, taking everything I could possibly need as well as all manner of items for purely sentimental reasons. I took all my art equipment and nearly all my clothes. I took a dysfunctional alarm clock because I thought it was better than none at all. I took my new camera and all the books that I wanted to discuss with Piet. My suitcase and sling bag felt as if they were filled with lead.

Micki had told me how to get to her place from the station in Münich, because she couldn't leave the baby alone in the house in order to meet me. The suburb of Neu Gilching in which she lived wasn't really an urb at all. It was a couple of two-storey flats strung out along the side of a minor roadway with only a slender street lamp to keep them company on the road. It was the first week of April and the air still smelt of snow.

Micki was waiting for me, looking welcoming but tired. It was just a week since she had returned to the house since the birth. We had spoken on the telephone only once, from London, when she had given me the directions. She had forgotten that I was nervous in the presence of babies, so when she showed her daughter Leila to me, I didn't need to worry that she would be offended by anything I said or did. Like anyone who has recently produced a living being, Micki could not imagine that I was anything but as enthralled as she was.

The apartment she was living in had a floor plan similar to those diagrams for plotting the golden mean using only a setsquare and a compass: one large rectangle with a square along its short end. The kitchen, pantry, dining room and living room were accommodated in the rectangle. The bedroom and nursery were in the square. The bathroom was out on the landing and was split into two separate spaces, one for a toilet, the other for a bath, shower and washing machine.

Despite its austere functionality the flat had a gladness that made it a happy place to be. The bedroom had a furry rug on the floor. When Kurtz came home, he and Micki would spread a silk scarf on the rug and set out a ceremonial tea, brewed in a brown clay teapot, with a fitted cosy under its arching bamboo handle. It was served with poppy-seed cakes from the local bakery. Kurtz would have changed into an embroidered cotton kurta and would play plaintive Western tunes on his sitar. Leila would lie on the furry rug, listening with a rapt, wondering expression. Kurtz was studying to be a homeopath. He was away from 9 in the morning till 4.30 in the afternoon. Until she could go back to work, the strain of running a household while caring for a newborn showed in Micki's pale skin. Since she had to take the child in a pram wherever she went, her option was to wait until Kurtz was home to do any shopping. Any daytime trips which were too arduous to undertake with the baby in tow were out of the question. She was looking forward to having me around, she said, because it meant that she could go into the city and get some of her essential paperwork done.

I had thought that my presence would be a nuisance and had therefore not planned to be with her any longer than it would take me to get a visa for Holland, perhaps a couple of days. But I was very grateful that she had agreed to have me at all and it was nice to feel wanted. I found myself asking, instead, if a month would be too difficult, given that there wasn't enough space for me in her flat. She said that we'd have to see how to manage.

Immediately after I arrived we went out with the baby in a pram, to get ourselves the makings of a fresh salad and sandwiches for lunch. We came back, ate, fed the baby, saw her safely off to sleep in her cot and only then did we allow ourselves the luxury of a chat.

'Okay! Let's hear it,' said Micki. 'What's the story?'

The silence around us was unnerving. I had thought that the place where Radzie lived was quiet, but perhaps in the US the atmosphere is so saturated with radio waves that even in complete audio-silence our brains pick up subliminal hummings from the ether. In Neu Gilching it felt as if a sonic-blotter had been turned on, so that even when we spoke, our voices did not linger in the air but seemed to be siphoned away, like everything else of consequence, by the big city over the horizon.

It was a tremendous relief, finally, to be able to discuss my secret plans. I made it as brief as I could.

At the end of my telling, Micki said, 'I want to get this straight: you're going to Holland for a month? To spend time with . . . two? Okay, one, Dutchman, maybe two though, whom you haven't known for more than three months – okay, not even three months – in Bombay?' She stopped, looking at me quizzically. 'Just like that? And there's really no reason?' I shook my head. 'None at all?' she asked.

I shrugged. 'If there is, I don't know what it is.'

She smiled ironically and said, 'Well. I suppose that you *have* considered the possibility . . .' She stopped.

I said, 'What?'

She sighed, exasperated. Micki was one year younger than me, though in the same class at school. She had always been smarter than me and more mature. 'Even *you* must have asked yourself whether . . . Oh, for goodness' sake! I mean, are you in love!?'

I flinched and said, 'Oh no! Not that.'

She said, 'How can you be so sure?'

I shrugged and said, 'Because!'

She said, 'No. You're not being honest with yourself.'

I said, 'I am.'

She said, 'No one – *no one!* – travels halfway across the world, on her sister's money, being sure not to tell her family what she's doing, just to shake hands with a man!'

I said, looking her in the eye, 'It's already gone beyond shaking hands – '

She said, 'And then!'

I said, 'Then nothing. I want to spend some time with him. That's all. Really, that's all.'

She stared at me. 'How long?'

'About a month,' I said. 'Maybe a little more. Two, perhaps.'

'Doing what?' she asked. 'Surely not . . . shaking hands – continuously! – for two months?' She grinned. It would become our euphemism for a while. 'I should think you'd get a little tired of it!'

I laughed, but said, 'I'm – I'm looking for cosmic truth. I think he can help me find it.'

She stared at me with frank disbelief and said, 'Oh! Don't be ridiculous!'

I thought about Zero, the loss of my room, the loss of my personal space back in Bombay. I felt bleak waters closing over my head. I hadn't told Micki about those problems yet. Or about Prashant. Or about Piet's girlfriend. Or that I didn't have a return ticket. Nor money to buy one, unless I left right away. By comparison with these problems, it seemed to me, the search for cosmic truth was practically child's play. I said, 'Really – '

'But you've never been interested in that sort of thing!' she said.

'I am now,' I said.

'You can't be!' said Micki. 'You're too – too – *normal* to be chasing after something so abstract and – you know – *daffy*. . .' She was shaking her head, in exasperated concern. 'I think you're in love with this man and want to marry him and want to live happily ever after –' she was good at being blunt – 'and that you can't bear being associated with anything so ordinary and straightforward, so you're refusing to admit this very simple fact, even to yourself.'

I shook my head violently. 'No!' Then added, with some heat, 'I don't understand why you find it so difficult to believe that I would be interested in something other than – you know – whatever – '

Micki snorted a little laugh and said, 'Because you're the one who's just finished telling me that the reason you're going to Holland *is* this man!'

'He was the medium through which I began to question my reality,' I said. 'It's not at all daffy – in fact, there's nothing less daffy to think about than cosmic truth, if you see what I mean – '

But she was twitching the corners of her mouth down, 'Oh – *please*! Don't treat me like I'm an idiot. You know as well as I do what I mean. How long have I known you? Since we were in school together, since you were fourteen – and in all that time I've known you, I never suspected that you were a closet mystic in the making – never! Quite the opposite, actually . . .' She grinned and I grinned too, ruefully. 'You've always shown a tremendous fondness – if I might say so! – for the worldly sphere!'

I said, 'Yes, okay, so – but – surely a person can change? I mean, even suddenly? Isn't it possible that I, at almost twenty-five, might have really found something more to be excited by than – just – you know, food?'

Micki tilted her head to the side, considered for a moment whether or not to speak her mind. 'Well,' she said, 'if there were no man involved at all, it would be a bit easier to believe what you're telling me. But there IS one and he *is* the reason why you're going. So . . . I'm sorry, maybe you don't want to hear something like this, but it looks to me like you're fooling yourself.'

I said, 'Micki, you're saying that if I'm seeking out a man, it has to be because of, like you said just now, wanting to live with him or marry him – but that *isn't* my reason!' I shook my head in irritation. 'Why is it so hard to believe that I might be fascinated by someone and be desperate to spend time with him and be willing to go to great lengths to make it possible and yet it isn't now, nor ever will be, what everyone else calls romantic love? Isn't it possible that there are more kinds of magnetism than just this most obvious one? And isn't it possible that some of us respond to fields and currents other than the typical kind?'

Micki said quietly, 'Okay, maybe it's true and maybe you *do* have some reason that goes beyond ordinary . . . forces . . . but if so, you haven't shown me proof that that is so! According to me, you're behaving just like someone who is ordinarily "magnetized" – except that you refuse to give it the same name as everyone else – '

Leila, who had been sleeping since her last feed, woke up now and made little snuffling sounds to indicate that she would like some attention.

I said, 'Piet has a girlfriend. I know about her and I don't plan to take her place. I don't believe in stealing people away.' I would have gone on to remind Micki that I didn't believe in marriage and child-bearing, but felt it would have been indelicate considering the recent events in her life. 'I just want to be with him a *short while*,' I said. 'It must be possible to imagine a *connection* with someone which is intense as well as brief?'

Micki was shaking her head, but looking around, towards Leila. 'Yes,' she said. 'It's possible to imagine it. All of us talk about it, we describe it and we pretend to believe in it. And yet I think it just . . . doesn't happen. I don't know why . . .' She got up, as Leila gave out an exploratory hiccough, tuning up for a yell. 'I don't think human beings are wired that way – '

'It's because we're conditioned to think that any strong emotion must also be long-lived,' I said. 'Nowadays, we can afford relationships which don't need to include reproduction – so we don't need to think of the long-term – '

But the baby had claimed Micki already and she was no longer listening.

It was decided that I would spend a couple of days with Micki and Kurtz in their apartment but that my continued stay in Germany would depend on whether friends of theirs, who had agreed to consider the proposition, could have me over for the remainder of the month.

The friends lived in a spacious condominium in the centre of Münich. Micki and I went to visit them. They were two couples, living together in what they called a 'Kommune'. They were Anne-Marie and Charlie, Margot and Franz, all four of them university students. Only Margot spoke any English, because she had an American father. She and I bonded quickly, which wasn't surprising considering she was the only one with whom I could actually talk.

They said that they would try me out for a few days, on the understanding that if I didn't suit them, they could ask me to leave without anyone's feelings being hurt and without explanations needing to be offered. I was to contribute to basic food expenses but nothing else, as they didn't want to think of my stay as a commercial transaction. There was a bathroom with a toilet, tub and hand-held shower. And there was a toilet room with just a toilet. In the kitchen was a table set with four wooden chairs painted red, where everyone sat together to eat. They added a spare one, however, to include me.

Each of the four rooms was occupied by one member of the Kommune but in practice Charlie shared Anne-Marie's room and Franz shared Margot's room. In theory they took turns to do the cooking, but in practice whoever felt like it could do a turn at the gas-range. Only the evening meal was ever cooked, mashed potatoes and salad being the norm. But there were always fresh vegetables in the fridge, with bread, cheese and the occasional sausage. Milk was not a high priority and orange juice was my regular contribution.

I spent my days with Micki, returning to the Kommune in the evenings. I was amused to hear, from Margot, that I wasn't to imagine they were typical Germans. She wanted me to know that it was considered highly irregular just to live together in this fashion, Germans being normally much more convention bound. What amused me was that, despite these disclaimers, if the four 'Kommunistas' made an appointment to meet at the kitchen table at seventeen minutes to 4 o'clock, by golly, there they were with four and a half seconds to spare! Even in their irregularity, they could not forsake the deep conditioning of being punctual.

WAITING

THE GIRL AT THE visa desk at the Dutch Embassy wasn't happy with me, because of course Indian passport holders must get all their visas before leaving India. But in the end she stamped my passport and said, in a tired voice, 'All right. One mons. Tourist.' I had spoken to Piet on the telephone a couple of times.

He seemed remote, though apparently looking forward to my visit. I booked my ticket before calling again. There was a train which went directly to Utrecht, where he lived. It was a big city by European standards. I confirmed the date and time of my arrival. He said he would be at the station to meet me.

After the phone call, I found that several times in the day I had to pause to breathe carefully. The air around me would suddenly fill with sparkles. Till that moment, the final phase of my journey had been very much like a daydream. But now, with the visa finally in hand, it *was* going to happen. I had made a plan, it had seemed unlikely and irresponsible, it had had many opportunities to fail but now it was coming to fruition.

But Micki was worried for me. She was not alone. Kurtz, whom I met only occasionally in the evenings, expressed his concern too. According to him, my descriptions of my Dutch friends suggested that they were unstable characters. Kurtz said, 'Do they take drugs, at all?' He spoke English well, but didn't like to, he said. If he was making a concession for me it was because I was Micki's special friend.

I said that I had asked Piet about drugs. He had said that they certainly experimented with this and that, but weren't habitual users.

Kurtz looked very sceptical and remarked that dharma-seekers and drugs went 'how do you say . . . hand in foot? Hand in hand.'

My Kommunistas smoked marijuana, which is how this conversation about drugs with Kurtz and Micki arose. In India, grass and ganja are so commonly used that no one I knew even referred to them as drugs. I had smoked ganja a few times, but never as a habit. I didn't like it. It either did nothing for me or it filled my mind with uncontrollable hallucinations. On one particular occasion, after rehearsing for a play I had rashly agreed to act in, I hadn't been able to get my regular ride home. So I accepted the invitation of one of the other members of the cast to crash at a two-room bachelor pad in Warden Road.

The flat was on the sixth floor and two other men shared it. All three of them used the bedroom to sleep in and told me that I could have the drawing room to myself. The place was reasonably clean and there was a mattress on the floor that doubled as a divan during the day. But the fuse had blown at the junction box downstairs and one of the circuits was 'out'. It meant that I would not have lights or a fan to use in 'my' room. I said it hardly mattered, since all I was going to do was fall asleep. We had returned from our rehearsal at 2 a.m. and I was ready to drop. But just before we went our separate ways, the boys wanted to know if I'd like to share a joint with them in their bedroom. It would have seemed unfriendly not to, so I accepted a few puffs and pushed off to my quarters.

Such a low dose would normally have had no impact on me at all. But this time, perhaps because it was a more potent herb or I was in a more receptive mood, it blew the lid off my psyche. I couldn't sleep at all because my nerves seemed to have become tripwires on which every sound within a 200 mile radius of that little flat registered as flashes of tangible light. If someone dropped a metal plate on a terrace ten houses away, I felt purple sparks crackle across the surface of my skin. If a car honked on the street I felt blinding cascades of shock all across my body.

My hearing had become so sensitive that I was picking up signals below my normal audio threshold. I was convinced, for instance, that I could hear a cockroach breathing inside the pillow my head was on. But because I couldn't turn the light on, I couldn't check to see whether I was right or wrong. Meanwhile I could hear it scratching the back of its silly head, wondering why there was this oppressive weight bearing down on it from above.

As for spirits, well, the air was so thick with them that it felt as if I had blundered into an otherworldly conference centre. It was an idiotic situation to be in. I was paralysed with fear of the supernatural and irradiated with unnatural sounds but if the only remedy was to wake up the three men sleeping in the neighbouring room, well – I wouldn't do it. If I had sought refuge in their room, and if they were as smashed as I was, then it would have been positively rude of them not to outrage my modesty just a little. And I would then have had to make the effort of either repulsing these efforts or succumbing to them, neither of which I wanted to do. So I passed a sleepless night, vowing never to accept casual smokes again.

For the Kommunistas smoking grass was more a rite of belonging to their unconventional lifestyle than a means to being stoned. They used branded cigarettes to make joints by emptying the tobacco out of a cigarette, mixing the tobacco with grass, then stuffing the combination back into the delicate paper shell of the cigarette. It was an intricate and time-consuming manoeuvre and the resulting smoke was extremely mild. It did not affect me at all and it amused me to see how much mileage my hosts got out of a sensory excursion that was only slightly more intoxicating than leaning out of the first-floor window of their own flat.

Micki did leave me to look after Leila a couple of times. Everything had to be explained to me. Measuring out the powder for bottle feeds, storing the bottles in readiness after taking them out of their sterilizing cold-storage tank, washing and putting them back in again. How to hold the baby so that she didn't choke or resist. How to pat her back so that she would burp on schedule. How to change her nappies. It was like being introduced to the secret lore of mothers, first discovering an entire repertory of astonishing problems, then being given the tried and tested solutions to them.

Micki and her friends were opposed to the throwaway nappy concept and so she used disposable pads in combination with the traditional cotton nappy cloths. She was proud of hers, which had all come from India. 'You can't believe how expensive these things are here!' she said. They were 2 feet square, sturdy and white. They were used up at the rate of five a day. The washing machine was in constant use and Micki always had one load of clean white squares to hang up on the line in the backyard downstairs, and one load to take down. She showed me how her mother-in-law had taught her to overlap the corners so that effectively twice the length of the line could be utilized.

I had watched her clean and change the baby several times before venturing to do it myself. I was surprised to find that it wasn't especially unpleasant, just unfamiliar. A baby whose feed is almost entirely milk produces only a very mild-tempered mush at the other end. Micki's approach to cleaning had been taught to her by the midwife who had assisted with the birth which had been at Kurtz's family home half a day's journey away by train. First the baby was laid flat on her back on a flat rubber-sheeted surface and the nappy opened up from being knotted on either side: 'There's the safety-pin concept and the knot concept,' said Micki, 'but Kurtz and I felt we didn't like the thought of something sharp and mechanical so close to her skin so we use knots.'

Holding the feet up and drawing the nappy and pad away was the tricky bit, because it was easy to forget to keep a wad of cotton, liberally soaked in Johnson's Baby Oil, handy. If one had forgotten, then one apologized to the baby, got one's act together and started afresh. If one had remembered, then it was a moment's effort to swab the baby's operational area, then lower the whole assembly down on a fresh pad and nappy which had previously been readied and kept accessible for this purpose. After that there was the dusting with talcum powder and the knotting up of the sides of the nappy, just like the one that had been removed. Through all of this the baby watched with grave, unsmiling attention, as if bemused at the change of attendant and not at all sure that she approved. But she never actually raised an objection.

I felt fiercely self-conscious under that sharp gaze and usually performed my duties while mentally holding my breath. She was at an age when her perceptions were like photosensitive paper. Even the weight of an eyelash would register and be processed, to become part of the foundation of a sane and healthy life. Or the gate-pass to an asylum. Or any of the conditions in between. Everything she encountered, good, bad or indifferent, would become part of the eternal record of her personality. I was anxious not to let her down, while feeling hopelessly inadequate all the while.

On one occasion, Micki and I went into town together, with the baby in her pram. Micki went off ahead of me to visit her office for the first time since giving birth, while I continued onward to the condo, with the baby. I didn't want Micki to panic, so I didn't tell her that I was overcome with terror at the thought of the fifteen-minute walk across busy city streets and alongside traffic, with the pram and its precious cargo. It is an extreme responsibility to be left with someone else's child. I was very glad to have done it just that once.

I noticed, however, the warm and friendly glances I attracted from other women as I pushed the pram along. Normally, I attracted no attention at all, as if I weren't there in quite the same way as everybody else. But with the baby, waiting for the lights to change at zebra crossings, the otherwise carefully neutral expressions of the citizens around me softened at first sight. One or two people stopped to lean into the carriage, to exclaim at the sweet sight of a sleeping infant.

I soon got used to handling her and no longer felt awkward about picking her up or holding her. Sometimes, looking at the little face with its hazel eyes and enquiring, intelligent expression, I caught glimpses of the reasons why people looked forward to being parents. But however much I approved of the warm, breathing bundle in my care, I was glad not to have one of my own, glad that I never would.

Having children meant taking on anxieties, tensions and heartache twenty-four hours a day, every day, until whenever the offspring chose to be independent! The miracle was that most people not only consented to such a fate but actively sought it out.

In the past it was considered the greatest blessing to have many children because that was the simplest way to ensure survival. Families needed to stay together for long enough to ensure security throughout the slow years of child-rearing. The conjugal bond was a survival tactic, romantic love was a breeding strategy.

But life is no longer so uncertain. Quite the opposite. If we are threatened by anything now, it is not annihilation by plague or war but by our own reckless population growth. Women need no longer behave like passive flowerpots into which male gardeners can plant their seed. More than at any time in human history, today's women have the means to control reproduction to suit our own purpose.

Very few of us do.

WALPURGISNACHT

ONE AFTERNOON, MARGOT BLEW in with the wind from the streets still caught in the blouse she wore over a T-shirt. 'Listen!' she said to me. Tonight there is going to be a big, big, demonstration! Would you come?' Then her lively face filled with bewilderment. 'But! I have forgotten the word!' She couldn't tell me what the demonstration was against. 'How do you say it – when a – a man and woman – when they – och!' She threw her hands up in exasperation. It turned out that the word she wanted was 'rape' which in German was 'vergewaltigung', a word I had never heard. We were both amused that our high-school language courses had not seen fit to include such a word in our vocabularies.

She explained that the occasion was the ancient observance of Walpurgisnacht, the Sabbath night for witches and others who consorted with the forces of darkness. The demonstration was formally entitled 'Give Us Back the Night' to highlight the fact that women were corralled in their homes after dusk, for fear of men's aggression. I had never marched in any sort of demonstration before and it seemed to me that this was a fitting one to start with. Anne-Marie and Margot both prepared for the evening by painting black crosses on their faces and wearing their oldest and shabbiest clothes. I didn't have to make any particular effort, as my clothes were fairly shabby to begin with.

We set off together. I had the idea that the evening would be spent wandering about the streets in an orderly procession, perhaps shouting slogans. But as we approached the venue, I realized that in scattered groups or individually, the women walking alongside us were dressed in bizarre, outlandish costumes, behaving in a markedly non-Teutonic manner. Raucous, unbridled. Young men, too, were moving in twitchy patrols, bushy-tailed, pumped up, on the prowl or standing on the pavements, in their tight jeans and boots, with their hands thrust into their pockets like guns into holsters, or tucked into their armpits, emphasizing their biceps. One man happened to be near us as Margot said, 'They will haff to watch out for us!' in English. And he whipped around and said, with a vicious, avid expression in his eyes, in English, 'No! *You* will have to watch out for *us*!' It was too late to bother with feeling anxious, so I didn't.

At the venue, the gathered women already numbered a couple of hundred. Burning brands were being handed out. Margot bought one for herself and one for me, 3-foot-long tapers made of cheap wax, skewered on to short, rough-hewn, wooden rods. Anne-Marie, who was normally very serious, was actually smiling as her taper was lit, dimples appearing in the black crosses on her cheeks.

At seven o'clock precisely, loud shrieks rent the air at the forward end of the procession. It was an unfamiliar sound, a high-pitched yelping, and it took me a few minutes to recognize what it was. Margot had not said anything to me about screaming! I wondered if I could be exempted from this part of the demonstration because I thought I would feel very silly afterwards. The cries rippled backwards along the whole length of the broad ribbon of marchers. Soon I could see the women in front of us putting their heads back, baying and whooping. Then the strangers directly around us, then Margot and Anne-Marie began to do it too. And a few moments later, so did I.

It had begun. Later we would hear that over seven hundred women marched that night. We moved like a living tide through the streets that had been cleared of traffic for the march, screaming continuously all the while, shaking the torches in the air like flaming lances. Linking arms once the brands had burned out and jogging forward. I never thought it was possible to scream so much. A few people attempted to sing songs now and again, but the screaming was far more successful, sometimes taking the form of police-car sirens, sometimes ambulance whoops, sometimes tribal ululations, sometimes just ragged soprano roars. Starting out on an 'EEEEEE . . .' then progressing through 'AAAAAA . . .' till the air ran out. Stamping one's feet and jiggling about. Laughing wildly at the men who stood at the edge of the action, grinning uncertainly at us, not sure whether to be excited or depressed. Chivvying the policemen who walked sedately alongside the procession, pretending that for the purposes of this day, this time, they were not men but only police.

It was violently exhilarating.

We got home feeling like unexploded bombs and talked through the night about feminism, the oppression of women, the need to take control of our lives. My throat felt hot and swollen and I thought it would be like a wood-rasp the next morning, but it wasn't. According to Margot, that's what came of good, healing energy. 'If you were frightened or angry the screaming would hurt you, make you lose your voice. But yesterday the vibrations were so good, you could not get the harm.' Whatever it was, I felt as if we had conquered oppressors and stormed the fortress.

I was looking forward to telling Micki about it, but when I did, she said, 'And so?' smiling faintly. 'You marched. You think something will change? In one night?' She had declined the invitation to come because of the baby, but it seemed to me that she wouldn't have come anyway.

I was instantly deflated.

She said, 'I didn't think you were such a committed feminist – '

I felt stung by this and said, 'I've been one for years!'

Micki made a little moue with her mouth – she had an attractive, full mouth and used it expressively. 'Well! For a feminist, you're not being very considerate, are you?'

I must have looked perplexed, because she said, 'Piet's girlfriend. She's a woman too, isn't she?'

I wriggled uncomfortably, regretting having spoken about her to Micki.

'Or doesn't that sort of thing matter? To a feminist?' said my friend, looking at me with her head cocked to one side. She added, murmuringly, 'I should have thought even being attracted to men was rather suspect . . .'

I knew that she was teasing me but I couldn't stop myself from rising to her bait. I said, 'It's very old-fashioned to believe that feminists are anti-men . . .' But as I thought about the demonstration of the night before, I had to acknowledge that the charge of energy released that night was certainly unfriendly. 'Feminism is also about liberating women from preconceptions about, you know, what's "nice" by the standards of conventional society – '

'And your own standards?' I looked away. She said, 'I thought you didn't believe in . . . you know, infidelity – other people getting hurt?'

'I don't,' I said. 'It's part of all the things I can't explain. It's like I'm trying to destroy the foundations of what I myself believe in, to see what's real and what's fluff.'

'Of course,' she said, 'you might be destroying someone else's life while you rattle about testing your foundations.'

I said, 'It's not a strong relationship – theirs, I mean . . .' Piet had hinted as much and Japp had said it in so many words.

But Micki just aimed her ironic smile at me, sideways. I felt chagrined.

She was right. What mattered was what *I* believed, regardless of the standards of the others involved. 'But it's not for long,' I said weakly. 'From my side. That's my ultimate argument, you know? I'm not planning to *steal* him. Just to borrow him, very briefly. And maybe not even that.'

I told Micki that I had felt, in the handful of conversations I'd had on the telephone with Piet since leaving India, that there were distances between me and him which were not accounted for by mere geography. 'So his house will really be just an address to stay at. I probably won't see much of him at all.'

I could say this and I could try to believe it. But I didn't actually hope it.

Micki and I spent pleasant afternoons, wandering in the English Garden with the pram and going on forays to the supermarket. We talked about my plans ahead. I called my parents in Calicut, my sister-in-law and Prashant in Bombay and my sister in the US from public telephone booths. I gave them Micki's number as my contact. However, I asked her not to tell them where I was if they called while I was in Holland.

She reminded me that she wasn't happy with what I was doing. 'It's such a risk, and for what? You say you don't even love this man.' She added, a little wistfully, 'You could just stay on here a little longer, maybe we can find work for you to do . . .' But we had tried that with a couple of magazines and drawn blanks. Language and culture, as one man explained, kindly, over the telephone, were important to making cartoons come alive for readers. Without a shared culture to refer to, my work would not strike any responsive chords. It was an argument I knew well. Even in India, my work did not strike responsive chords.

I said, 'I've chosen a twisted path. I know it. But having chosen it, I owe it to myself to see it to its end. Or I'll never know. I'd have to live forever wondering what would have happened if I had gone all the way. I know that I might regret it, but I'd prefer that – '

'You can't *prefer* regrets!' exclaimed Micki.

'I meant, I'd prefer that regret to the other one,' I said.

'What other one?' asked Micki.

'Returning home without trying to stick it out,' I said.

THE MISSIONARY

MY DEPARTURE WAS DRAWING nigh. I gave the Kommunistas caricatures of themselves as parting presents and they were pleased in the uncertain way of those who suspect they are being made fun of but know that it's not cool to object. We swore to stay in touch. Anne-Marie gave me a small vase made by herself. The three weeks for which I had been part of their unit had brought a closeness that surprised all of us, I think.

I went over to Neu Gilching early the next morning. Micki walked me to the local station of the suburban line, with the baby in her pram. I had been living out of my sling bag for the duration of my stay with the Kommunistas, but now I had my heavy suitcase. We walked slowly, along the same route I took every day to and from the station, except that today when I got off at Münich Central, instead of walking out into the city, I would go inward to where the transcontinental trains were parked, searching for the one that would terminate in Utrecht. Micki and I said our goodbyes at her local station as if I were a soldier going to the front. She was convinced that I was treading a spiralling path towards self-destruction. I had been infected by her fatalistic belief and felt doomed, a traveller bound for nowhere.

Ticket, passport, money. By 11 o'clock, I had located my seat on the train, the ticket had been checked and punched, I was told to keep my passport ready for the border and then there was nothing more for me to do but wait to reach Holland.

I had brought along a book to read, *Shogun*, recommended to me very highly by Piet. I couldn't concentrate on it, however. It had been five months since I had last seen Piet. For the month that I had been in Germany, I had not been able to find any freelance work at all. What were the chances of finding enough work in Holland not merely to afford living there but to buy myself a ticket back to India? Dim.

The person sitting next to me was a woman in her late fifties whose gauntness was set off rather badly by the dull red sweater she wore over pale creams and greys. She smiled at me as I took my seat but something in the quality of her smile caused me to make an instant and negative assessment of her. I could not define what I didn't like about her and since I could not define it, it annoyed me even more that she was friendly.

Once the train had picked up conversational speed, she reached into a pannier tucked under her seat and brought out a greaseproof paper packet. It contained sandwiches. She turned to me and smiling encouragingly said, 'Please! Will you have one?'

I thanked her and took one, knowing that to accept a gift of food on a train is the fee for agreeing to talk. It was a warm cucumber sandwich.

She said, 'Ah . . . excuse me!'

I said, 'Yes?'

She said, 'Are you . . . von Pakistan?'

I said, 'No, India.'

'Ah!' she said. 'India! It is a vonderful country, is it not?'

I said, 'Well . . .' I could describe India in many ways, but wonderful would not be one of them. I smiled, however, to show that I didn't mean to be unfriendly, even if I sounded that way.

'So?' she said. 'Are you going to Holland for a visit?' I said I was. I had concluded that she was Dutch, not German. The accent was different and her skin had a transparency, a light-expanding fineness. Her eyes bulged slightly and their colour had a watery pallor as if centuries of saving the Netherlands from the North Sea had rinsed out the irises. 'Ah! And how long you will be dere?'

I said, 'Three months.'

She raised her pale eyebrows high. Why did I get the impression that she was an unmarried woman? 'Three months!' she exclaimed, apparently aghast at the thought. 'That is a ffery long time!'

I was nonplussed. I had not expected such a pronounced reaction from the lady. I would have preferred it if she had remained within character, slightly fussy, but with no very defined views on anything. I said, 'Is it?'

'Yes!' she said. 'For instance, where – how! – will you stay? Holland is ffery expensive!'

I said, 'I – I have friends.'

'Friends!' she said. 'But it will be ffery difficult voor them! Are you sure this is right?'

I wondered if I had wandered into someone else's film script. 'I – uh – *they* said it would be all right. I asked them,' I said, conscious of the fact that it was only in my final conversation with Piet that I had specifically mentioned three months. 'My friends are quite rich. Very rich, actually.' Piet had told me this several times. It was the one reason that I did not have any qualms about staying with him. I assumed that my presence would not be a financial burden to him and would cost me nothing because I had already warned him that I would not be able to pay.

'But, still! It is a long time!' persisted the lady. 'It is a big responsibility – three months!'

I thought it extremely odd that she was willing to make such personal observations. Was it a Dutch trait then, to be so outspoken, even with a complete stranger on a train? I said, 'Oh, but – he – they – stayed in my house for three months in India, so I thought – ' Of course, they had been Govinda's guests, not mine precisely. I felt self-conscious about these dislocations of the truth, and aimed my annoyance at the lady for bringing them to my attention.

She clicked her tongue rapidly, shaking her head sideways in denial. 'Ah no – it is not the same, in Holland! We have not the servants that you have in India! It is different for us, to have a guest inside the house!'

This was undeniable. I didn't have an answer for it, but it gave me an opening to extend the conversation in a less personal direction. I said, 'So . . . you've been to India?'

She beamed and said, 'Once! To South India. An ash-ram. It woss extremely educational!' She said she belonged to a missionary society that went on regular tours to countries where the message of Christ had not yet been properly installed. 'And we attended a public lecture. By Mr and Mrs Gandhi. They are doing wonderful things for the country. It is so tragic that they lost the election.'

'You mean, that *Mrs* Gandhi lost – '

'Ye-es,' she said, hesitating only slightly. 'Mrs Gandhi *and* Mr Gandhi. They are both such vonderful personalities – '

'Mother and son, you mean? Or the son and his wife?' I didn't want to be pedantic, but it seemed to me important to know which pair she meant.

'I mean, the vonderful man vith de glasses and de spinning wheel! And his beautiful wife. I saw only her. With the white –' she drew a graceful plume in the air above her own head, with her hand, to signify the characteristic streak in Mrs Gandhi's hair – 'you know, in de haar.'

I drew in a deep breath. Did I dare to reveal that there was no relationship, marital or otherwise, between Mahatma Gandhi, the visionary revolutionary, and Mrs Gandhi, the politician and ex-prime minister whose party had so recently been ousted from power?

But she went on. 'It is a shame. De good peoples all over de worlt are losing everywhere and de bad ones, dey vin – '

I said, 'Excuse me, but I can't agree with you – ' She looked at me, her eyes widening in pained shock. 'I mean, about Mrs Gandhi. I think it was *great* that she lost the election. Maybe the only good thing that's happened in a long while. I was in Bombay when it happened; it really felt wonderful at the time. To think that the poor and helpless citizens of a country like India could actually take control of their fate like that – '

The diluted blue eyes misted over with distress. 'No, no!'

whispered the lady. 'She was *good!* I heard her talking to the people! She spoke about her father, her ideals! And she has saved so many of the sad, unhappy tigers. She told us, you know, at that public lecture, that when she went to the forests some years ago, there were only two or three liddle cubs. And now there are two tauzend tigers, again. All because of her good policies . . .'

She had been facing me at the beginning of the conversation, but as our discussion progressed, she was less and less inclined to look at me directly. By the time we reached the tiger cubs, she would have, if it had been possible, reclaimed the cucumber sandwich I had eaten. I felt a twinge of shame not to have left her to her illusions, but I couldn't control myself. If there was one moment when I had felt an involvement in Indian political events, it was at the time of that election, the previous year. It had seemed such a vindication of what was possible, given the will to make it happen. I couldn't bear it that even in some corner of the globe so removed from India as a train speeding towards Holland from Germany, there should be someone misguided enough to imagine that Mrs Gandhi's reign had been a gentle and peaceful one.

AN ANXIETY ATTACK

WHEN THE TRAIN REACHED the lady's station she departed without a backward glance. In the vacuum she left behind, I began to brood over what she had said. Three months. Was it true? Was it too long? It had not occurred to me for one instant to think about who would be responsible for domestic activities in Piet's home. I had not thought about his family's possible reactions to me right up till this moment.

The countryside outside the train's windows was a brown-green blur. The windows were sealed. I began to feel hot. I looked around me, wondering whether there were other equally uncomfortable passengers. But no one else seemed to be distracted by the heat. Some people were lounging in their seats, some were reading books, some were talking amongst themselves. I appeared to be the only person aware that we were hurtling towards the Netherlands in a travelling sauna.

I got up, hoping to find some air elsewhere along the length of the train. But it was the same in the corridor, a stifling, panic-inducing heat. My heart was hammering, my pulse was buzzing in my ears, I found it difficult to breathe or to swallow. Reality was shifting and cracking. I could hear harsh sounds within my head, like the grinding together of different and mutually exclusive spheres of my life.

For five months I had stalked a particular fate like a conscientious hunter, creating a trap, setting it, covering my tracks and leaving it to be sprung in my absence. But now that the time to check on it had come, my skin was crawling with unexpected terrors about the nature of my quarry.

Supposing Piet didn't come to the station? I knew that I could call him at his home or wait at the station, in case he was on his way. But what if he didn't show up at all? What if he had died between my last phone call and my imminent arrival? Or worse: what if he simply didn't want the responsibility of having me in his house?

But that was only the first and most basic level of my anxieties.

If he didn't come to the station, my options were straightforward. I had already thought them through. I had enough money to return to England. Once there I would call Radzie and tell her that I hadn't been able to find any kind of work in Germany. I might try to hang about in London, looking for freelance illustration jobs. Or I could ask Radzie to send me a ticket back to Bombay right away. It meant returning to my brother's flat with nothing gained from my travels but the wan satisfaction of knowing that I had actually managed to touch base with Piet's home-town. It would embarrass me to have to fall back on Radzie's generosity yet again, but I was conscious of being fortunate to have that option to fall back upon at all.

I would return to Bombay chastened. And I would never see Piet again.

Just admitting this thought to my mind caused the second level of anxieties to unspool within me, like bright snakes, slithering around my neck, tightening their coils around my ribs, waiting for me to breathe out, before their fatal squeeze.

I realized as if for the first time, on that overheated, airless train, that the thought of never seeing Piet again was an abomination that I could not face. It shocked me to see this. I had apparently been bottling an extreme emotion within me, without the slightest idea of its potency, like someone who has made preserves out of radioactive plums and is astounded to see them months later, glowing malevolently in the dark of the pantry shelves.

I tried to calm myself. Keeping oneself calm takes energy, however, and I had none to spare. Instead, I heard Micki's questions and I saw her face, as she asked if I wasn't deluding myself when I claimed that I was not merely pursuing love.

I looked up and down the corridor, seeing only the smooth glass and steel surfaces, the neat, spare structure of a flying shuttle, carrying pastel-shaded human threads across the loom of Europe, with one irregular dark brown strand amongst them. I had considered feminism a peg on which to hang my resistance to romance, but Mrs Prasad the psychiatrist, with her droopy eyelids and her laser vision, had cut through my flabby rhetoric: she had shown me that much of what I did and said was an expression of my non-acceptance of a woman's destiny. Feminism was supposed to celebrate femininity whereas I could not face the straps and buckles of female domesticity. I did not rejoice in any but the most superficial aspects of being female.

The price of romance for heterosexuals is the enormous expenditure of energy and resources which goes into getting married and raising children. If I wasn't willing to pay that price, then in a real sense, I couldn't afford to be 'in love'. Yet here I was on a train hurtling towards Holland, realizing that if I didn't see Piet, I would be in an awful state. I felt confused and frightened.

I could see my reflection in the glass of the windows along the corridor. Particularly when the train passed by the mass of a building or a clump of trees, the image would sharpen as if in a dark mirror, then fade out again the moment the background vanished. I looked perfectly unremarkable. My face showed no sign of distress. No one would have guessed, from looking at my surface, the turmoil that lay just beneath it. I felt like a sack from which all the organs had been emptied, passed through a blender and then poured back into me. I did not feel substantial any more, even though every part of me was still, in terms of physical mass, present.

Maybe the reason I was planning to shorten my life was that I realized I was too much of a freak to survive very long anyway. Maybe the desire to diet was actually a yearning to step out of the suit of soft, fat-filled female clothes that I had been given to wear at birth. Maybe if I had been given a free choice, I would have chosen to be something else. I couldn't imagine what, however. Not a man, for instance. It was idiotic even to contemplate it. I didn't think of men and women as being so different that their bodies created their destiny. The society in which a person is immersed might do that, but not the body itself. I could easily imagine how violently unhappy I would have been if I had been a man. I could imagine hating the responsibility of having a wife and dependent children just as much as I hated the idea of being a wife and a mother of children.

Another passenger entered the corridor, acknowledging me with a slight nod as he passed behind me, a young blond man, a student by the looks of him. I glanced enviously at his retreating back. I felt greedy for the ease with which he had been able to put together a personal appearance that was so complete and decipherable. I looked back at the ghost image of myself in the mirror-windows and saw that even at the level of clothes I was undefined. I wore baggy jeans, a loose shirt and a loose corduroy jacket over it. All in neutral colours. My hair was short, my face was bare. I could be anything and for that reason, in practical terms, was nothing, was nobody.

The ghost image in the windowpane was about as insubstantial as I myself was, I thought. It depended on its backdrop in order to be seen. On its own, it was transparent, invisible. Just like I, on my own now, on a train with no one who knew me. There was a pain in my throat, as if it were bulging with unexpressed emotions. I didn't know what to do with this. A course of action suggested itself: perhaps I should see if I could throw up? I thought it might unblock the constriction in my throat.

I entered the toilet at the end of the corridor, locked the door and turned towards the mirror. I found it difficult to meet my own eyes and stood there with my head bent down for a few seconds, before looking up, embarrassed. *What are you?* I would have liked to ask, *What would you like to be?* Except that it was, of course, ridiculous to speak out loud to myself. Then a thought crossed my mind. It was surely even more ridiculous to be afraid of speaking out loud to myself when there was no one else to observe me at it. I was struck by the logical loop. A person could not really be caught in the act of talking out loud to herself because, if someone else were there to observe it, the potential soliloquist would not technically be alone.

I saw that a smile was beginning to form on my mirrored face, a small, familiar, ironic smile. 'You silly twit!' I whispered to myself. The words were a trigger. My eyes filmed over with tears and when I blinked they slid down my face. I continued to stare at myself, not allowing my face to crumple. It was a trick I had learnt long ago, to avoid grimacing or making a sound when I cried.

I looked at myself in the mirror, seeing all that was familiar and aggravating about myself, but feeling a powerful, painful fondness. It was like being a child who knows the reasons that its parents do not love it and but who, when faced with its own self in the mirror, could not appreciate those reasons. I felt like sobbing uncontrollably, in sympathy for myself, but the sounds wouldn't come. I turned on the tap and washed my face. I drank some water, feeling the unpleasant sense of breaking deep-seated taboos because, of course, in India, the first commandment was never to drink the water from a tap, any tap, for fear of infection. I heard someone knocking on the door and finished up quickly. I checked my face in the mirror – yes, I was back to being inscrutable. No trace of tears now showed anywhere.

I left the toilet, nodding to the person who was waiting to use it after me. I went back to my seat feeling composed. I picked up my copy of *Shogun* and applied my mind to reading it.

In a couple of hours, the other passengers around me began making those winding-up gestures that accompany the end of a journey. Hand luggage was brought down from overhead storage, odds and ends which had been taken out during the journey were packed away. A few people were starting to push their cases into the corridor. The train began to slow down.

Outside the windows the track-bed widened out like a river delta. New tracks materialized from the void, crossing and recrossing, like live steel zippers, writhing, scissoring together, then scissoring apart again. The central station was approaching. Another train clattered past ours, overtaking us, pulling on ahead. Another few minutes passed before the platform appeared, flowing alongside us, bordering the left-hand margin of vision. The train's momentum slackened still further.

Then it slowed, it began to jerk.

Anxiety began to grip me again, but it was no longer nebulous. It had a specific focus, like a collection of disease symptoms whose unique source has finally been identified. In a scattering of moments, I would know once and for all the answers to questions that I'd had five months to stew over. The encounter, which I had played and replayed in my imagination, was finally imminent.

The train jerked sharply as it braked once and then once again, but it continued to move forward, slowly and musingly. There were muted squeals and shrieks from the springs and rivets of the train. Outside the windows, now, there were faces and sweater-clad torsos and happy cries, fragments of greetings. The train slid forward just a few more feet, gave a final violent wrench and died. A complete halt. A blasting hiss of pressure was released from the brakes. A breathy gasp of air broke from the tight-sealed doors as they bumped open. I stood up and reached under the seat for my suitcase. I hauled it out, concentrating on nothing but the precise moments left to me before I must inevitably look outside the train, to know in which way my personal dice had fallen. I shouldered my sling bag. I checked that my passport was still in my handbag. I picked up my suitcase.

Then when I could put it off no longer, I glanced out of the windows.

And he was there.

HOLLAND

THERE

HE LOOKED DIFFERENT. HIS hair had grown out. Cold-weather clothes made him look bulkier than I remembered him. He was scowling slightly, glancing in through the windows of the train, with that expression of concentration common to anyone sorting at speed through the infinite permutations of noses, mouths and eyes offered by a crowd of disembarking passengers, waiting to be tripped by the one pattern which is familiar.

For just those first few seconds before he saw me, everything that I had been thinking about, fretting over, fearing and dreading for five months ceased absolutely to exist. It was a moment precise and perfect in itself, a peak.

Then I got down from the train, he caught sight of me, we hugged briefly and I said, 'My suitcase is *very* heavy . . .'

He hauled on the handle of the suitcase, testing it and laughed, saying, 'Yes, it is heavy!'

The everyday quality of this exchange should have calmed me, but instead it felt surreal. I could feel the fabric of my expectations stretching and tearing, like the wrapping around a package which must be removed to reveal what it contains. But there was a silence where there should have been a sound. I could not understand what it meant.

Piet heaved the suitcase up on to his shoulder. The sky was quilted over with low, soft clouds. Fine pinpricks of rain peppered my skin. We had crossed two streets and started down a third before I realized that the plan was to walk all the way to Piet's home. The metalled road changed to cobbles set in a fish-scale pattern. Piet pointed to places of interest along the way: the church where Japp was christened, the mile-high tower called the Dom, the statue holding a victory torch which he said was called the Ice-cream Cone.

He said he wanted to stop along the way. He chose a small café and ordered two espressos. He sat with his back to the wall while I faced him across a tiny table with a ceramic-tile surface. He was wearing a loose, hand-knitted sweater, pale fawn. Underneath it was a white shirt with a round-necked collar, a bit of which showed over the top of the sweater. 'We . . . should talk,' he said.

'Yes,' I replied, thinking that as observations went this was not the most profound.

His forehead creased. 'No,' he said, 'I meant . . . we need to talk before we get to my house.'

'All right,' I said.

'There's a problem,' he said.

'To do with my stay?' I asked. I felt a breeze whistling in through my gut, as if a hole had been punched into me somewhere. 'It's difficult? It's too long?'

'Yes . . . no.' He smiled, embarrassed. 'It's not difficult at all. Not really. That's not what I'm saying. But . . .' He stopped, as the coffee arrived, two demi-tasse cups in heavy white ceramic, with one powdered creamer, two sugars in sachets, and a cellophane-wrapped cookie on each saucer. The coffee sent up a tart, rich scent. I picked up the cookie at once, wanting my first taste of Holland to be sugary. But it was dense, granular and not very sweet.

Piet was hunched over the table, looking around the room. When he was ready to speak, he said, 'I told my family that I was bringing an Indian guest home. And . . . that's all . . .' He looked back at me, a complex appeal written into his expression. I felt sure that he was telling me that I couldn't stay with him for more than a few days, so I said, nodding, 'I think I understand . . .' while telling myself, internally, that I should be prepared to leave in a couple of days, back to Germany or to the UK.

He said, 'No . . . it's not what you think. It's not . . .' Then he shook cobwebs from his head and tapped my wrist. We were both sitting with our hands on the edges of the little table. 'I can do what I want, you know? It's my house. So you are staying with me as long as you want because' – he shrugged – 'because I say so. And that's all right. But that's not the point. The point is, you're just *staying* . . . okay?' He opened the palms of his hands.

'Yes,' I said, 'I understand.'

I believed that he was telling me that my stay would be a chaste one. The cold breeze inside me had turned into a gale, tearing wounds and fissures in the warm substance of my interior. But my face betrayed nothing. I told myself to focus on the idea that my visit to Holland had been inspired by a philosophical enquiry into the nature of reality. This was the reality. The aerated feeling inside me was something I must learn to ignore. And that was all.

His expression relaxed and we left the café shortly afterwards.

Presently we entered a curving street bounded by a canal on the right. I saw the name of the street and recognized the address. 'Ah,' I said, 'we're getting close!'

A narrow channel marked out by a yellow stripe designated the bike-lane, with a longitudinally distorted diagram of bicycles painted on to the cobbles at regular intervals to remind passersby that cyclists had right of way. Piet pointed to the legend and said, 'Look – you don't have these in India – you must watch out! Or you will get run over by a mad cyclo. Holland was the first country to invent the bike-lane.'

Spaced at regular intervals along the left side of the street were the front doors of homes. Some had the characteristic Dutch stoop with the three steps and a dainty wrought-iron guard rail surrounding them. Others were at street level. Some were painted and had smart brass knockers, others were less ostentatious though well maintained.

The number of Piet's home was 37. We entered the street in the 80s. So his door was still far enough away that I couldn't guess by counting forwards which one would be his. I looked ahead, nevertheless, with a sense of anticipation, as at the opening of the first window on an Advent calendar. A posh black door seemed a likely prospect, but we passed it by. Then there were two ivory-white ones in succession with their mouldings picked out in gold. But they weren't it.

There were still enough doors ahead that I couldn't estimate without stopping to think about it which would be the correct one. Amongst the several possibilities was a remarkably dilapidated entrance, painted green. It was completely out of character with the quiet street, seeming more suitable to a garden shed than a front door. Its paint was peeling. Its letter slot was a bare slit in the wood. It had no beading or brass to dignify it.

It was the one.

'Here we are,' said Piet. He was smiling slightly as he leaned my heavy suitcase against the wall, fishing in his pocket for the key. The facing for the keyhole was the only bright new surface in sight. He fitted the key into the lock and said, 'Welcome to the zoo!' In the instant that he pushed open the door, a humid, living stench had poured out, a clenched fistful of animal scents, claws and feathers, warm furry bodies and tepid pools of piddle. It was a challenge to all that was quiet and orderly elsewhere in the neighbourhood.

Then he picked up my suitcase and went in ahead of me, along a short passage rather like a tunnel. I followed him, feeling like Alice trying to keep up with the White Rabbit, unhappily aware that holes, once they have been fallen into, are quite difficult to get out of again. I noticed, however, that the door worked more efficiently than its raffish appearance suggested it might. It had a self-shutting mechanism and a deadbolt which closed with a smooth, well-oiled *snick*. Perhaps reality would prove to be neatly sandpapered and polished after all, if I would only wait long enough.

THE HOUSE AND FAMILY

WE EMERGED FROM THE tunnel into an open-air space. It was perhaps 30 feet wide at its greatest extent. Ahead of us was the main house. On either side were the high walls of neighbouring houses and behind us was what must once have been the gatehouse, built over the front entrance. Five people stood in the front yard, momentarily frozen by our intrusion within their midst. Piet nodded a greeting to his family. Then he turned to me while pointing to the oldest person present and said, 'And here, on my right, is my grandmother!'

She had been speaking when we appeared and, after the initial instant of silence, resumed from where she had broken off, addressing Piet now, in Dutch. She was a short, wide, sturdy-looking woman, with blunt-cut white hair and a lively expression in her brown eyes. She wore a long dark skirt and a white cardigan over it. She was holding a hosepipe, directing the stream of its water towards a watercourse fashioned out of cement between the boundary wall and the flagstones of the yard. The channel was neither broad nor deep enough to contain the water, which was, as a result, flowing in every direction. Waddling with fussy dignity in this artificial tide were a pair of mallard, three barred geese, two white ducks, one Peking duck, two skittish jaçanas and a huge white gander, hissing grandly while attempting to outrage the modesty of the Peking duck.

'She's complaining that I have not made her bird sanctuary properly,' said Piet, translating for me from his grandmother's speech. The rest of his family had glanced towards me, acknowledging me noncommittally. Piet made perfunctory introductions: his mother; Juliana, the anorexic sister; Erik the third brother; and Jani, the youngest.

Then Piet moved forward in his long unhurried stride, past the group and into a cavernous interior space. The floor was made of marble slabs, some of them cracked and broken. I would learn later that they owed their breakage to the hooves of Nazi horses, during the Occupation. On the left, just by the entrance, was a broad wooden stairway with a regally proportioned balustrade on massive, turned-wood supports. We went up the stairs and reached a landing. All the woodwork was exposed, revealing beams so thick that though the house was indeed as big as Piet had described, most of its interior was taken up by the wood of its construction.

Piet said, 'I'll take you on a tour later, but just now we'll go to the room.' He swarmed up a steeply angled wooden companionway that led from the landing to the next floor. An unlit passage led off the landing of this second floor. It ended abruptly with two doors at right angles to one another. The one painted red was Piet's.

He showed me a key as he pushed it into the lock, saying, 'I'll get one of these made for you tomorrow.' Then he opened the door and went in.

The room was so dark inside that for the first few moments I couldn't see anything from where I stood, except for a threadbare Afghan rug on the floor, a few feet from the entrance. It lay in a pool of light spilling out of an orange plastic bucket. A weak cheeping emanated from the bucket.

'Chickens,' explained Piet, following my gaze. He put the suitcase down and took me to look inside the bucket. 'They're very young, you see.' A bobble-headed lamp had been turned on and clipped to the rim of the bucket. Inside were three adolescent chicks crouching in the manner of young birds who are as yet suspicious of the rumour that their legs might be used for standing up.

'I keep the light here on so that they don't die of cold?' said Piet, forming a question in response to the one I had not yet asked about what we were looking at. 'But unfortunately the light keeps them awake, as well! So they keep . . . you know . . . *cheep! cheep! cheep!* all night long.' He followed this with, 'Don't worry, you'll get used to it – '

'Oh!' I said. I looked around me. 'Isn't this your room?'

'Yes,' he said, nodding. 'But you will sleep here.'

'Won't that be inconvenient?' I asked, puzzled. 'Where will *you* sleep?'

'Here,' he said tranquilly.

My eyes were adjusting slowly to the gloom. I looked around and saw the bed, a brass queen-size, with gleaming rails and spheres. Just above it, the roof slanted sharply, like a canopy, before levelling out. He shrugged and said, 'It's big enough, I think, for both of us . . .'

There was a blank space inside my head where I would like to have seen a simple explanation for this turn of events. I had thought that the point of the conversation in the café was that my visit was to be platonic. I had assumed that this would not include any sharing of nocturnal quarters. In fact, I had assumed that regardless of what our personal equation was to be, I would certainly have a room to myself, since he had said it was a big house. But there was no time to ask questions. There was a knock on the door, which, like the street door downstairs, had been fitted with a self-closing mechanism and had therefore locked itself shut behind us.

Piet opened the door to find that it was Erik with a message about someone having arrived.

Piet turned to me and said, 'Ah – that's my girlfriend. We must go down.' His expression was neutral, giving no indication of whether he would prefer that I remained upstairs or not.

I followed him once more to the first-floor landing. On the way, he showed me that the toilet was tucked into a tiny triangular space under the stairs. Beside it was the entrance to the kitchen. Next to the kitchen door was one that led to his mother's room. Beyond the landing was the dining area. Tall windows with small glass panes overlooked the entrance yard.

The table was made from one giant plank of oak, borne on wooden supports each the girth of a healthy young oak tree. The rest of the family was already sitting down, talking animatedly. The grandmother was missing, as she lived separately in the gatehouse over the street entrance of the property. Amongst those whom I had already met, there was now one more person, sitting with her back to us as we entered the area.

When I had moved around the table I saw that she was slender and tall, her hair cut in short curling wisps framing an attractive pixie-face, sharp featured, with light, up-tilted eyes. She was wearing a short-sleeved denim vest and a matching skirt, with a fine, pale cardigan thrown lightly over her shoulders. She had just purchased a tiny sachet of perfume with the Charlie trademark embroidered on it in white against denim, made to be worn as a pendant. She was showing this to Juliana and giggling over it as I moved around the table and into her range of vision. Piet stood just behind her chair, as if he were undecided where to settle down.

She looked up to see me, smiled and said, 'Willkommen!' Her eyes crinkled and her cheeks creased in long dimples. But a wave of pain and resentment slapped across to me from her. I recognized that it was not something intentional, maybe not even conscious. Just her raw instinct. I felt a gasp of shock within me. I had never before been in a position to hurt someone by my sheer presence yet here I was now, doing it. Just by being where I was, I was causing a blade to turn within another person, slicing soft organs with every breath taken in my presence.

Piet said, 'This is Anneke . . .' as he sat down beside her but in the distant manner of someone who wished to discourage her next action, which was to smile and lean towards him. He put his hand on the back of her chair for a few moments, then removed it.

I had arrived in Utrecht at 4.30 in the afternoon and it was now almost two hours later. Outside, the sky was still light. I was told that Juliana had made dinner in my honour and that she was now ready to serve it. The family's reserve at the moment of my arrival had evaporated and I felt warmly included. All of us continued to sit where we were, while in an adjacent room the TV murmured to itself. Directly over the table a single light with a broad-brimmed lampshade had been switched on. The effect was of sitting on a bright raft floating on a sea of lapping shadows.

Juliana brought in the main dish, a dumpling stew. I looked at her curiously, trying not to stare. I had read about anorexia nervosa in the US and was now very keen to know what it was like to be someone who had taken the path of weight loss almost to its terminal conclusion. But there was nothing obviously unusual about her. She was as petite as Piet was huge. Her hair was orange-blonde and she had large sweet caramel-brown eyes, with strongly marked, black brows. But when she smiled, I saw that she was missing two incisors, one above and one below, from her set of teeth. I knew that it was a mark of her period of starvation.

Plates, bread and cutlery were brought in as they were needed. The conversation was largely in Dutch, but with English additions. Piet translated for me part of the time, while his mother said, laughing at herself, 'We . . . understand more easily than we speak!' Her voice had an attractive yodelling quality. She had a virile, square-cut face, with elastic skin and strongly marked creases, good-looking in a characterful, unpretentious way. Her dark brown hair was caught up in a chignon from which a few strands escaped over her forehead in an impromptu fringe. Her eyes were grey-blue and held an expression of willful good humour.

Aside from the family, there were three cats and several obese guinea pigs present in the room. Two of the guinea pigs were actually on the table, creeping about like animated sandbags. There was also a lone dog who sat some distance away. She bore a long-suffering expression on her face, as if unable to bear the anguish of having to live peaceably alongside so many prey animals. Her name meant 'mouse' in Dutch and she was low-slung but broad. Her distinctive feature was that she had been born without a tail, making her the only example of a Manx dog that I have ever encountered, before or since.

In the course of the dinner, Jani went upstairs and fetched the young chicks down from Piet's room. The young birds stood unsteadily on the tabletop amongst the plates and dishes, their spindly legs wobbling dangerously. The overhead light probed pink highlights through their thin skin, as yet patchily feathered. They looked around with that expression of professional contempt one sees on the faces of senior politicians: eyes bright, brows drawn down in frowns, the lines of their juvenile beaks already hardened into sneers. And then, each with its neck bobbing like the thread-guide on a sewing machine, they made a cautious circuit of the table, stepping into the butter dish, over a snoring guinea pig or two and into our plates, scrambling to regain their balance as their claws lost purchase on the crockery, before pecking at crumbs of food.

It seemed very exotic to me, to be accompanied at the table by living creatures. I felt more than ever like Alice but not in Wonderland so much as Through the Looking Glass. Instead of being on the plates and waiting to be eaten, here were animals trotting in and out of the plates, waiting to be fed. It seemed only a matter of time before one of them made a little unwelcome deposit on someone's plate. What was the correct etiquette, I wondered, in such an event? Did one coolly eat around it or could one be excused to go and throw up in the toilet?

I didn't have the opportunity to find out. As the meal ended, Juliana began whisking the plates away while Anneke protested that it was her turn to help. I felt too awkward to make any offers in this direction. Claiming travel-weariness, I bade everyone goodnight and went upstairs to Piet's room.

THE FIRST NIGHT

I WANTED DESPERATELY TO sit alone by myself to think. The moment of my arrival, when I saw Piet at the station, had been a peak. Ever since then I had been slaloming downhill.

Why?

The only explanation I had was that I was too accustomed to plotting a course for myself on a campaign map marked with little flags and coloured pins. This situation, hurtling at breakneck speed through uncharted territory, was the equivalent for me of stepping through a door and into thin air.

In the café, it had seemed clear to me that Piet wanted me to be the sort of just-good-friends-nothing-else guest he had told his family I was.

But when he showed me into his room and revealed that we would be sharing his bed, I didn't know what to think. Surely, from his family's point of view, the fact that we were sharing a room, never mind a bed, must look just a little suspicious?

Or was this some feature of European life that I, as a foreigner, did not know? Maybe it was a completely ordinary phenomenon, a practice common to all Dutch homes. Visitors to a house were to be accommodated in their hosts' beds. Maybe no one in his family was interested in what we did behind closed doors, maybe I had misunderstood the point he had made in the café.

Maybe I misunderstood everything about reality and had no way of knowing what was or was not the right way to breathe, or eat or think.

I could not say if I was glad or sad, or what my feelings were at all.

I could not locate the centre of my perceptions. My thoughts were waving like streamers around my face, blotting out any clear vision of the events taking place around me. If only I could sit still long enough to sort each strand out, smoothing creases and disentangling knots, I would perhaps be able to plot a course based on the new information coming into my possession minute by minute.

But I had barely opened the door to Piet's room, wondering where the light switch was, when there were boisterous sounds from the first-floor landing. I heard farewells as Anneke prepared to leave, then the sound of a huge figure pounding up the stairs to the second floor.

It was Japp. He barrelled into the room, greeting me with whoops and cheers, lifting me off my feet in a hug before settling down in one of the two armchairs in front of the gas fire. He said that Piet was just seeing Anneke out but would be up, shortly, with coffee for all three of us.

Japp had changed little except for his hair which had grown out in pale blond strips straggling over his forehead. 'So-so-so! You are heeeeere!' he said. 'Piet said you were coming today, or tomorrow, or yesterday . . .'

His rubbery pink mouth was stretched to maximum. He seemed intensely happy to see me. 'How long are you here for? What will you do? Have you found yet the Trooth?!' He was dressed in heavy black pants, a white shirt and a dark grey jacket.

I said, 'Of course! I declared it when I crossed the border – '

'Ah,' said Japp, 'and did they charge you the famous Dutch Trooth Toll Tax?'

'It was duty free,' I said. 'No charge for imports from the Third World – '

'Ah!' said Japp. 'So now you can hold the Trooth camps for us poor white savages and show us the Liiiiiight!' He was in a wild and boisterous mood. He stayed for three hours. Piet brought in the coffee, balancing three clear glass cups one above the other, each with its own saucer. We laughed and talked raucously, like drunkards, though we had nothing stronger than caffeine to sustain our spirits. No one disturbed us. We may have been in a tree house isolated from the world, from families and from all claims upon our time.

All the time that Japp was in the room, thoughts about what could happen after he left obsessed me, like mosquitoes homing in on the heat generated by my curiosity. I hated the continuous whine of these thoughts which could be neither silenced nor ignored. I wanted to be a cool-headed person, controlling the flow of emotions in my life like a policeman controls the flow of traffic. I would like to have believed that it was in my power to decide what would happen once Japp left, rather than to know that I was in a foreign country, with very little money, in the company of someone whose behaviour I couldn't predict or understand.

Piet went downstairs to see Japp to the door. I continued sitting in one of the two armchairs by the fire, concentrating on breathing calmly. When Piet came back into the room, he said, 'Well –'

And I said, before he could continue, 'I really should have a bath. A shower.'

He took me to the kitchen, to show me how to light the gas-jet that guaranteed an unlimited hot-water supply to the shower. Back upstairs on the second-floor landing, he showed me a shower stall standing beside the washing machine. Beside it was a sink for brushing teeth and washing hands.

While he demonstrated the virtues of a good shower nozzle, with its luxuriant cascade so unlike the one in the guest bathroom at Palm View, which had produced at best a fitful trickle, the only thought in my mind was, *There is no bathroom!* No little sanctum within which I could lounge in blessed privacy.

A flimsy-looking plastic curtain prevented the water spilling out of the stall on to the landing and that was all. According to Piet, it was entirely sufficient. Then he gave me a towel and left me alone.

I felt extraordinarily uncomfortable removing all my clothes on an open landing. The rest of the house was in darkness, there was no risk that I would be disturbed and I knew that Europeans thought nothing of nudity. But that did not help me in any way overcome my own prudery. So I removed my socks and shoes, stepped inside the shower stall and tore my clothes off as quickly as I could manage. I wondered all the while whether I would feel more embarrassed to be discovered in this pathetic attempt to preserve my modesty than to be seen naked and shivering on the landing.

The water was as gloriously hot as promised, but the moment I turned it off icy fingers of cold air parted the clouds of steam and scraped my skin. I had never realized before how profoundly attached I was to the concept of a bathroom. It was not merely that it offered physical privacy, but that it was like a meditation cell, in which a body and a mind could collect themselves in isolation. By contrast, on that exposed landing, I felt as if my mind was clogged with conflicting ideas, impressions and emotions.

I toweled dry and threw on my long nightie, warm only to the extent that synthetic materials usually are. Barely pausing to brush my teeth at the sink, I ran back to the room. There was a gas fire in the grate, but earlier in the evening, I had noticed that the window across the room from the fire had one pane missing, with a sheet of paper stuck over it. Whatever heat the gas generated, it was lost via this noisily vibrating membrane. In contrast to the icy landing, however, the room was positively cosy.

Piet had changed and was sitting up in bed wearing a T-shirt. He was lying near the right-hand edge, tucked under two layers of blankets, reading one of his psychiatry textbooks.

A lamp was angled so that it could shed its light precisely on to the pages of the open book. He glanced up and smiled as I entered, then returned to the book.

The sheet of paper masquerading as a windowpane was breathing in and out as if all the ghouls of night were standing outside and sucking on it. At the far end of the room, there was an Olympic-sized aquarium with an air-pump which growled rhythmically every half hour for ten minutes at a time. During Japp's visit the chicks had been returned to their orange bucket and were *cheep-cheep-cheeping.*

I clambered over Piet, with all the grace of a three-toed sloth. I slid into my side of the bed wishing I knew the drill for situations of this sort. *Dear Ann Landers, what rules of etiquette govern the sharing of a bed with a man with whom there has been one exchange of intimacy which, however, is not going to be extended?* Should I engage in polite conversation? Should I pretend that we were actually in separate sectors of the universe and fall asleep? Should I leap on him and seduce him?

But Piet was the chief of protocol. Turning to me, he showed me his textbook and said, 'This is the kind of thing we're studying about – '

The pictures on the page looked like line drawings of shrivelled morning glories.

'Flowers?' I asked, puzzled.

He smiled, shaking his head, 'We-e-e-ll,' he said, 'you're almost correct. I mean, if you tell yourself that flowers are the sexual parts of a plant, then . . . yes, these are also flowers – but of the human plant – ' They were diagrams of female pudenda in varying states of excitation.

It seemed a rather spicy topic for discussion between two people of opposite sex who happen to be sharing a bed in a platonic, companionable way. But I nodded as if it were completely standard fare. I did not, after all, want to behave like a savage recently arrived from the outer darkness of civilization, where men and women rarely exchanged words on any subject except as a preamble to leaping at one another.

We talked about the practice and pedagogy of psychiatry till my mind was cottony with sleep. I begged leave to retire from consciousness. I rolled over on my side saying, 'Good night!' and Piet murmured an appropriate response.

But I couldn't sleep.

The room was dark during the day. At night, however, even after Piet had switched off his reading lamp, the light from the aquarium, from the chick-bucket and from the gas fire on the side, were like lasers, boring holes through my eyelids.

It is not easy for two people, neither of them midgets, to share a queen size bed without coming into contact with one another. But I was determined not to allow any part of me to stray across the invisible line that distinguished his territory from mine, which meant that I did not dare to toss or turn or so much as twitch, because it was a spring bed and it registered the slightest movement of either of its occupants.

I lay like a corpse upon whom rigor mortis has yet to settle, tense with the confusions of the day still raging within my mind. My thoughts were wriggling about like eels. I could not command them to stay still so that I could examine them. I could not so much as catch any of them. When I finally fell asleep, it was only after I had noticed that the patch of sky I could see through the gable-end window at the far side of the room was no longer black but pearly grey with dawn.

ERASURES

WHEN I WOKE UP I saw that I was alone in the room. I lay still for a while, trying to identify the thing which had made this awakening different from other awakenings in my recent past. It was several minutes before the answer occurred to me: it was that I had woken direct from sleep into consciousness, with no dreams or fantasies to buffer my sleeping self from the wakeful one. I sat up, looking around me. Everything around me was completely unfamiliar.

Sunlight entered via the gable-end window, screened by the gigantic leaves of potted monstera plants. The glass coffee cups of the night before remained where we had left them. The house was quiet. There were no voices that I could hear and no sounds of city traffic.

I got down from the bed and moved thoughtfully around the room, trying to get acquainted with it. But it resisted me. I could find no echo of myself in it, as if I were a space-traveller, newly arrived upon a planet which had never known my species before.

I should be happy, I told myself. *I set out to achieve something and I've succeeded.*

But another voice in my head demurred. *This is not success,* it said. *This is nothing*.

It sounded like the combined voices of all my teachers in school, my professors in college, my peers, my sister, my brother, my parents.

It's taken me an enormous effort to reach this place, I told the voice in my head. *That's quite enough in itself.* But the voice was implacable. *If that was the case,* it said, *you would be jubilant right now – and you're not. You would be feeling relaxed and confident – and you're not.*

It was true.

Standing amongst the leaves at the end of Piet's room, instead of feeling like an explorer whose struggles to reach the heart of the Congo have met with glory, I felt like a fruit bat which has managed to fall asleep in a bunch of fragrant young bananas and been inadvertently included in a shipment bound for European supermarkets. I crouched down amongst the leaves, trying to feel a sense of comfort from their giant tropical shade – and almost cried out loud. There was already someone sitting there! In the split second it took to realize that it was only a life-sized wooden sculpture of a squatting boy, his slanted eyes suggesting a Balinese or Malaysian origin, I had leapt up and fled back to the centre of the room, in front of the gas fire, my heart pounding.

I felt as if I had stepped into one of those carnival rides, where nothing was what it seemed and every shadow concealed something that would twitch or leer. I looked around me, trying to calm myself, but could not. Everywhere I looked there was something which confused or disturbed me. For instance, above this part of the room, over the place where the two huge cuboid armchairs faced the gas fire, the ceiling boards had been removed, revealing the attic above. Across the gap so created, stretching between the two main beams of the room, was a broad plank of wood, with a sturdy leather strap passed around its middle.

What was it? I couldn't imagine a solution to this riddle which did not involve something perverse and unnatural.

Across from the fireplace was the window with the paper pane. Beside it was a generous desk, with cubby holes and study books stacked in tiers on its top. Above the window were three or four rifles, with rusting barrels and worm-eaten wooden stocks. Behind the desk, facing the door, was a pedal organ. I had noticed it when I first entered the room, but hadn't been able to examine it until just now. I tried to understand why it was there. It was small enough to look like something custom-made for a ten-year-old child. Could it have been bought for Jani, perhaps? But no – several of its ivory keys were broken, suggesting that it was not in functioning order. And it looked very old. Why, then? Why keep such an object in a bedroom?

I looked around for my suitcase, finding that it had been pushed under the bed. I pulled it out to look inside, feeling like an intruder to my own life, pawing through possessions which no longer felt recognizably my own. These were things with which I had been living for the five months it had taken me to reach this place, yet now they appeared to be more like a fossil record. These clothes, these undies, these toiletries, were irritations to me. They kept me pinned to my previous definitions, they reminded me of who I used to be.

If I were brave, I told myself, I would throw everything away. I turned each separate item over and over in my hands, my passport, my wallet, my slender wad of traveller's cheques. If I cashed the cheques, I told myself, I would have no further need of their plastic carrying case nor of my passport. I could buy a new wallet which would not be freighted with the private gallery of personal photographs inside it.

Amongst my possessions was a small mirror that I always carried in my handbag. I drew it out now. It was a dainty little thing, oval in shape with a black cloth backing and a pattern of pink roses in needle-point decorating it. It was something my mother had given to me many years ago, part of a little vanity set. I may have been fifteen when I got it. I felt astounded that a small item like this, so easily lost or broken, had the resilience to adhere to me, enduring through so many reversals and changes in my life.

I did not dare turn it over and look into it. The oval-framed portion of my face that it would reveal to me would be like a window into that other world I belonged to. It would show me the face of someone I recognized as the person I used to be. Unless of course I had changed between this moment and the last time that I had seen myself in a mirror, which had been on board the train to Utrecht. In which case I might not recognize myself or I might catch myself in a moment of metamorphosis and be dismayed.

I looked around me, suddenly realizing that there were no other mirrors in this room. I hadn't seen any downstairs, in the passage way or over the sink. I smiled at the idea of going mirror-less. Yes, it would be appropriate and fitting not to see my own face. It would be an excellent primary exercise in self-forgetting. I put my mother's mirror away without looking inside it. No use tempting fate.

Since I did not yet have a key to the door of the room, I got dressed before going out to brush my teeth at the sink in the passage. I didn't want to get locked out of the room wearing only my nightie, in case Piet had gone away somewhere.

I washed my face with the corner of the bath towel Piet had given me the night before. I told myself that I could decide, as I went along, whether I was the sort of person who preferred getting bathed before putting on fresh clothes for the day or not. After all, for the three years that I had lived in a boarding school in Kodaikanal, it had been cold enough that we were allowed baths only twice a week. If a pattern can be broken once, it can be broken twice.

I decided that I would have to stop wearing my contact lenses because I didn't have a secure place to set up the kit, with its fussy little bottles, its sterile fluids and its heating equipment. I thought it went with the changes I was programming into my life. Lenses were part of that other self, the one who wore makeup and worried about self-beautification. The time was long overdue for me to give up these vain pursuits.

The house appeared to be deserted.

But when I went down the wooden companionway, I found Piet in the kitchen. He had a huge pile of chopped mushrooms on the sideboard and was preparing to shove the lot into a frying pan in which a lake of butter had been melted, smoking mildly and fragrantly. The two youngest boys were in school, Ma was at work and the third brother, whom I had not met yet, was at university. Juliana lived on her own, separately.

The fragrance of mushrooms cooking in butter inspired me to decide that my concerns about weight-loss might soon be relegated to the list of erasures. I was bursting to tell Piet about the morning's revelations. He portioned the mushrooms out onto two dinner plates and said, 'The bread's on the table – '

We settled down to eat. I said, 'There's something I must tell you – '

'Okay,' he said, 'but first . . . let's decide what we will do for this day.'

'Okay,' I said, stifling a surge of impatience. I found myself wondering whether my new persona was the sort which agreed passively to having plans being made for her day or whether she was the sort which resisted. It was difficult to decide, at short notice.

'To begin with, we need to make a key for the room and then also for the house,' said Piet, ticking off items on the fingers of one hand. 'And . . . that's near the place where I can buy some paint for my motorcycle – you remember? The Harley? Well! I've got it completely stripped down – ' Talking about the bike took twenty minutes. We ate through a whole loaf of dark brown, nut-flavoured bread, progressing from the mushrooms to cheese and then to butter with chocolate sprinkles, a novelty for me. At the end there was coffee.

'But we were making a plan,' said Piet. 'We need to talk about what you will do when you are here,' starting a new count on his fingers. 'Maybe you need to buy some things or meet some people, huh?'

I nodded, not wanting to interrupt him to tell him that in my newly reformed state it was difficult for me to make any predictions about anything. It may take me several few days of experimenting with different selves before I could be sure who I was. For the sake of being practical, however, I told myself, I might need to appear as if I hadn't changed for a little while.

'Then we need also to go to Amsterdam one day to meet, you know, Kay? The Dutch Boddhisattva?'

I nodded, but thought to myself that what I really needed to do was to inform Piet that I wanted most of all to spend several days, a week maybe, just talking to him.

There were so many thoughts and ideas backed up in my head, of which the concept of treating my life as if it were a lump of clay waiting in moist anticipation for me to shape as I wished, was just one. But there had to be the right kind of gap in the conversation.

'Then maybe we could go to see a film. Or to a bookstore.' He shrugged. 'Though I have my classes also, at the university. I won't be free for a little time until the holidays.'

My mind was like a blank white page. Everything was equally possible or impossible. So I nodded. He said, 'It's easy to rent a bicycle here and then when you can find your way about, you can use it.'

Here I found I had to say something: 'Oh! But I don't ride.'

It was Piet's turn to look blank. 'That's . . . very strange,' he said, finally. 'In Holland, riding a bicycle is . . . is like *breathing*!'

I shrugged. 'I've tried it a few times,' I said, 'but I couldn't ever get my balance.'

I didn't add that, as a child, I had never been encouraged to explore the world outside the secure walls of the various residences in which I had grown up. After the first return to India when I had been so shocked by what I saw of my country, I myself rarely wanted to leave the compound. It was a state of mind that had survived to adulthood.

He said, 'Ah – but never mind: I can teach you. It's very, very easy. Even my little brother is learning to ride.'

I felt obscurely annoyed. The implication was that I was deficient in a particular area and would surely want to improve myself. Supposing I didn't? After all, I wasn't planning to live in Holland. But I couldn't decide yet whether it was the sort of annoyance which was worth mentioning or not. So I didn't.

The doorbell rang. Piet showed me that there was a button to press in the kitchen which activated a buzzer which released the latch on the door for a few seconds. Piet said, 'We don't have the door-microphone like in the apartment buildings so we can't find out who is coming in – maybe one day it will be the terrorists and we will have to shoot them – *pah-pah-pah!* – as they come up the stairs!'

As he spoke, the person who had rung the bell came up the stairs. It was a slight young man, with blond-brown hair, washed-denim eyes and a smile which combined diffidence with an alert, friendly attention. This was Simon, the eldest of Piet's younger brothers, nineteen years old. He greeted me warmly, then vanished up the stairs.

The day was mild as Piet and I walked out of the house.

We went to the locksmiths. We went to a café. We checked out a local hardware store for spray cans of khakhi paint and after much debate decided that the best course was for Piet to mix the colour himself and to apply it using a spray gun. We bumped into two friends of Piet's, a couple. The man, Henk, was dark-haired and the same height as Piet but lean while his girlfriend Ramona was petite and white-blonde. They bobbed and nodded at me, then moved on.

Piet said, as we strolled under an avenue of luxuriant elms, 'It's interesting. That girl . . .' He paused as if considering whether or not to continue. Then he asked, 'What did you think of her?'

I had spent only just long enough with her to register that she was pretty in the way of a fresh tasty fruit, her skin supple and her hair bright with youth. So I shook my head, puzzled.

'Would you say . . . she is intelligent?' he asked.

I said, 'I don't know. I didn't have enough time with her to find out – ' But if he had pressed me, I would have said that based on something as superficial as the Barbie-doll bangs on her forehead, I would have been willing doubt it. I felt ashamed for having that thought. I knew perfectly well that it was judgemental in the most conventional way, based on nothing at all.

'Okay, I'll ask you another question,' said Piet. 'If you had a choice to be an animal – or, no, let's say that you *are* an animal – what sort of animal do you think you are?'

I have never had the slightest doubt about answers to questions of this sort. 'A tiger,' I said, smiling. 'I mean, that's what I'd like to be, in some ideal jungle where there are no humans to be hunted by. But why? Why d'you ask?'

'Because,' said Piet, 'when I asked *her* this question, she said – you know what she said?' He didn't wait. 'She said she was a . . . *koala bear*!' He screwed his face up, expressing incredulity. 'Can you believe it? Can you believe that anyone would call themselves a koala bear?' He shook his head, amused at the memory.

Then he continued, 'The strange thing is . . .' He paused, considering his words before continuing, ' . . . the strange thing is, some weeks ago, she came over to my house and she had some acid, you know? LSD. So we had some together. Normally I don't do that stuff, you know? But with her it was . . . very interesting. Very sort of . . . brilliant. And she was so – *smart*. She could understand everything! About reality and the universe and relativity. Everything. Whatever I said, it was really reaching her, like in some way, she already knew it. It was like she was telepathic. I couldn't believe it was the same person . . .' He continued in this vein for a while. As he talked, I found myself experiencing a familiar dislocation. I remembered it from our conversations in Bombay. It was as if I were listening to a tune from which crucial notes were missing. I could hear the sounds but no coherent melody. Was it only my cynicism that made me think there's nothing at all astonishing about feeling mystic empathy with one's acid partner?

'She is not my girlfriend and I have never felt especially attracted to her. But that day, she just came into my room, we took the acid and – *paf!* – it was fonthasthique.'

I felt suddenly as if my shoes had been turned to stone. Every step was an effort. I hated to realize that Piet had been to bed with this Barbie-doll person. I hated to find that I hated it. As far as I was concerned, this was one of the most erasable features of my previous existence. A being who could be knocked over by every passing gust of emotion was not worth much in the tempest-driven climate of reality. I did not intend to include vulnerability to the list of characteristics I was developing for my new persona. Yet it seemed to have sneaked its way in.

Piet and I continued walking.

I felt that I was justified in suppressing my reaction on the grounds that I did not want to dignify emotions of this sort with any attention. It was most annoying to find that I could not stop myself thinking about it, however. I made a mental note to examine the whole issue thoroughly when I had a moment alone.

I said, 'I've never done acid.'

'Oh you should try it sometime,' said Piet. 'It's very interesting – '

'I don't know. I've heard it's dangerous,' I said. In my mind, I heard Kurtz's voice. I saw his mocking expression. But we just kept on walking.

Piet shrugged and said, 'It's dangerous to cross the street.'

'I'm afraid to try it,' I said, preferring honesty to any abstract argument. 'Many years ago, I saw a programme on television in Iran – the US Armed Forces Radio and Television Service. They were the only ones broadcasting in English in that area and they had a programme which left a deep impression on me – '

I had been fourteen at the time and in Teheran. My father was posted there as Ambassador. I remember the program vividly. A carefully neutral man of middle years, perhaps a sergeant, looking directly into the camera, spoke in a tone of quiet authority about the facts as he knew them: that drugs mutilated the brain; that soft drugs led to hard drugs as the user chased ever higher highs; that there had been some people for whom just one bad trip had left permanent psychological damage.

'I'm not even curious,' I said.

'Yes – but – ' said Piet, 'it's nothing so bad. You should try it. Really. It would – I don't know. Massage your kundalini. Open your third eye. You would really like it, I think. Well, of course, I don't know. It's important to be with someone who can lead you the correct way. In the wrong company, of course, it's no good. It's terrible.'

I shook my head and said, 'No. I know what my mind is like and I don't want to experiment with it.' I described the experience with the joint in the bachelor pad. 'Maybe my grip on reality is already too shaky. I don't feel confident about placing any further burdens on it.'

We had a burger at the local McDonald's. We passed by a quaint old-style tobacconist in a three-cornered shop and on a whim I bought a packet of Dunhill Menthols. Piet said, 'Ah – you smoke now?'

I said, 'No, but I like to pretend I do.' I've never been a confirmed smoker, but there are periods of time when the people I associate with are smokers and during those periods I become a smoker. Then I move out of their company and I never have the motivation to go out and buy cigarettes for myself.

In Germany, however, I discovered the uses of cigarette-vending machines. The anonymity of the machine, the plaintive appeal of its wares displayed invitingly in display panels, available for the price of just one Deutsche Mark, spoke to me. I chose Dunhill Menthols because the whiff of mint had pleasant associations with peppermints. To inhale the cool, breath-freshener smoke of a menthol cigarette was a bit like sucking on a mint minus the guilt of sugar.

We went home. The bright sunlight of the morning had clouded over. The first fat drops of rain were starting to fall as we entered the front courtyard. The grandmother was there as we entered, awash in her water birds. The gander hissed and flapped his wings at us.

Piet said, 'Ah – you said you wanted to talk about something?'

But there was a tapping sound and we looked up. Behind the tall windows of the dining room, I could just make out Japp's large features leering at us through the narrow windowpanes. I couldn't hear what he was saying, but it was clearly an encouragement to hurry our way up.

'Oh – ' I said, 'it'll have to wait till some other time.'

SIMON

THE NEXT MORNING I woke feeling disoriented once more. Hearing footsteps on the floor beneath the one I was on, I dressed quickly and went downstairs thinking it would be Piet.

But it was Simon. He flashed his open friendly smile, and asked me how I was doing.

I returned his smile and said, 'Fine. Sort of.' He looked a question in my direction. I said, 'Well, I woke up this morning feeling confused about who I am.'

He nodded as if to say, 'Ah! Completely normal then!'

He had a message from Piet. 'He has gone to the university for his class,' he said. 'He wanted me to tell you, if I saw you, to help yourself to food for breakfast, you know? From the fridge?' He showed me where the bread and other vital supplies, like cheese, butter and chocolate sprinkles were kept.

Simon was very easy to speak to. He said the same to me about myself. According to him, this was a clear sign that we had shared a previous incarnation together, maybe as brother and sister. I said I didn't believe in reincarnation. He thought I was joking but when I told him I wasn't, informed me in all seriousness that I was wrong. There was no question about it, he said, 'It's the only explanation for everything.'

He suggested that we go for a short walk around the neighbourhood, as he had some groceries to pick up for his mother. So we did that, talking all the while about reincarnation, Simon's past lives, my lack of faith, the guru in Bombay. When we came back, Piet had still not returned. Simon invited me to come up to his room, his door being the one that shared the end of the passage with the entrance to Piet's room.

We had coffee and then he rolled himself a joint. He did this in the way that another person might take out a cigarette and light up. I watched the automatic movements with which he cleaned the grass, mixed it with a little pouch tobacco, extracted a leaf of cigarette paper and rolled a slender, tightly packed cylinder. It was obviously second nature to him, unlike with the Kommunistas for whom it had always appeared to be a ten-thumbed novelty.

I hadn't decided whether or not to accept a smoke as I watched Simon take his first few puffs. Then he offered the joint to me and I heard Kurtz's voice in my head, warning me about my Dutch friends and the high likelihood of their addiction to drugs.

But I accepted the offer. Within a few minutes or an hour or three hours, it was hard to tell because time had assumed the consistency of warm taffy, I began to feel that Kurtz's objections were just another reason that I was in Utrecht and not, for instance, in Münich.

I felt the tensions easing from my mind like wrinkles on a piece of linen straightening out under a hot iron. A warm golden haze descended upon my skin, enveloped the back of my neck, entered my throat and stopped there, as if a mouthful of sunshine had wrapped itself around my vocal cords.

Conversation was extremely difficult. I felt as if I would emit sparks if I opened my mouth. Words became like messages in a bottle, each one discrete and separate from all its companions in a thought.

It was thus only with the greatest effort that I could make myself say, 'This . . . is . . . really . . . potent . . . stuff!' Every syllable had such a gigantic range of meanings that I felt like bursting into tears at my own eloquence.

When Simon replied I realized that there were two geniuses possessed of astounding verbal skills in the room. What he said was, 'It's . . . very . . . good . . . huh?'

It seemed all but miraculous that two such divinely gifted people should be together in the same continuum. We spent the rest of the afternoon listening to Mussorgsky's *Pictures at an Exhibition*, until Piet returned from the university.

SLEEP

IT WAS IMPOSSIBLE TO find a time of day for having a chat with Piet. I was too spaced out with Simon's grass to remember what it was I wanted to talk about. And in the evenings Japp would come by or Piet would go out with Anneke or everyone would sit together for dinner. Before I knew it, the clock's hands would be pointing to the wee hours and it would be time for bed.

The sleeping arrangements remained as they were. I continued to find it difficult to fall asleep. I lay awake in the fitful darkness of Piet's room, listening to the chicks in their bucket and thinking about the pros and cons of sharing a bed chastely. It certainly seemed to suit Piet, because he fell asleep easily. Did it suit me, I would ask myself. Did I really mind it or was that merely a habit of thought, based on typical situations? And if I didn't mind it, why couldn't I fall asleep?

I could, for instance, tell myself that there was something beautiful about lying next to a person to whom I was attracted, listening to the sound of his slow, sleeping breath.

I could feel satisfied with the idea that my function in that space and time was to be a guardian spirit watching over my friend as he lay vulnerable in sleep. It was a privilege, after all. Not many people could fill such a position. The average person who entered the bed of another person did so with a specific intention and that intention sometimes resulted in ugly scenes and dishonourable behaviour.

By contrast, this relationship between Piet and me, since it was not using physical entanglements as the coin of its exchange, was unusually pure. The fact that he could entrust his unconscious self to me suggested a degree of intimacy that I could feel flattered by.

I did not allow myself to look at him as he slept, however. That, in my opinion, would have betrayed the unspoken contract that kept me in my sector of the bed as much as touching him would have. Listening to him was different. That was involuntary. If his unconscious self chose to communicate with me, it could not be held against me. So I listened to him.

Sometimes he talked in his sleep. The words were slurred, muttered in an urgent undertone. The first time I heard him, I thought he was saying something to me and that perhaps I had started to lose my mind, because I couldn't understand a word of what he said. Since there's very little to be done about discovering that one is losing one's mind in the middle of the night, while sharing a bed with a mumbling companion, I merely lay very still, wondering for how long I would remain sane enough to recognize that I was becoming insane. It was only the next morning that I realized he must have been speaking in Dutch. I was so unused to hearing him speak his own tongue that I mistook it for gibberish.

Sometimes I would find that our breathing would fall into step. I tried to avoid this, but it happened involuntarily. The reason I wanted to avoid it was that it would begin to work on my mind and gradually I would become convinced that there was a single shuttle of air being passed back and forth between our lungs. This would make me feel breathless. Not only was his lung capacity larger than mine, so that he seemed to be getting the lion's share of the breathing-shuttle, but I felt sure it had to be unhygienic to be recycling air in this fashion. The thought that it might be unhygienic convinced me soon enough that I wasn't getting my full quota of oxygen with each intake and that if I wasn't careful I might be brain-dead by morning.

I would then be desperate to break free of Piet's rhythm. But he, or to be more precise, his sleeping body, would not let me. With each powerful intake, he would suck air out of me, and with each luxurious exhale pump the same air back up my unwilling nose. Then I would begin to worry that the real problem had nothing to do with Piet but was actually an asthmatic attack. The fear of starting to wheeze in this situation, with not enough air to go around between us and no drugs to control the attack once it started, was itself enough to trigger an attack.

Whole nights might be passed with me gulping for air like a lungfish on dry land, while Piet lay beside me, breathing serenely. Restless and slightly delirious, on such nights, I would find myself questioning the rightness of my situation. Wondering whether it wasn't rather cruel of him, since he must surely know that I was attracted to him. Whether he didn't worry that I may just be a little bit peeved by his lack of interest in my person. Wondering why the initiative was necessarily his. Wondering why I couldn't afford myself even a little quota of annoyance, at being ignored in this fashion. Surely it was something of an insult? Surely it suggested that my attraction quotient was at an all-time low?

On such nights, I wanted to know what Piet's family felt about the sleeping arrangements in his room; what Anneke felt; what he told her; whether she knew that there had been an encounter of the physical kind in Bombay. I wanted to know whether the reason we were observing chaste relations was moral or physical or merely circumstantial. Whether there would be some other time and space in which it would not be so. Whether there were words in which such matters could be discussed. Whether to feel desires of this sort were what most people called love or whether I was right in calling it short-term infatuation. Whether it made any difference either way.

On especially exhausting nights, I could find myself becoming convinced that it was unhealthy to feel desire in so unrequited a fashion, and that my psyche was suffering gross wounds as a result of it.

At times like this, I could find myself thinking that it would be a good idea to shake Piet awake and tell him that we needed to have sex for purely therapeutic reasons. Men frequently stated therapy as the reason they needed to have sex.

Surely it must be true for women too, even those as unwillingly female as myself? Surely he should be sympathetic, considering that he was hoping to find work as a psychiatrist? There could be no guilt attached, after all, since it would be practically the same as a medical consultation. Three doses of clinical intercourse, no sugar coating please.

Why should anyone mind? I found myself wondering about the whole nature of possessive relationships, the folly of them, the pointlessness. So much anguish and heartache wasted on encounters which did not, of their own accord, amount to much more than a dose of aspirin taken to ease an erotic headache.

In this mood, I could think back to my distress when Piet told me about his encounter with Ramona and consider it entirely childish. I could tell myself that if Piet's family expressed no curiosity about the sleeping arrangements in his room, it was because they were more sensible than I was and that I would do well to learn something from their example.

JAPP

IT CAME AS A surprise, therefore, to learn that I was wrong about the lack of curiosity.

One evening a couple of weeks after my arrival, Piet was out and I was in his room reading *Shogun*. It was something of a struggle because of the jerky bestseller format in combination with the gracious dignity of the medieval Japanese setting.

Then it began to rain fit to make the original deluge seem like a spring shower. The cold grey water entered my spirit and I had to put the book down to sit in front of the inadequate gas-fire in Piet's room and concentrate on keeping warm.

While I was thus occupied, I heard footsteps bounding up the stairs and, in the next moment, Japp had banged on the door to the room, demanding admittance.

He came in saying, 'So! You are alone?'

'It doesn't look like it now,' I said.

He went back down to fetch two cups of coffee and showed me that it was possible to turn the gas-fire up a few notches. The temperature in the room improved from sub-zero to zero. When he had draped himself onto one of the two armchairs he said, 'All right! Now I want to hear efferyfing!'

I made a face at him.

He said, 'No, no, it's all right! You can tell Dr Japp – '

'There isn't anything to tell,' I said.

'Then why do you look so sad?' he asked. 'Is it because of Piet? Is not he beingk kind to you?'

'Tch,' I said, feeling annoyed to be so transparent.

'It's better to let your feelings flow-oooooo – ' said Japp, howling the final word. 'Don't worry. Efferyone is in loff with Piet. It don't matter – '

'I'm not in love with Piet,' I said.

'It don't matter,' said Japp, 'because he don't loff nobody. Or else maybe he loffs efferyone the same. Which is maybe worse, huh? *Tja* – maybe is worse.' He shrugged. 'It's jus' the problem with Piet.'

I frowned and looked away. 'Well – he's not the reason I'm here, so I don't see why you're telling me this,' I said.

'You come to Holland for somefing else?' said Japp. 'Not to see Piet?'

'Of course not to see Piet!' I said, haughtily.

'So – for wot? To lose some fat by not eading dinner? To chust to sit in front of Piet's fire and listen to de Chickens Chorale all night alone?' He grinned, his mouth stretching like pink rubber across the whole width of his face.

I was silent. Just because it was absurd didn't make it easier to handle. Japp reined in his broad features and, in an effort to be serious, made his eyes bug out and his forehead pucker, 'Is it becose the world is a dark place?'

I snorted a laugh, but said, 'No! The world's okay. It's me. *I* am a dark place. No, wait: it's worse than that: I don't know what I am. I don't know what I want to be.' Would he be understanding or would he make it worse? 'I don't like myself. I feel uncomfortable being me. I want to be someone else – but I don't know who or what.'

He was silent, looking at me thoughtfully. Then he said, 'No . . . you haff to explain to me becose I am too stoopid to understand on my alone: is you are sad becose of being too fat? Or becose Piet don't loff you?'

'I wish you wouldn't reduce everything to its most idiotic level,' I said. 'I'm trying to discuss a serious identity crisis here.'

'So where did you sleep anyway?' said Japp, with a mischievous expression on his face. 'Last night?' And then he grinned again. 'Dot's wot efferyone is interested in – '

'What do you mean?' I said.

'You know – Ma, Oma, Julianna – and, of course, Anneke – and me – '

'You're lying,' I said. 'No one's interested. I don't believe it.'

'Of course they're interested,' said Japp. 'They're humans. They're interested. They don't care so much, maybe and it don't matter anyhow – but that's not the same as not being interested. Of course, Anneke is more than chust interested. She cares. But she don't say nuffing. Piet don't like to be asked too many questions.' He trailed off. 'Of course I told them, it's okay. Piet is a goot boy. If he says somefing, then it must be trooth.' He half shut his eyes. 'Unlike me. I am not such a goot boy.'

It was hard to know whether or not to believe Japp. He was hardly anyone's idea of a reliable witness. At the same time, I felt an odd pleasure to hear about this interest. It made me feel less invisible. 'What did Piet say?'

Japp smiled lazily and shrugged, 'Of course, it don't matter to you at all, huh? Wot he finks!'

'It matters to me to know what the people in the house believe is true,' I said.

He was lolling back in the soft embrace of the armchair. 'First you tell me, den I will tell you,' he said, teasingly. He had long since finished his coffee but had not put the cup down yet. There was some sugar still at the bottom of it. He held the cup to his face now, looking at me over the rim while sticking the wet pink slug of his tongue inside, visible through the clear glass, to lick away the lingering sweetness.

I took a deep breath and said '*I* slept in the bed.' What would Piet have said? I couldn't quite believe that anyone would ask him. It wasn't the kind of question that would come up. Nevertheless . . . if it did, what would he say?

Japp continued to look in my direction with his foxy expression. 'And?' he said taking his face out of the cup momentarily.

'And what?' I asked.

'Where did Piet sleep?' The way he was grinning, it was clear that he knew that these were highly objectionable questions. The kind that wouldn't or shouldn't normally be asked.

I said, 'Over there, of course!' tilting my head towards the split-gut horsehair sofa. I did not dare to look at it, because I was so sure it couldn't be large enough to contain Piet even in theory.

Japp nearly bit through the glass cup as he lurched forward in his seat, his giant limbs folding at awkward angles to accommodate the movement.

'Reely!' he said and I felt surprised relief wash through me. This must have been the story that Piet himself put out. If so I was very pleased to be able to confirm it. It allowed me to imagine that we were of the same mind. 'He woss on de sofa – de *whole night?*'

I smiled and nodded, while mentally patting myself on the head for what I believed was superb piece of trooth-modulation. I hadn't said the lie out loud, I had merely tilted my head. Japp's reaction made it clear that he would carry this piece of information outside the confines of this room. In which case, though the specific detail was wrong, the point of it would be right: Piet and I had been in the same bed but the effect was the same as if he'd been on the sofa.

Japp pouted his huge mouth forward and curled down the corners in mock chagrin. 'Wal! Piet reely ISS a goot boy, huh?' Then he shrugged. 'Iss goot. Anneke was feeling ffery sad for some days before you came, huh? Now . . . I fink, maybe she won't feel so sad.'

'I'm glad to hear it,' I said, primly.

'And for you?' he said, refusing to give up. 'Is okay? The arranchement?'

'Why not?' I said. 'I told you, I'm not here to be with Piet.'

'Yes, but I don't haff to belief efferything I heer,' said Japp. 'I can also belief wot I see. I can see you are sad. Maybe it is becose of Piet, he sleeps on de sofa – '

'Japp!' I said. 'Maybe it's *becose* I have some other kinds of problems!'

'So, so – I am trying and trying to understand wot are dose problems!' said Japp.

'I'm not happy to be what I am,' I said. Then, feeling reckless, I added, 'For instance, I don't like being a woman.'

I glanced at Japp, challenging him to make something of this statement. For me it was the equivalent of being an orthodox Muslim willfully eating a whole side of ham in public.

He shrugged, lightly and said, 'So wot?'

This took the wind out of my sails. I said, 'Well it's a problem, you know? It's difficult to look like a woman while living in a world where being one is considered a drawback – '

'You mean, in brown-rat countries or . . . anywhere?'

'I mean anywhere,' I said. 'It's difficult to be a woman who doesn't want to behave like other women.'

'Yes,' said Japp, a little dreamily. It was not of real concern to him.

I stopped caring whether or not he understood what I was talking about. There was a certain pleasure in being able to say out loud the sort of things that would have got me drawn and quartered in a feminist court of law.

'Women are considered an inferior species in most parts of the world. I don't think I'm inferior, so when I am alone in a room, I'm fine. But the moment I am with other people, even other women, I can feel their minds pushing me down, forcing me to be the same cow-like type of being that women are expected to be even when it's obvious that we're not.' I stopped, feeling breathless. 'I don't want to be pushed by any thoughts or expectations. I want to be the way I am without having to feel that I'm a freak just for being a little different. I want to be different and ordinary at the same time!'

'Yes,' said Japp. 'I understand. I have a same feeling, sometimes – about being human.'

'It's *not* the same,' I said, irritated with him for being so obtuse.

'Because "human" is what we all are. We could all be feeling bad about that, but we can't communicate with any other creatures, so we don't have any idea about the alternatives. But men and women *can* communicate to one another.'

'I *can* communicate with animals,' said Japp. 'When I am alone, I am a bat. I hang upside down and I fink bat-thoughts. But when people see me, they talk as if they fink I am also human, like them.'

'You're just making a joke about this,' I said.

'It *IS* a choke,' said Japp. 'A bad choke. On efferyone. So it don't matter, huh? Becose efferyone is in de same choke.'

'You're not listening to what I'm saying!' I said. 'It's a serious problem. I don't know how to live my life when I can't feel comfortable with what I am!'

'I'm listening. Wot I'm hearingk is dot you're not comfortable with you, but you're also chust grabbing hold of your uncomfortableness and keeping it *so*,' he hugged himself tight. 'Like he was your lover.'

'I'm not *doing* anything,' I said. 'It's just my condition. It's in the script I was given – '

'So – you can throw it away,' said Japp.

'Throw away my body?' I asked, feeling sad. *That's what I am planning to do*, I thought. *It's on my agenda already. In six years from now. Less.* It was nearing the five year mark.

'No, chust the *script*,' said Japp.

'It isn't possible to throw away scripts,' I said, feeling that the lack of fluency was becoming an impediment to comprehension.

'It is,' he said, and proceeded to tell me a story about an experience he'd had in an encounter therapy group.

'We woss doing this exercise, you know? Efferyone stands in a line, two-and-two, one in front of de other. So de exercise is, each one who is in front must fall back into de arms of de one standing at de behind, ready to catch him. So we had all done it once and then we changed places, de . . . catchee becomes de catcher. So I was standing with my partner, de catchee, you know, she was maybe forty years old and she seemed fine and efferything. All de catchees were falling nicely. Came our turn and – my catchee couldn't do it! Oh, she screamed and she cried and she told us her whole life story . . . how her parents died when she woss too young, and she never got over it and she can't trust no one. And all de time we woss telling her, fall, fall fall! But she couldn't fall.

'So den the instructor asked her to stop and fink about why she woss afraid of falling back and she said, because she knew that I would not catch her. She chust knew it. In her life, she woss always trusting people and they woss always letting her fall. So she couldn't trust nobody any more. And we all told her, no, no, don't worry, nothing will happen, he will catch you. And she said, No, no, he won't! He'll let me fall and I'll break my neck! I'll die, I'll die! So we all said, No, no, no – he'll catch you, you won't die.

'So it took, I don't know, maybe haff an hour, before she said, Okay, so I try. So we all stood up, and she woss in front and I woss in back and efferyone woss calling out, Don't worry! Don't worry! And so finally, finally, finally, she fell. And I . . . *stepped aside*!'

All through this story, I had been waiting for him to tell me that he had caught her and what a difference it had made to his life to prove himself dependable and trustworthy. But when he said that he let the lady fall, I realized that my Pollyanna notions about the world had betrayed me as usual. Of course he didn't catch her. She had been right all along. He was a sadistic, feelingless lout.

I gasped and said 'Oh *god*, Japp! No! You didn't!'

And Japp said, 'I *had* to! She would have learnt nuffingk if I had caught her. The big lesson is that she *will* fall some day and she *will* die and that's chust reality. No-one can go crying all the way to the box, you know? The grave-box.'

'Yes – but – ' I said, feeling helpless. 'What about *you*! You need to know that you can catch people too, that you can be kind and caring – '

He shrugged, with a quizzical expression on his face, '– so, I already *know* that, huh?'

Outside, the rain had intensified and the draft was causing the paper-pane to crack and snap. The gas-fire hissed. The chicks were cheeping in their bucket. I felt desolate. He was silent as well. I felt his eyes on me, but I didn't look up because I didn't know what to say. Finally I asked him, 'So . . . what happened to that lady? What did *she* think?'

He said, wrinkling his nose to make his glasses ride higher, 'Oh . . . I don't know. Maybe she broke her – ' he indicated ribs ' – you know, one of these bones, maybe becoss of the falling. I don't know later wot happened. Efferyone woss mad at me, so I didn't stay in de group. I heard sometime that maybe she killed herself, but I don't know.' He looked at me, boldly.

I couldn't meet his eyes. It was such a dismal story. 'I don't why you've told me this,' I said. 'I don't see the point.'

'There is *no* point,' said Japp. 'That is the point.'

'No. What I was saying before.' I could barely find the thread myself.

'It's chust *scripts*, you know? Her script woss she would fall and so she would die. So. *She* made it happen. Becoss it woss her *script*, you know? Not becoss it was reely the trooth – but she made it trooth! You know? She had faith in her script and so she made it trooth. I didn't do nuffingk – I chust helped her, is all. I became part of her script. Is like you too. I don't know how you said it exactly, but you are also talking about scripts. So if you don't like your script, it's your choice, you know? To throw it away. Or not.'

The gas breathed heat out. I stared across the short space of the two armchairs to where Japp's pale bulging eyes were gazing at me. He was smiling very faintly, that slightly mad smile of his.

I felt as if I'd been running all day long. I wanted to sleep. I said, 'Japp, I think it's time you should go. I . . . need to think.'

He nodded and got up, grinned, waved and went out the door. Then he turned around, blew a kiss in my direction and went out again, closing the door behind him.

KAY

THE NEXT DAY, A Sunday, Piet came home in the morning, convinced that he would be able to teach me to ride a cycle. I protested but the lure of spending an hour alone in his company was a powerful one and in any case, the word 'can't' did not exist in his vocabulary. He borrowed Simon's cycle in the hope that the seat would not be too high for me – though it was – and said, 'It's so easy. You just push with your feet on the pedals and when you want to stop, you pedal backwards – '

I could have told him what was going to happen and it did, almost: I cycled forward with every sign of confidence for a few yards, but when I had to turn, my feet flew off the pedals of their own accord.

Inside my head, a red light had flashed on, informing me that I was far too incompetent to remain in balance and that I MUST fall off. This was what had happened, routinely whenever I had previously tried to learn. My own certainty that I wouldn't succeed guaranteed that I didn't. Normally, taking my feet off the pedals would cause the bike to topple to one side and I had become an expert at hopping off before I or the bike came to any harm. But this time, to my surprise, the bike stayed in balance and my forward momentum kept me going.

I and the cycle flew down the short road, then across a main thoroughfare, over the road divider, up onto the opposing pavement and *bump!* into the wall of the building on that side of the road. All of this happened in the time it took for my mind to process the idea that I had not succeeded in toppling off the bike in the usual manner. Piet's panic-stricken shout to avoid the main road reached me only after I was already across it. He caught up with me fast enough that he was able to grab the carrier on the back of the bike just as I bumped into the building that had halted my gliding progress.

His face was white with shock as he said 'It's a *main road*!! You could have got *killed*!' But it was a Sunday and there was no traffic to speak of. I shrugged and smiled, wondering why he found it so hard to see that since I was unharmed, there was nothing more to agonize about.

'I told you, I'm hopeless!' I said.

He nodded slowly, his face registering unbelief. 'I can see what you mean now,' he said. 'You are not ready to ride. It's strange . . .' We walked back to his house in silence. I felt I had let him down and berated myself silently for not having made the extra little effort that might have kept me going. At the same time I felt curiously exhilarated. Later, when I could examine my mood, I realized that despite the negative result, I was crowing over the fact that Piet had, for once, been wrong.

I saw little of him for the rest of the week. His routine was fairly tight. In the morning he went to the university for his classes, in the afternoon he came back and worked on his motorbike. In the evenings he either attended a study group or went out with Anneke.

The rain was relentless. It dripped directly into my mind, the dank wetness drenching through my defences, finding cracks in my confidence. I couldn't focus on anything, I couldn't make any plans. I had no idea what I wanted to do. I could no longer remember what kind of bright assurance had guided me through so many twists and turns to this one particular spot in the universe. Inside my head there was a grey blanket as thick as the clouds bearing down on the rooftops of Utrecht, just as soggy, just as coldly unreasonable.

I spoke to Micki on the telephone a few times. 'How's the search for cosmic truth coming along?' she asked. I said it was thin on the ground, but that I was persevering. I knew that I sounded more positive than I felt, but I didn't want her to worry. I told her that I would write letters home that I would send to her to post from

Germany. But I never got around to it. There was nothing to say and I didn't have the stomach to actually fictionalize the events of my life.

I kept to myself, sitting in Piet's room, listening to his music or sometimes sitting with Simon in his room. He smoked joints all through the day, rolling them reflexively without even looking at what he was doing. He told me that it was a great honour to be permitted to operate Piet's music system with its sleek black turntable and stack of sacred records. Sometimes I shared a joint with him, telling myself that the weather was affecting my ability to think straight in which case the joints would have little effect. They seemed not to.

I told myself that just as soon as the weather cleared, I would pound the streets looking for drawing assignments. But whenever the clouds thinned enough to let a diffused glow of sunlight through I felt like drowning myself in the fish tank rather than face the challenge of making any decisions. When someone, Japp or Piet or Simon, asked me what I was doing, I said I was 'watching the cobra'. I knew that this was considered an impeccable way to pass the time, so there could be no argument.

The family only ever met for dinner and, even then, only the core group of Ma and the two youngest boys. On the average day, Juliana came in, made dinner and left. There was always cheese, bread and salads in the fridge to eat during the day. I had asked Piet what I should do to help around the house and he had shrugged the question aside saying that it was upto me, if I wanted to, but that between Juliana and Ma there was no real need. I went with Simon on shopping expeditions during which I shared some expenses and bought a few items specific to my needs, such as orange juice and low-fat buttermilk.

Piet made an appointment to visit Kay on the second Sunday of my stay. I had heard enough about Kay to realize that meeting him was going to be an important node in my stay in Piet's company. At the same time, I had noticed a resistance in myself, not just to the meeting but to Kay himself. It was hard to explain, considering that I had not met the man. If I had mentioned it to Piet or Simon, I knew that they would interpret it in some mystic way. Past-life disturbances blinking like Belisha's Beacons in the ether. A tidal wave of bad karma engulfing me on the eve of my encounter with a Luminous One.

I told myself that I must suppress my reactions in order to be impartial.

We set off in the morning, Piet, Simon and myself. I was glad of Simon's company. Of all the people I had met so far, he was the single one whose friendship was pleasurable in a simple and uncomplicated manner. The three of us took an intercity bus to Amsterdam and, when we got there, boarded a local to Kay's house. I began to get the change out for a ticket, but Piet stopped me. We were sitting in the rear vehicle of a trailer pair.

'It's free,' he said. Then he grinned. Simon, who had said very little on the journey so far, caught his eye and smiled but, it seemed to me, there was an element of embarrassment in his response. They were both a little jumpy. I must have looked puzzled because Piet leaned towards me and said, in a breathy undertone, 'It's a wonderful system, the Dutch public transport. All passengers standing on the rear bus can travel without tickets.'

I said, 'Really?'

Simon was laughing silently, but said nothing. Piet smiled and looking away.

We got off a little later. I wanted to know how the city could afford to offer a free bus-service. 'Is it subsidized?' I asked.

Simon said, looking a little shame-faced, 'We have student identity cards. It's only your ticket that needed to be bought.'

Piet said, shrugging, 'The passengers are supposed to go up to the driver and pay the ticket. But if you're in the rear bus. It's too much trouble, huh? So, unless there's a ticket collecter, no one bothers.'

'What would have happened if I got caught?' I said. My voice was calm but within me a thunderhead of anger had boiled up, like storm clouds out of a blue sky. Alarms flashed like sheet lightning inside my head: My one-month visa! My tourist status! 'Would I have had to pay a fine?' My dwindling dollar resources!

'You should read Carlos Castaneda,' said Piet, coolly. 'Fear is the only danger. If you're sitting there, you know,' he mimed a horror-struck face, chewing his nails to the bone, 'thinking *oo, now they come, now they come*? Then you draw them to you, huh? It's like, do you remember what he said about the power walk?' It was one of the first exercises that Castaneda's Yaqui spiritual guide, Don Juan, taught him: a style of walking or to be more precise, running, which had to be performed in pitch darkness, ideally along the margins of perilous cliffs, with the knees pumping high and no thought whatsoever of danger. The only way to avoid a fatal plunge, according to Don Juan, was to develop a state of mind that was absolutely without fear. It was an intrinsic part of the training that he imparted. In such a state, the safest route between two points would be created, moment by moment, as one ran.

I nodded, but the turbulence continued inside my head. I couldn't make it settle down. I felt that Piet had done something extremely irresponsible given my precarious position as a tourist and I couldn't feel all right about it. At the same time, in my head, a team of lawyers sprang up in his defence. They jeered at me for ignoring the crowds of free-loaders who travelled ticketless in India. 'It's nothing special at all! It's just a little prank!' jibbered Piet's lawyers, to me in my head. 'It's you and your boring, four-square, bourgeois upbringing that's outraged! You're afraid of identifying with the ticketless-travellers because they're LOWER CLASS!!'

I endured these internal taunts and I said nothing to anyone. We were at a zebra crossing. Once again, as it was a Sunday, traffic was sparse. Piet demonstrated the power walk. He took off across the road, raising his knees chest high, his back straight, his shoulders up around his ears and his arms stiff at his sides, hands deep in the pockets of his WWII surplus jacket. As he ran, he yelled over his shoulder, 'Basically, it's something like this!' He looked manic and very funny. Simon's shoulders were shaking with laughter. I was smiling, but stiffly. I was still stuck on the bus, fretting about the unpaid ticket.

Kay had retired from government service, said Piet, as we neared the house. He had devoted the rest of his life to being a full-time Boddhisattva. The first time I heard this, back in Bombay I had not paid it much attention. But now I asked, 'Who decides when someone is a Boddhisattva? I mean, was it Kay or someone else?'

'Oh, it was Kay,' said Piet. 'When you become a Boddhisattva, you just know these things.' His expression was disengaged, in the way of someone who answers out of politeness, even though he knows the question to be gauche.

The house was a ground floor apartment in a tidy and self-contained complex. We entered through a narrow corridor. In the kitchen at the other end, I could see that Japp, who had also been invited, had already arrived. He, along with two others, Hans and Adrian, was in the kitchen. They were cooking lunch in the style of three tornadoes who believe that if enough food is kept circulating in the air, a meal will eventually thicken into substance.

Kay called out from somewhere inside to say that we should make ourselves at home. Piet showed me into the drawing room, whose small size was compounded by the number of Oriental artifacts arranged on its walls, on shelves and on every available horizontal surface. The predominant colour was bronze, with red accents flaring from the eyes of small Sri Lankan demons and bright blue accents from the turquoises adorning the innumerable representations of Tantric figures locked in writhing, multi-armed union. There were batik decorations hanging on the walls and a pair of small, dark Persian silk prayer-rugs on the floor. A perforated brass lamp cast its intricate shadow from atop a gleaming brass ceremonial platter. But the atmosphere in the room was tense and stuffy. I felt uneasy, rather than at home amidst all the familiar Asian textures.

Then Kay entered the room and I realized at once that he was the source of my unease. He was a man of perhaps fifty-five and his demeanour was that of someone who has swallowed a pinch of white dwarf matter, causing his whole interior to implode. All his vital fluids and every calorie of human heat had been sucked down into an infinite interior void. Just being in the same room as him was an effort of resistance, because the emptiness at his centre exerted its influence even outside the boundary of his own body. I felt like turning tail and running out of the room, away from him and the vacuum he contained. I was stricken to think that this man had been such a profound influence on all my current friends.

He despised me on sight, reciprocally. He knew at once that I was not the sort of Indian who could augment his prestige amongst his brood of young acolytes. My clothes and appearance instantly proclaimed that I was not traditional.

What he said out loud however was, 'Ah! The genuine article!', in the cultivated English accent that many Dutch have. 'A real Indian!' Then he pronounced my whole name with careful concern for getting the inflection right before cooing again, 'And a South Indian too! Welcome, indeed.' His tobacco-brown eyes flickered coldly over me, like the tongue of a snake reviewing the heat-profile of a potential victim. 'I have heard a lot about you.'

With Piet sitting silently by my side, I stammered my way through a miserable inquisition about Govinda. How long had I known him? Where did I meet him? Had I known his parents? Which gurus' salons did I frequent? What did I think about the philosopher Radhakrishnan? And so on. When he asked me where I was from, Piet looked knowingly in my direction and Kay, intercepting the look, demanded to know what it was about. Piet said, in English, 'She's been telling me about how that's such a cliché question amongst Indians, how she hates to be asked that.'

'Ah – you don't like that question?' said Kay, raising his eyebrows. 'Well, I'm sorry, then. I didn't mean to insult you and, of course, what a foolish question. Your name should tell me everything . . . yes? Padmanabhan. A Brahmin, then, if I'm not mistaken?'

I said, angry with the question, angry with the circumstances which brought forth the answer, 'No, not a Brahmin. My name is misleading.' I took in a breath and said, 'I was brought up to believe that casteism is wrong. So I reject that way of thought. But if you want to believe in it, you can call me an untouchable.' I hoped that my tone of voice told him that I didn't care what he thought, because I didn't care about the thoughts of people who believed in caste.

He raised his eyebrows again, 'Ah – a modern,' he said. But I sensed his guard relaxing. He was someone for whom the inflexible hierarchies of traditional societies are a source of comfort, not distress. My statement had told him that I was too far beneath his contempt to be of harm to him. If I was not firmly rooted in my own culture then I could not challenge his knowledge of it. I could not threaten his authority with authenticity.

I said, 'I'm not religious.' I blurted this out as if it were a guilty confession. 'My parents brought me up to be liberal. Three of the schools I went to were convents. In fact, if I had to choose a religion to follow, it would be Christianity.' The Sri Lankan demons blinked in astonishment to hear such words

'So that explains why you speak English so well,' said Kay. 'The convents?'

'No,' I said, 'I grew up outside India. It's the only language I speak.'

Kay's large, heavy-lidded eyes were magnified by the glasses he wore. He watched me intently. I felt I was being passed through the gut of a large, slow-moving organism, which would gradually assimilate all my essential juices before discarding the remains with a contemptuous squirt.

PRIVATE JUNGLES

WE HAD LUNCH SOON after and despite the shambles that the three cooks had left the kitchen in, it was a pleasant meal. Towards the end of it, Piet leaned towards me and asked if I wanted to see a film. *A Clockwork Orange* was showing. It was a great favourite of Piet's and I hadn't ever seen it. I agreed readily.

We left the others at Kay's house, saw the film and got back to Utrecht together. Simon had elected to remain in Amsterdam along with Japp and the others present at the lunch. For the first time since I had arrived in Holland we had the sort of conversation that had animated so many rainy afternoons in Bombay.

We talked about state repression, psychology, the ethics of punishment and of mind-control. We ate hamburgers at McDonald's. We got home after the rest of the family had had dinner.

When we were once more in his room, Piet asked me what I thought about Kay.

I had a brief moment of doubt in which I considered saying something neutral, before deciding to be honest. 'I didn't like him,' I said.

Piet was watching me intently.

'I'm sorry. I know how important he is to you.' I tried to focus on what had disturbed me so much about the man. 'He's – I'm sorry, it's a terrible thing to say about anybody – but I felt he was like a psychic leech.' I felt immediately better for having got these harsh words out. 'Whatever he gives to you is nothing compared to what you give to him. It's like he lives off you. And the others.'

The room was lit only by the chick-bucket, the aquarium light and the thin gas-fire. Piet was sitting at his desk, leaning his head down on his folded arms. I was lolling in one of the armchairs. He turned his face towards the paper-paned window beside the desk. He was silent for so long that I began to feel I may have insulted him beyond recall. But at last he turned his head towards me and said, 'It's interesting . . .' He broke off before completing his sentence. When he continued it was along a different thread. 'I can see a little of what you see. Just a little. I'll have to think about it.'

He went on to tell me about how he met Anneke. She had been one of Kay's first disciples. Piet had met her at Kay's house. 'She is seven years older than me,' he said. 'She was always interested in the dharma search. She met Kay becose she went to a lecture by him. She's very sensitive to energies. The first time she met me she told me that my energy is very special. She was the first to notice it. She said it is sort of refined. She thinks that I should definitely become a psychic healer. That kind of thing.' He shrugged.

'She told Kay to be interested in me and for some time we were' – he held his hands together in a tight bond – 'all very close. He helped me to look inside myself. To see where the problems were stuck, you know? In my chest, in my stomach. Anneke had learnt yoga and she said that would also help me. She began to teach me some yoga. She said I was very good, my attention was very focused, etcetera. But then she began to be more interested in me than in Kay. And then, slowly, that began to create problems between her and Kay. And then . . .' he shrugged again. 'She became my girlfriend.'

Japp had not come by that evening so I had actually been alone with Piet for a considerable stretch of time.

I could hear the faint sound of music from Simon's room. He had a girlfriend called Mandy, a pretty but brittle brunette whom Simon said he was hopelessly in love with. He had told me that she didn't reciprocate the intensity of his feelings and he feared she was just playing with him. She had, however, agreed to spend Sunday evening with him so for the moment he was happy.

Piet was looking pensive. 'Anneke says she loves me,' he said. 'She loves me very much. She hasn't had good relationships with men before this one. She says she is sure we were together in our past lives.' He raised his shoulders in a shrug. 'But I don't feel sure of anything. It's too soon.'

He had brought the head-lamp case from his Harley up to his room to work on. He had hammered out dents where he could, but there were a few patches where he had filled over the unevenness with epoxy resin. He had waited for it to harden in order to sand it down which was what he was doing now, as he talked. He was aiming to get the filler-patch to match the curve of the rest of the case.

'She says she was a, you know, a king's mistress? A courtesan. In her last life. I was her lover, a prince. She has seen me in her dreams.'

Presently he stopped to flex his arms. Then he put down the head-lamp case, stood up and stretched towards the plank in the ceiling. With a smooth, elastic motion, he swung himself up into position, upside down, with his shins threaded through the leather strap, supporting him. He had shown me before that this was the purpose of the plank. I had tried hanging upside down, but felt uncomfortable, especially since the plank was too high for me to reach it or dismount from it on my own. He said it was a yoga exercise and that it had taken him a week to get used to it. Now he could hang there as long as he pleased, feeling completely relaxed.

I had changed into my nightie and was sitting on the bed, listening to Piet and watching him. I could understand why Anneke felt what she did for him. He was handsome in the way that a healthy young animal is handsome, with its skin loose and gleaming, its muscles proportioned for maximum efficiency. He was intelligent and he was self-sufficient, capable of being the supporting member for his family, attacking any task he took up with bright assurance and supreme competence. But what did I feel about him? I pushed the question out of my mind.

We played the 'Which Animal?' game and I said that I saw him as an elk, a great tall creature with a giant head of horn, silhouetted against the sunset, alone on a peak in the Canadian Rockies.

He laughed, his voice breathy from his upside down position and said, 'I like that!' He said he thought I was a type of bird, large, with plumes of some sort, but not a predator. One of the big storks or herons. I wasn't sure that I liked this description, particularly since I was so sure I was a tiger. He said he had never been clear what he was. Perhaps a horse, a big draught animal with huge hooves and a luxuriant mane hanging like white curtains from its thick neck. We both agreed that Japp was a wolf. We didn't talk about Anneke.

I asked if he had answered that series of questions which starts, 'Imagine a forest . . . describe the forest . . .' He said, 'You mean, *When a tree falls in the forest* . . . That one?'

'No,' I said.

'But did you know about that one?' He dismounted from the plank.

I said, of course. A tree falls in the forest when there's no one and nothing to hear it. Is there a sound?

'You know what the correct answer to it is?' he asked.

'What?' I said.

'It depends on how you define the word "sound". If you mean sound waves, then there is a sound. If you mean something that someone hears and recognizes as sound, there's no sound.'

But who or what constitutes a valid someone, I wanted to know. After all, how could there be a forest so theoretical that there were no creatures in it, none at all? And if there was even one creature within hearing range, then there was a sound.

'Of course,' he said, 'but that's not the point. The point is the idea of reality – is there reality outside the context of consciousness?' He stripped away his outer layer of clothing.

'It's still a question of how you define consciousness,' I said, turning around so that I wasn't looking at him, but getting in on my side of the bed.

'That's not the point,' he said, getting in on his side.

'Because everything depends then on what you're accepting as the foundation of your reality. After all, the forest could be in a vacuum – in which case, there would be no sound waves either!'

'That's ridiculous – there can't be a forest without air – '

'So then there can't be a forest without creatures – ' I said.

'For the purpose of this enquiry, the consciousness of creatures doesn't count!' he said.

I laughed and said, in that case, that's what I had always thought was the problem with that question – it implied a view of consciousness that I did not accept.

He turned off the light in the chick-bucket from the wall. The chicks had grown up enough to be shifted out from Piet's room to their permanent home. The bucket had remained. The aquarium light was off and its air-filter was in the silent phase of its cycle.

'What is the other questions about a forest,' he asked, whispering, his voice close to my right ear.

I said, also whispering, 'It starts like this: Imagine a forest . . . describe the forest . . .'

'A forest . . .' he said, his voice little more than a modulation of breath ' . . . is dark. Ffery dark. There is no light nowhere . . .' Then after a pause he continued, hushed, as if he were not actually saying the words, but merely thinking them, 'And no sounds. Nevertheless . . . there is some consciousness!'

Two pairs of consciousness.

A heron, an elk, a tiger, a horse: sharing warmth in the wilderness of a bed. There was some baring of tusks, some mingling of breath. Some tumult, no speech.

He asked in whispers if I was thirsty. I said that I was, but we had cleared the coffee cups from his room just that evening so there wasn't anything in which to fetch water from the washbasin on the landing. I wasn't thirsty enough to go down to the kitchen for a glass.

He said, 'Wait,' and left the room. I thought that maybe he had decided to go down to the kitchen himself. But when he came back, he was empty-handed and shivering slightly against the cold because he had left the room naked and barefoot.

He jumped under the covers, saying nothing, so that I wondered why he had gone out at all, but then he turned immediately towards me and, holding my head steady in his hands, transferred one mouthful of cold water from his mouth to mine.

THE PEACOCK

THE NEXT MORNING I came down to find Piet sitting at the dining table. He seemed pensive. I sat opposite him and one of the cats jumped up and into my lap. I stroked her and tickled her under her chin. She purred and began kneading me with her paws.

Weak sunlight entered through the tall windows, constrained by the small panes, falling on the table top in pairs of glowing rectangles. The angle at which the light entered was too steep to penetrate the rest of the room which remained as a result awash in sepia shadows.

I said, 'Ouch!' to the cat, who looked up, surprised that I should object to her claws as she kneaded.

'You know why they do that, don't you?' said Piet.

'Because they're happy,' I said, 'because they're remembering their kitten days, nursing at their mother. The kneading is what they do to keep the milk flowing.'

Piet picked up another of the cats and reversed it onto his lap, so that it lay with its paws in the air, practically growling with pleasure. 'Cats are very special, huh?'

I agreed.

'I have a theory,' he said, 'that cats are telepathic. They listen to our thoughts and sort of amplify them. So if we are in a calm mood, they can pick up that mood and amplify it. That's what this sound is – this *rrr-rrrr-rrrr* – it's the sound of our own peaceful mood.'

I smiled and said it was a nice theory.

There was a silence. The house was so quiet it was almost possible to hear the sunlight as it came in, as it touched surfaces with its radiant energy, causing atoms to stir and hum.

Piet said, 'You said the other day that there was something you wanted to say to me.'

It seemed like such a long time ago. I shrugged and said, 'Oh. It's almost unnecessary, now.'

'Tell me anyway,' he said.

I struggled to recover the sense of revelation I had felt at the time. 'It's just that I woke up that first morning, thinking that just by being here I am freed to be whoever I want. Not just whoever, but also *what*ever.'

He glanced up from the cat and said, 'Like . . . a tiger?'

I looked away, feeling that the sunlight filtering in through the windows was filling directly into my brain making speech impossible, but managed to say, 'Yes.'

I was embarrassed by this direct reference to the night before. I had made an adjustment that I myself hadn't noticed till that moment, to maintaining a silence about any activity that took place between Piet and me.

From this new perspective I could look back on the time in Bombay when I had felt disturbed that he did not like making any public acknowledgement of a private connection between us. I could see now that the desire was childish. We shared a space and that was sufficient. It was fragile. It did not need discussion. It needed to live its secret life outside the realm of comment or conscious thought. It was my turn to feel annoyed that he had made a reference to it.

I continued, 'That's right. A tiger, a horse. Anything. Not necessarily human. I feel I can question my reality and look at many different answers, not just the one that everyone expects. In Bombay if you had asked *What kind of animal are you?* I would have said – '

He laughed gustily, 'You would have said, *He's crazy!*' making a screw-loose sign at his temple.

'No! I would have said, *I'm an artist, a woman, a feminist*. I would have answered literally. But now? There are no obvious answers.' I looked directly at him. 'I find that I am not comfortable being anything just now. Not an artist, not a woman.'

I felt I was exploring the outer margin of self-definition. Issues that used to be of such supreme consequence were fading and losing definition. I felt an interior glow. At that instant I could explain clearly why I enjoyed Piet's company: it was that he did not force me to conform to any existing definitions of myself. It was a quality that I didn't always appreciate. But when I could see it for what it was, I felt freed by it and wondered why I would want it to be any other way.

He was looking down at the cat on his lap and raised his eyebrows, to acknowledge what I said. 'Are you comfortable being . . . nobody?' he asked.

'I'm trying to keep my options open,' I said. 'I want to see what I will become if I don't make any effort.'

He was stroking the cat slowly and thoughtfully. 'Do you think it's because you are *here* or because you are away from anything familiar?' he asked.

I said it was quite definitely because I was *here*. 'It's difficult to be anywhere without being identified as a particular person. Even in a hotel, though you're a stranger to the staff, they know who you are, at least in terms of your outer shell. They know your name, your passport, your room number, your appearance. All the things that matter the least to your inner being and yet can become a prison, in the wrong circumstances. It's only here, because you make it possible for me to live in your house without forcing me to BE someone, that I can experiment with my own definitions. Your family – I'm not sure that they see me at all – but they don't seem to mind. I am free to be invisible.'

The thing that had bothered me at the time of my arrival was now something I felt grateful for.

He was holding the cat up, burying his face in its belly, as if it were a living face ruff, blowing warm air into its fur. 'Is it because you don't like being yourself or because you want to be someone else? There's a difference, huh?'

'I don't like being myself,' I said. 'I don't like all the baggage that goes with being this particular person, "me". I say I want to lose weight but that's a symptom, isn't it? When you want to lose weight, it has to mean you don't like yourself. Or the other way around: you don't like yourself so you add layers to your body by eating too much, in order to forget the one that's underneath.'

'You should ask Juliana about that,' said Piet. 'She knows a lot about losing weight.'

'I'm talking about cultural weight too,' I said. 'The baggage that comes along with being a – a – liddle brown rat, like Japp would say.'

'You don't mind?' asked Piet looking at me, over the cat's boneless form.' When Japp says those things?'

'I think he's saying out loud the things that many outsiders think when they come to India,' I said. 'Some people say they like being there. But I think there are many who are just the same as Japp, except they don't say so.'

'Yes – but –' said Piet.

I said, 'I mean, I know I'm "liddle" and I'm brown but I'm not a rat. So I don't feel the description on my skin. And I remember walking around with Japp, in Bombay. I remember seeing what he saw: the crowds, the mess and the horror and . . . yes: millions upon millions of small, scurrying forms, whipping themselves to run, run, run all the way from birth to death, seemingly blindly, just helter-skelter down the tracks set for them by fate and tradition, as fast as they can go.'

I felt breathless and depressed just to recall that moment of insight. 'The traditional way is to avoid thought, and to follow the path set for you. Lose yourself in the pattern. Give up your personal identity.'

'Just what *you* are doing now – ' he said, challenging my position.

I met the challenge. 'Yes. I'm giving up my liddle brown rat personal identity because *liddle brown rats are not encouraged to have a personal identity*!'

We both smiled.

He breathed into the cat for a few moments.

'But you know,' he said, speaking thoughtfully, 'it's not so different with us. We're not brown, okay and we're not disorganized – but so what? We're . . .' he sought for the words, 'white . . . ants? Termites. We're so *precise*, you know? And rigid? And marching in long straight' – he trailed his hand along the edge of the table to suggest columns – 'armies, you know? March-march-march, with our little shopping trollies, you know? And our little cars and buses and trains – march-march-march! To the office and to the school and then the college and then maybe once a year we go marching all the way to the holiday resort and then marching back again – it's just another kind of racetrack!'

He wiped the surface of the table top, as if clearing it of soldier ants. 'So maybe it is more precise. More neat or more clean. But it's *still* a track.'

The mood in the room was shifting. I said, 'Okay, but look at – okay, you and Japp. You're not on a track. You're both outside.'

Piet frowned slightly, his forehead lacking a natural crease, so that it merely folded up without a line. He said, 'Me . . . not yet, but that's just for the moment. And Japp – well.' He shrugged and shook his head, as if trying to rid himself of a bad notion. 'He's outside *everything*. There's no point being Japp.'

'Why do you say that?' I asked, surprised.

He looked away before saying, 'I'll tell you but not just today. There's something else I want to talk about.' He considered his statement carefully, before continuing. 'When we were at Kay's house?'

'Yes,' I said. 'I was very uncomfortable.' I believed I had understood the problem. 'He looked at me with the kind of eyes that Indians use for seeing other Indians. That is, when he looks at me, he recognizes that I'm not following the pattern that is set for me. And his first instinct is the same as it would be for many Indians, that is: to squash me down and force me to sit in the little box that they believe is the right one for me. Except that it isn't. Boxes are suffocating. No one should be forced to sit in them.'

Piet nodded then said, 'Kay called me today.' As he said these words, I should have felt something, a shift, a premonition. But I did not. I was too well-protected by my desire to see what I wanted to see.

He looked far away, out of the windows, the cat limp in his hands, in a pleasure-coma. 'He wanted to warn me about you.' Piet paused, then continued. 'He said you had the wrong kind of energy. Unformed. He said you could be destructive for me.' I could hear the sunbeams making their way to the tabletop. A pale, golden hiss. The air sharpened into fine needles. I felt myself go numb inside.

'And what do you think?' I asked.

Piet resumed breathing into the cat's belly so that it finally stirred and gave a little purring groan of protest. He put it down on the table. It stretched, flexed its back and then as if it had had a surfeit of delight, leapt down from the table and stalked away, its tail in the air. 'I don't know,' said Piet, his voice low. 'I don't know.'

There was a long silence after. Then the mood shifted once more.

'I understand . . . very *exactly* . . . what you mean when you say that you are unhappy with being you,' he said, presently. 'I used to be like that. Not just unhappy – I used to be like – *angry!* All the time. It was part of my, you know, everything. My life. I mean . . .' He looked away. 'Before I got into all this, you know, guru-business, I used be like a, like a – I don't know.' He laughed in a disjointed way.

'Angry about what?' I asked.

'I hated my father – ' but he glanced at me as he said this and we both laughed shakily. It was such an obvious cliché. 'Yah! It's sort of so – so – pathetic, you know? You read about these things in textbooks and before you know it, *paf! Me too, Lord!* But the point is, I really, really did hate him. He was such a, a – *shitty* person. You know? And at the same time, I wanted his approval too. And he never gave it. It's all so classic. He sort of hated me too – I mean, he even said it, sometimes. And at the same time, it's understandable, what he felt.'

'Understandable?' I asked.

'They got married because of me – my mother and father, I mean,' he said. 'My father was a very intelligent man, he was a scientist, he was a free-thinker. He never wanted to be married or to be tied down with anything so . . . so *basic* as a family, you know? So when my mother told him that I was on the way – I mean, I don't know what she said or how she said it, I wasn't there but I think he sort of, you know, couldn't run away. At the same time, he couldn't stay either.

'So maybe he did both things. Sort of. He would come and spend some time with us and we would be happy, you know? And then my mother would get pregnant again and he would go away again. When I was small I couldn't understand any of it, I just felt that he was rejecting me. I felt it was me, personally. He seemed to be all right with the others, but not with me. Maybe because without me the others would never have happened? He was always fighting and pushing me around and insulting me. Making me feel stupid. I used to hate him, really hate him sometimes. But I wanted him too. You know that feeling? It's all very standard stuff. Classic textbook stuff.

'And then when I began to grow, you know? I grew so tall and *big* – I was really pleased with that, you know? Like he couldn't push me around any more. But then he . . .' Piet shrugged, smiling through pain. 'He didn't stick around long enough for me to get it out, to let go of all that *junk*. He just went away and then after some time with no news, comes the news that he has died. Of a heart attack. He was very young. Just fifty-something.

'So then I was just, you know, *stuck*. With all that stuff, that anger, that violence, just sort of like a . . .' He formed his hands into a knotted ball, held against his chest. 'Like this kind of big, big *bunch* just here, just in my chest. And I was like that right until I went to see, you know,' he paused and looked away. 'Kay.'

He was telling me why Kay was so important to him, such a crucial part of his life and his recovery. He was explaining that he would not be discarding him any time soon. That whatever I had said about him would not affect his respect and love for the man.

Then he began talking of other things. He told me about his mother's father, an artist, a sculptor, a wonderful man. He and the grandmother, Oma, had lived in this house we were in, that had belonged to Oma's family. When Piet's parents could not keep their troubled marriage together, the mother had moved in to this house with her small children.

On an impulse, he took me downstairs and through the marble courtyard to the half-glazed door in the rear wall. Passing through it, we were in the back yard. It was a long narrow stretch of grass, defined on either side by high walls. A stone-flagged path led to its further extremity, where there was a toolshed and a wooden gate.

On the other side of the gate was the sound of traffic. The passing cars were not visible from where we stood. Close by the door through which we had passed, on our left, was the entrance to a glassed-in construction, like a greenhouse. On the right was a tall wire cage. In the cage was a peacock.

I gasped and said, 'Oh!'

Piet smiled at my surprise.

'As you know, my grandmother likes birds.'

I went up to the cage and stared at the gorgeous creature, so succulent in his finery that he drained colour from the world around him. The sun shone on the south face of the house but did not rise high enough to touch the backyard. The clouds overhead brooded grey, the stones beneath the bird's feet were grey and even the low shrubs around him were grey. In this setting he burned like a living jewel, sapphire, topaz and emerald, with white fire limning his eyes. I felt blinded by his beauty.

He peered at me, then hopped up onto a covered shelter that had been created for him within his cage and he stood there, trying to preen. But the cage was not big enough to contain his tail comfortably.

'Oh – ' I said again, this time because I felt a sharp stab of pain at the bird's plight. 'His tail – look – '

Piet nodded, absently and said, 'Yes. We have been telling my grandmother that she must let him go to the zoo. But she loves him too much. She always says, *Next week, next week*!'

Turning, Piet opened the door to the glassed-in shed. It was the studio that his grandfather used to work in.

It had the neat, spare quality of an artist's workspace when the artist is temporarily away. The shelves, floor and tables were covered with shapes swaddled in soft grey cloth, from beneath which shiny folds of dusty plastic showed, suggesting that the pieces had been kept in storage for several years just as they were. Only a few smaller pieces were uncovered. Piet showed me one.

It was a maquette in plaster, like a 3D sketch, not much more than a foot in height. The lines were smooth and angular with one or two patches where the plaster had been churned up, looking like miniature bushes interposed between tiny tree trunks. It had the easy vitality of a piece produced by someone confident of his craft. Piet was obviously proud of his grandfather, speaking in whispers while we stood in his room.

We went for a long, directionless ramble after that. We ended up in a park, had an ice-cream and returned home via a stationer's shop where I bought paper as a first step towards getting down to some work. We didn't talk much. When we were back at the house, Piet went to work on his motorcycle while I went up to his room.

I sat down in one of the armchairs in front of the gas-fire, feeling as if the inner lining of my spirit had been curetted. A day that had started so well was now down the tubes. I could tell myself that it was the weather. Clouds were once more pressed low over the rooftops, squeezing out their cold grey juice that drained into me like acid.

But it wasn't just the weather, of course. It was what Kay had said to Piet.

However much I thought of Piet as a hook onto which I could hang my problems of self-definition, I had to recognize that he himself was hooked onto another person whom I disliked and who disliked me.

As I sat there my attention was caught by a plaintive mewing honk. I had heard it before, I realized, but this time noticed that it came from outside the gable-end window. I went to the window, pushing aside the monstera and realized that I was looking out over the backyard.

The sound was of the peacock, calling.

I wondered why it was making the effort, considering that it had neither a mate nor any competitors in sight. Then I understood. The cars on the busy street on the other side of the garden gate occasionally honked their horns. The peacock called whenever it heard the sound of a car-horn.

I felt my spirit shrink with pain. In the peacock's fate I glimpsed a parody of my own. I too was responding to signals which were not intended for me. I had followed Piet to Holland, thinking that I would be able to find clues to the puzzle of myself by studying the lives of others who seemed similar to me.

When I felt upbeat it was because I believed that I'd done well by myself and had made the right choices. But at other times, I saw that I was as confused and ignorant of the true nature of my companions as a captive peacock mistaking car horns for the calls of fellow peacocks.

DISCOMFORTS

LOSING THE MORAL HIGH ground I had been occupying in reference to Anneke was more unpleasant than I expected. I now felt embarrassed to be in the same room as her.

I told myself that in an ideal world, it would be possible to sit together on a park bench in the sun and say, *Well, the fact is, I AM now physically involved with Piet – but you mustn't feel concerned about it. It doesn't mean anything. And you have nothing to worry about, I do not intend to take him away from you!*

But the world is not ideal and in my more lucid moments, I realized that there was no question of having such a chat. I would clear my conscience perhaps, but for her there was only the bitter option of having to accept my presence in her life, whether she liked it or not.

I did not pretend to care very much for her either way, but that didn't mean I wanted to harm her. That wasn't in my character at all.

It was very strange to be in the position of the much reviled 'other woman' of slushy novels. I did not feel in the least suited to the part. I was not glamorous, I was not a gold-digger, I did not anticipate any concrete gain.

I did not think of myself as passionate. I believed that, compared to the molten river of lust that other people describe at the core of their emotional lives, what I had was a slender thread, a strand of cool but witty desire which I liked to wind around a man rather like the cord which is wound around a top to make it spin, just for the duration of the encounter, just for the light, electric playfulness that resulted from the contact.

Living in a house where there were quite enough women for me to be friendly with, I nevertheless found it much easier to align myself with the male faction. I told myself that the ladies had their well-established routines into which I would probably not fit with any competence. It was a very convenient logic. Like Piet, I rarely ate meals at the table and this eased any guilt I might have felt about being unable to cook or to help out in the kitchen. I occasionally bought food of the kind that I regularly ate, adding it to the stocks in the fridge.

I had no job to complain about, no oppressive boss to resist, no husband to nag, no children to fuss over or even to look forward to, since I did not plan to have any. I could not swap recipes or laundry detergent tips or compare the price of potatoes in the way that, I believed, other women did when they met their sisters from other parts of the planet. The fact of bearing children or managing the 'menfolk' gives rise to an ease of communication that crosses most linguistic and cultural boundaries between women. But I did not share those reference points.

The only person with whom I had anything in common was Juliana and that was in the realm of dieting. She seemed to have completely got over her anorexia and since she didn't live in the house I did not notice what her eating habits were like. But once, we got into a conversation about something I was wearing. It was a silk blouse, one of several I had. It was loose-fitting, long-sleeved and ended at hip height, a very familiar design of a short kurta. It was embroidered just around the neck and down the front on either side of the button-facing. I said, not pausing to think of the consequences, that I liked these somewhat shapeless clothes because I was too fat for anything else.

It was as if I had pressed a button.

Juliana became instantly animated and said, 'Fat! Oh yes, it's such a problem being fat, isn't it?' The normally gentle expression in her eyes glazed over. 'I'm so sick of being fat!'

I was taken aback and said, 'Yes, but you're not fat at all. Not like me – I'm *really* fat, you know? I mean, I have a really big belly,' and patted it, to prove it.

Juliana was so tiny that two of her could have fitted comfortably inside one of the legs of my jeans. But my remark affected her like a bee sting. It frightened me to see the hectic intensity of her belief in her own obesity.

She whipped off her light sweater to display her waist and said, 'Look – look at this!' There was hardly enough flesh there to pinch between her fingers, but she plucked at it anyway, saying, 'Fat! Totally fat! Disgusting!' And she looked up at me smiling wide, her soft caramel-gold irises shining like haloes around the enormous black pools of her pupils.

I smiled while backing away, afraid that if I said anything more, she might take a carving knife to herself. I knew there couldn't be any real discussion between us. She was for all practical purposes a professional in the art of weight loss, compared to whom I was the merest amateur. She had starved herself, Piet had told me, to the point where her hair had fallen out and her teeth rotted in her gums in pursuit of the goal of perfect weightlessness which, taken to its logical conclusion, had to mean death. I could not match that kind of dedication, nor did I want to try. She made me feel positively healthy to be overweight.

But identifying with the men in the group produced its own peculiarities. Once, while out with Piet and Japp, we had collected takeaway Chinese packets, intending to wander down to a canal-side patch of grass, and eat a picnic lunch. The flimsy wedge-shaped containers of chop suey noodles were beginning to disintegrate even as we carried them away.

As we walked, I became conscious of a sound like intermittent shouting. It became louder as we crossed one narrow street to enter another. It reminded me of the Walpurgisnacht demonstration but I dismissed this idea as ridiculous. It was the middle of the day and there wasn't any amplified shrieking of the kind there had been in Münich.

Yet the sound of a demonstration is familiar to any urban-dwelling Indian and my ears were attuned to recognize it.

Japp heard the sound too. He said, 'Wot's that?'

I said, 'A protest march.' By naming the thing that I did *not* want to see, I was hoping, by reverse magic, to avoid seeing it. I did not want to encounter the marchers while I was in the company of two huge men, my hands tied down with soggy containers of Chinese takeaway. I was in no mood just then to throw my shackles aside to join the march.

Japp said, 'Nah. We don't haff protest marches in Holland. It only happens in brown rat countries. Or America. Or even in Münich, like you told me – but not here!'

We turned a corner and entered a long street bordering the canal. The sound of the marchers grew louder. I was praying that we might cross the street and get to the canal before they appeared. But in the next moment, a column of young women popped out of the side street ahead of us, stepping smartly four abreast and shouting slogans. It was indeed the Dutch chapter of the Walpurgisnacht demonstration.

'You're right!' muttered Japp. 'Protest marchers!' Our path took us alongside the women for a certain distance and then we had to cross them at right angles to get to the break in the chain-link fence through which we could access the canal.

I *burned* with embarrassment. Piet and Japp, striding along in their WWII surplus fatigues, were revelling in the situation, the three of us with our lunch containers, awash in a tide of bouncy-breasted girls, squeaking in high registers, like an army of rampaging mice.

The only act that could have redeemed me in my own estimation was to have flung my noodles at the male oppressors on either side of me and joined the march. Instead, I closed my mind and ears to the women around me and walked across their rowdy ranks as if they were a hallucination brought on by the fine weather. Whatever claim I had to calling myself a feminist, I lost it then. I was a traitor to the cause, a partisan, a deserter.

I and Piet made it through the demonstrators with no mishap. But while Japp was still mid-stream across the column, his takeaway container burst. 'Lucky for me, I put my hand under it,' he said when he caught up with us, 'or it vould haff all spilt out and I vould haff, you know, to lick it off the road like a dog!'

Japp's accident made him the cynosure of all the marchers' eyes. By the time he joined us with half a kilo of noodles dripping from his hand, it was with the full force of Utrecht's fighting females yelling slogans at his back. He loved it. He waved and yelled back, with the noodles held aloft.

Even when he had settled down with us, the continuing line of demonstrators aimed their remarks at him. He acknowledged them like a visiting dignitary waving from the window of his stretch limo.

Piet laughed and waved alongside Japp, exchanging goodnatured insults with the girls, while I sat looking the other way, pretending to be a hermaphrodite.

LOSING WEIGHT

EVERY TIME I SPOKE to Micki our conversation was shorter than the one before it. There was nothing I could talk about. I was in a fog of suspended animation.

Once she asked, 'And how about the . . . handshaking?' It took me a couple of moments to recall what she meant. Everything that had happened before my arrival in Holland now seemed to belong in some other dimension. I admitted there wasn't much in the way of handshaking, aside from the sharing of bed-space. She paused slightly before saying, in a voice that told me that she had not ceased to consider it a folly on my part to have gone to Holland at all, 'Well in that case, why are you still there?'

I said it was insulting to suggest that handshaking was the only valid reason I could have for being where I was. Micki countered this with, 'Oh really? But Piet was all you spoke about when you were here!' That didn't mean, I said, that he was my only interest. 'Why don't you wake up?' said Micki. 'You're fooling yourself. You're running after a guy who's not interested in you and you're too stubborn to face that fact.'

'You're wrong,' I said. 'There's something more to it than that.' But I couldn't say what it was and I knew she didn't believe me. I couldn't blame her. There were times when I didn't believe myself.

Micki asked me what she should do about a letter she'd got from my sister-in-law in Bombay, asking about my whereabouts. When I left Germany I'd said to Micki that I would send letters to her from me for my family, which she was to post from Germany, so as to maintain the fiction that I was there. But once I was in Holland I couldn't budget the energy for wholesale deceit and therefore had written no letters at all either to her or to my family.

I begged her to say anything she wished, other than where I was or with whom.

She agreed, though unwillingly. I knew that the burden of responsibility I was placing on her was growing heavier with every week I stayed out of sight of my world.

Time passed as in a dream, one day blurring into the other, so that it was difficult to tell where in the week I was, in which month, in which year. The hashish had something to do with it. But even without it I think I would have been in the same state of bewildered inertia.

I appeared to have little initiative, now that I had stripped myself of my familiar contexts. I watched my small hoard of dollars dwindling as I spent the money on hamburgers and ice creams. I told myself that this was the ultimate 'watching the cobra' exercise.

Once the hoard vanished, either I would also diminish and vanish, or I would survive to tell about it. Either way, there was nothing for me to do but watch the cobra.

When the first month of my stay drew to a close, I got my visa renewed for one more month. I maintained that my reason for being in Holland was that I needed to earn my way out by selling drawings and that until I had succeeded in this aim I could not honourably leave. I no longer had the funds to buy a ticket back to the UK, though I knew that at a pinch I could call Radzie in the US and beg to be bailed out.

Piet never asked any questions. The impression I got was that he avoided thinking about anything which didn't actually come up for review.

Anneke was never mentioned and I rarely met her either in the house or anywhere else. It was as if she weren't relevant in the scheme of this particular friendship, but then again, since it was nominally platonic, there was no cause for guilt. We saw films together. We went shopping for motorcycle spare parts. I sometimes sat with him downstairs in his workshop, where his Harley had been stripped down to its bare minimum, watching him as he painstakingly repaired the rusted and worn-out parts of the old machine, resurrecting it from oblivion.

Simon and I occasionally went out on a shopping expeditions together. On one such occasion, I picked up two cartons of low fat buttermilk. When he raised an eyebrow, I explained that I needed to lose weight. Japp had been reminding me ceaselessly of the effort he had seen me put into the diet when we were in Bombay. He said it was a waste of that effort to bloat out of control now that I was in Holland.

Simon grimaced and said, 'Yeh, yeh – but you should be a little careful about who you listen to! After all . . .'

I was puzzled. 'After all – what?'

'Look what happened to the last victim?'

He was smiling strangely as we walked along, carrying the groceries home from the store.

'I don't know what you're talking about,' I said.

Simon said, 'Juliana's anorexia! Don't you know it was because of Japp? He used to be her boyfriend.'

Click, click, click: finally, now, I understood the strained atmosphere in Piet's room at the time of Japp's first visit.

I told Simon what I had noticed. 'Is Juliana okay now?'

'Not completely,' said Simon. 'I bet you've never seen her putting anything in her mouth!' It was true. She made the food but she didn't actually eat it.

'He kept telling her how fat she was, that she was looking like a pumpkin and so and so. One day she just stopped eating. Completely. She wouldn't even drink water some days. He stopped seeing her then, saying that he was a bad influence on her. But she took it as a sign that he left her because she was so fat. She just starved. She became like a skeleton, with dark rings around her eyes, her hair fell out, her teeth started to fall. It was like some kind of horrible comic.'

He was smiling as he said these things, but I was growing aware of the different levels of smiling in his house. There was one kind of smile that was a mask, a shield against open pain.

'And Japp! Well, he just never said a word about it. He didn't try to help her, he didn't try to stop her. He said he had nothing to do with it.' That's why, he said, I should be wary of listening to Japp. 'After all, you're not really fat,' said Simon. 'You're just a bit, you know, *plump*.'

'Excuse me,' I said, 'just because I'm not anorexic doesn't mean I'm not fat.'

'But why does it matter so much?' Simon wanted to know.

'You're right,' I said. 'It doesn't matter.'

'Yeh, yeh – but you're still eating the low-fat buttermilk.' said Simon.

'Perhaps I like low-fat buttermilk?' I said.

'No normal human can like low-fat buttermilk!' said Simon. 'Low-fat buttermilk is the height of ironical – even the name is a contradiction – it's got butter but it's low-fat!'

'Are you saying that I'm drinking the butter-milk because of Japp?' I asked.

He said, 'All I'm saying is, be careful. Of Japp.'

RELATIONSHIPS

THE OBJECT OF OUR discussion came over at least once a day, if not oftener. He said he was on the dole 'Becose I am too crazy to haff a chob.' Then he would grin and add, 'I say it's becose I am too sane!'

On one such walk I asked Japp about Juliana. He shrugged as he said, 'Wal – we were together, you know?' He hooked the forefingers of both his hands together in a clinch, to make it clear what he meant. 'Piet wasn't happy about it. But he couldn't say that to me, of course, because I am his best friend. So – yah. It was quite intense. And then we broke up, after two years, three years.'

Japp shrugged and turned his head this way and that, a big shaggy wolf surveying the horizon. 'Piet wasn't happy when Juliana and me broke up. I mean, becose of the way it happened, you know? It made some problems between he and me. But we never discussed it. So,' he shrugged. 'I don't know.' He turned to me. 'And you. How about you? Haff you effer been in loff?'

I shrugged, feeling uncomfortable. 'Maybe,' I said. 'Once, I think.'

He laughed. 'If you haff to think, then – it's not loff!'

'I thought it was, at the time,' I said. 'I was sixteen and in my final year in school.' It seemed such a long time ago. Nine years. An eternity had passed since then.

'And he was ffery beautiful? A shining loffer?' Japp was leering from the side of his mouth.

We had wandered into a park and were sitting down on a bench. A row of elms in young leaf canopied us and the pale sunlight daubed soft green lights through the shade. There were geese waddling whitely on the grass, like living advertisements for superlative detergents.

'Oh, it wasn't . . .' I felt momentarily shaken by the effort of digging up this past. I preferred it to be something that only I knew about, on the rare occasions that I looked in that shelf of my mind's closet.

'It wasn't very physical,' I said. 'It was barely physical at all.' Then I added, in a rush, 'He was a priest. One of the priests at my boarding school – they used to come on brief visits, you know, to lead the Mass and take confessions. Sometimes the same person would visit over a period of time.'

How silly it now seemed, all of it. The violent emotions of youth detonated by a handful of private conversations under the eucalyptus trees of the school's campus. His name was Father Como, he was Italian and handsome in that artless way that makes the fact of being a priest such a waste of masculine potential. He was not a raw young man or unworldy and I think he regarded my immoderate pursuit of him with something between pity and amusement.

He wrote wonderful letters, in which he counselled me to be careful with my passions. Not to give myself away lightly and not to consider him a worthy vessel. He warned me against confusing my adolescent infatuation with the higher calling of love. He tried to show me that my fervour for converting to Christianity owed much more to my fixation on him than to an understanding of God. And that I must not cheapen the quality of faith by making a connection between the two.

But he failed in all his aims. In his final letter, he told me that it had been his own ego that had led him to allow matters to get out of hand and that he regretted the harm he had caused me by his attention. He told me that the only way I would recover from this encounter was to face towards the tempest rather than away from it and that I must not underestimate myself. In the way of advice it was more enigmatic than I knew how to deal with at that age. I heard nothing more from him or of him, ever. Japp said he'd never heard anything so hilarious. He couldn't believe that I had invested so much importance in an affair that did not include so much as a single kiss.

I felt my face grow hot. 'Well,' I said. 'There *was* a kiss. Just one.' This was a very difficult admission to make. It brought back the hopeless, reckless, keening ardour of that time and the immense waste of time and energy that hung upon the slender nail of that single physical contact.

It embarrassed me to acknowledge the large effect that such a small event had had on my life. How much easier it would have been, for instance, if I could claim to have been ravished by a team of bouzkashi players out on the Mongolian steppe! Anyone would understand that such an event might have left me somewhat discouraged. But *this*? Pathetic.

And yet, as I told Japp, it was on account of that one, very chaste, very spiritual love affair, that I wanted to ring down the curtain on all reality. Die, in other words. Commit suicide. 'I've given myself till thirty,' I said, 'and then, you know, the sharks, the tigers – whatever.' I briefly outlined my schemes for returning myself to the elements.

Japp was laughing so hard that passers-by began to glare at us for disturbing the peace. 'You're so full of bullshit!' he roared.

'I am *not*!' I said, feeling increasingly annoyed that he was refusing to see the tragic dimension of the thing. 'I WILL do it.'

'No, you won't,' said Japp. 'No one, not even liddle brown rats, can plan so calmly to kill themselves. It's chust a drama you haff made for yourself to make you feel proud, ya? It giffs you power to be able to say to Meester Death' – tuning his voice up to sound like a society lady – '*nyo thenk you! I'll* ffisit *you first, before you ffisit ME*! It's chust your mind games.'

'You wait and see,' I said.

'It's a waste,' said Japp. 'At least you should first find somefing reely, reely bad to happen and *then* you can go feed de wild life.' He began to laugh again, but said, after a while, 'Still. It's more interesting than chust having many liddle baby rats.'

I told him about my theory about monotheism and love. 'There's a connection. Believing in one true God is the religious ideal and being faithful to the one true love is its counterpart. That's why it's such a big thing in Western movies and books – it's a Christian model of love.'

'But in brown rat countries there is also the big loff movies,' began Japp. 'I saw one or two in Bombay. De hero is singing only of loff, loff and more loff.'

'It's not the same thing at all,' I said. 'Religion in brown rat countries is like a government bureaucracy. There are senior and junior gods and all their consorts and their godlets and peon gods and god-vehicles. Romantic love is just one of the minor portfolios in the Ministry of Family Duty. It's only tolerated if it doesn't destroy the family or the community. It isn't seen as something fulfilling on its own. In a movie, lovers who disobey their families are sure to die by the time the end-credits roll. It's always a very beautiful death and everyone is crying.'

'But if in de West we have the Christian model,' said Japp, 'that means not only the one true God, but also we have the one true Deffil.' He looked at me sideways, wrinkling his nose to raise his glasses up.

I said I hadn't considered this angle before but ad-libbed, 'Yes, so maybe that raises the importance for being faithful? Because being *un*faithful means to follow the Devil?'

Japp looked away, processing the thought.

Then he said, 'So: if you are in loff with Piet, it means that he is for you, Gott?'

I said, 'But I'm not in love with Piet.'

Japp said, 'Still he is sthleeping on the sofa, huh?' But he pushed his wide pink mouth out to show his scepticism.

I looked away and said, 'No. He's not on the sofa.'

Japp grinned with his whole body. 'So! Den you *are* in loff with him!'

'You're so childish,' I said. 'The sofa was uncomfortable. So we decided that as mature, consenting adults, there was no need to spend the whole night suffering, just because of some silly convention that requires people of different sex to sleep in separate beds.'

'But do you and he . . . ?' he cocked his head on the side.

I was completely nonplussed by his curiosity. I didn't expect men to be so interested in such things. I said so, adding, 'And anyway, why does it matter?'

'It's also the Trooth,' he said. 'It's to know the difference between the Trooth and the Not-Trooth.'

I couldn't tell whether or not he was joking.

'No!' I said. 'And anyway, it's none of your business.'

'Then it's my business,' said Japp. 'Because my business is finding the Trooth. Anyway, if you had nuffing to say, you would say nuffing. But you *haff* somefing to say and so! And so.' He grinned.

I looked away.

He ruffled my hair. I continued to look away. He said, 'Okay, okay, so it's too much Trooth for we to talk about it. So maybe you are an atheist and so you don't love nobody.'

I said, 'I belong to a pantheist culture. So there's no polarity. I neither have belief nor unbelief. Only monotheists can become atheists. They give up their faith in one true God in order to believe in one true No-God. It's the same thing as believing in something except that it's believing in NO-thing.'

'So – so – so –' said Japp. 'The atheist falls in loff like efferyone else, but he calls it . . .' Japp screwed his eyes up with the effort of conjuring the ideal term, 'Full employment!'

I laughed. We congratulated ourselves for being wiser than we knew what to do with and made our way homewards. When we reached Piet's house, I found that I had forgotten to take my key with me. We rang the bell, but no buzzer sounded to let us in. Japp said that there was a fail-safe system for opening the door if someone had forgotten or lost the key.

'It's in heere, a kind of thing,' he said, peering in through the letter slot. ' A string – a string to pull, you know?' he looked around, squinting at the quiet, tidy street. 'But I need somefing. Like a wire, a hook. To *grab* the string.'

For a moment it looked hopeless but in the next instant I said, 'What about your glasses?' One arm of his aviator frames could be pushed into the letter slot, hooked around the string and withdrawn, bringing the string out with it.

Japp looked surprised and pleased: yes, it would work. He took his glasses off and in another few moments, had got hold of the string and by pulling on it released the latch on the door. As we entered, Japp said, 'Sometimes the Trooth is like that: right in front of your eyes, but *still* you don't see it.'

There was no one at home.

In the living room was the latest addition to the family, a golden hamster. It was Jani's pet, a sweet and dainty creature, too defenceless to survive against the cats and the dog. So it had its own cage, which sat on the low table between the settee and the television. Japp and I watched it trotting industriously on its exercise wheel until it gave up in its abrupt rodentish way, to curl itself up in a tiny ball of champagne-coloured fur, its paws over its face.

It had enormous silvery whiskers which trembled delicately as it slept. Its ears were fragile cones of finest coral pink.

'Do you think,' said Japp, whispering as we watched the small dormant bundle, 'that he knows there is no experience without desire?'

POSTERS

ONE DAY WHILE OUT on a loaf with Piet and Japp, we passed a shop called 'PAGODA'. Piet stopped to look at the fine Buddha displayed in the window. As we stood there, admiring the rings, pendants and silver bracelets arrayed alongside the figurine, the owner of the shop came to the door and said, 'Hello?'

She was Indian.

'Can I help you?' she said in a voice that invited a positive response. She smiled at me, guessing that I was Indian too.

I smiled back, admiring her chic appearance. She was petite, with the sort of dusky beauty that was ahead of its time. A Naomi Campbell mouth and small, almond eyes expertly made up. Her eyebrows were plucked high and thin, giving her a permanent air of mild surprise. Her long straight hair was not quite black. She wore it so that it flowed silkily down her back.

Though the three of us did not have the least intention of buying anything, we entered the shop. It was larger inside than it seemed from outside. The lady turned immediately towards me and established my vital statistics: Indian, from Bombay, English-speaking. With every question, I felt the chains of identity wrapping themselves around me once more. It was like stepping into a suit of armour. Within a few minutes I was completely defined.

She nodded to herself with each of my answers, because I had confirmed her every guess. Her name was Sarojini, but her husband called her Jini, pronouncing it 'Chini'.

'Chini!' he called, from the back of the shop, then came forward when he saw that she was talking to customers. He was a small dapper man, rather like the supremely sociable estate agent called Jolyon in Tintin comics.

Jini introduced me to her husband as if I were a long lost friend. 'Freddie,' she said, 'What did I tell you? She *is* from Bombay!' They had apparently seen us and discussed me while we were still quite a distance away.

Freddie had sharp, intelligent eyes. He darted a glance at me which took everything in and, I could see, decided that I wasn't a threat of any sort. Perhaps even an asset. I could see him filing this information away for later use. He paid little attention to my companions, who towered over him, looking around the shop.

'So! How long will you stay in Holland? Just visiting, that's all?' he asked. There was a slight British slant to his accent.

'Well . . .' I said. 'Yes. Just visiting.'

'How long have you been here already?' Jini asked and when I told her, she opened her eyes wide, 'One month – oh that is a long time! For a tourist.'

'Wait a minute, Chini!' scolded Freddie. He did it in the manner of a man who is in the habit of engaging his wife in charming minor arguments, staged for the benefit of an audience as a way of making a point. 'Who said she was a tourist? You should never jump to conclusions about a customer!'

He turned to me with his most foxy smile. 'My wife, you know! Always she jumps too quickly without looking!'

'Yeh, yeh – ' said Jini, 'just like the way I married you, *henh*? Without looking!'

I was turned off by Freddie's type of man, yet they were an attractive couple, both of them together like star performers in a smart nightclub act. I found myself talking easily, explaining my situation. 'You're right,' I said, 'I'm here because I wanted to see if it was possible to find a market for my work as an artist. I don't want to live here, just pick up contacts for work as a cartoonist and illustrator.'

I went into my little spiel. When I got to the part where I said I was interested in creating poster designs but didn't know how and where to start looking for poster companies, Freddie laughed and swatted the air with his hand, as if dismissing my problems.

'Ah!' he said, 'you just didn't come straight to Freddie Hopp, that's why you have problems!' He turned and rooted around under the telephone stand, locating the telephone directory and the yellow pages. He ran his finger down the listings muttering, 'Posters . . . posters . . . posters . . . ah, here we are – '

It took another five minutes to explain to Freddie that I wasn't looking for billboard designers or banner-painters or advertisers. Simon had shown me the name of the leading distributors of posters in Holland, Verkerke Posters. I mentioned this to Freddie, who then located their name, whipped out a slip of paper, wrote a number down and handed it to me with a flourish. 'There you go! All problems solved! See, wasn't it easy?' I had to admit it was.

We left the shop beaming with smiles all around.

I felt this was the catalyst I had been waiting for. I needed only to call the number on the paper to be launched on a successful career as a poster artist.

A day later, I called the number given to me by Freddie. I thought it was for the Verkerke Poster company but it turned out to be another concern, called Melody Posters. They dealt primarily in record album covers.

But the owner, Willem ' – call me Willy – ' Haas was friendly and invited me to show him my work. We made an appointment and two days later, I had a commission to draw a poster of ABBA.

On the train, returning from my meeting, I was sitting at a window seat when a young man suddenly entered my field of vision by sitting down directly opposite me. The train was not yet full enough to justify his choice of seat. This meant that he was there for a purpose. I had even registered in a subliminal way that he had walked down the aisle, passed me, then passed back again looking over his shoulder at me before deciding to settle down.

Shogun was open on my lap. I stared down at the book. I could feel holes being drilled into me by the young man's eyes. He was staring unblinkingly. I willed myself to keep looking at the book though I wasn't able to read it. Why was fear my first reaction? Why couldn't I apply any of my mental exercises to block off the beam of negative ions flowing my way from the young man? It was as if he had a superior control over reality and it was his version, not mine that was prevailing over the situation.

When he spoke to me, I pretended deafness until he leaned forward and fairly shouted in my ear. Then I looked up with the blank expression of one who speaks no human language.

He was about the same colour as myself, but his hair was a fuzzy halo and the shape of his eyes suggested the Far East. There were Dutch citizens of former Indonesian colonies who lived in Holland. Some of them were militants calling themselves South Moluccans, demanding a share in the colonial spoils taken by force from their ancestors.

Some years earlier, a group of South Moluccans had hijacked a train full of nursery school children to bring their cause to the attention of the world, which of course it instantly did. The school children survived the rescue attempt but the world refused its sympathy to terrorists who would target the very young.

I decided this young man was Moluccan.

The first thing he said to me, when I looked up was, 'How much does that gold chain around your neck cost?' He spoke in Dutch but terror had sharpened my perceptions to the degree that I understood everything he said, while pretending that I didn't. I shook my head and looked blank.

He repeated his question, 'The gold chain, that thick one around your neck. How much does it cost?' I continued to look baffled and uncomprehending.

He cocked his head to the side. Then he called over to another passenger, a young woman sitting at the window seat across the aisle from us and asked her how to say 'thick gold chain' in English. He spoke to her in a tone of insolent menace.

She answered him without really looking up from the book she was reading. Though there were a number of other passengers in the compartment, from this girl's response I got the feeling that I may as well have been alone in a maximum security cell with the Moluccan.

He now repeated the question in English: 'The thick gold chain: how much?'

Feigning great surprise I said, 'Gold chain? What gold chain – oh! You mean *this* thing? Oh – hahaha! – gold! It's not *gold*! It's – it's *nothing*!' I said this in English.

He responded in broken English, 'Not . . . gold? Is no . . . price?'

'No, no – of course, no price!' I said, guessing that the boy was not familiar with Indians, because otherwise he would have known for sure that I was lying. Indians are notorious gold-hogs. And I was no different to any other Indian in this respect, despite feminism and my claim to wanting to reduce my personal decorations. I continued to wear four gold bracelets, the half-sovereign ring, one thin necklace with a tiny flat pendant, one fatter, longer necklace with no pendant and a pair of diamond ear studs as my daily jewelry. I never took these items off and for all my life till then had believed that what I wore was the bare minimum.

But my would-be mugger pursued his enquiries. 'And de . . . de diamonds in de ears – dey is diamonds?'

'Glass!' I said.

'And . . . the bangles – also gold?'

I said, grinning like a death's head mask, 'No, no. How can I travel wearing gold?'

The Moluccan had a puzzled frown on his face. Was I mad or was he mistaken by all the yellow glitter? Suddenly his face relaxed into a smile. Maybe he finally realized what a bore it was to conduct a mugging in broad daylight.

Leaning back in his seat, he said, 'So! You is . . . von India?'

I said, 'Yes! Von India. Very poor country! Me, tourist! No money at all!' Well, that was true.

He said, 'Movie films, von India, very fine!'

'O yes!' I said, 'very fine!'

He leaned forward again and cocked his head to the side. 'Ah! So, you will come? To see movie? With me?'

Eh, what? My comprehension reverted suddenly to Outer Mongolia. I shook my head in mute non-comprehension.

'You! Me!' he said, starting to frown again. 'Going see movie films. In Holland! Tonight!'

'Ah . . . nononono!' I said, shaking my head vehemently from side to side. 'Me no see movie films, nonono, never, oo no! Me mummy not liking movie film! Me daddy not liking! Whole family is not liking. Never seeing! Oo no!'

He thought deeply about this one. I took the opportunity to return to *Shogun,* worrying only very slightly that he might consider it strange that I could read a book in a language that I seemed to understand only intermittently.

When he had composed his next question to me in English he said, 'Where you living? In Holland – what is address?'

Once more it took me a long while to understand the question. 'Ah, address!' I said, finally. 'Oo – no! No address! Not knowing! I tourist only! Poor tourist!'

Suspicion flitted across his features. He looked like Jimi Hendrix. Shorter and a bit wider perhaps, but the same aura. If he had been Jimi Hendrix, I would have thought he was handsome. He said, 'So where you go, huh? After de train gets stop?'

I'd had time to work this out. I said, 'Straight to India!'

If he stayed by my side until the train stopped in Utrecht, I felt, at a pinch, I could run all the way home or fall at the mercy of the police.

He lost interest, then. Perhaps he had concluded that I was a dangerous lunatic from whom there would be no sport in removing a couple of possibly worthless chains. Two stations before the terminal stop, he got up, bade me a polite farewell and moved off.

I walked slowly back to Piet's house, feeling like a traveller returning from the far side of the galaxy. The sun was out in earnest and, all the way, young people were walking the streets with their shirts tied at the waist, their winter skins painfully white and their faces wreathed with summer smiles.

When I told Piet about my adventure with the Moluccan, he was unconcerned. From his perspective, nothing had actually happened to me, in which case, there wasn't much to discuss was there? He went down to his motorcycle.

Simon was a little more sympathetic. He agreed that it must have been disturbing to be accosted but he too felt that nothing was gained from thinking about the incident.

'What's the point? It's over. You have to learn to let go.'

I said that it was a little like having a ton of rocks dumped in one's backyard with no warning. It's all very well to suppose that they will gradually evaporate, but getting rid of them isn't a simple matter of wishing them away.

Simon shrugged and said that the last part of my statement was up to me. It was *my* backyard after all and *my* mind. If I wanted to wish the rocks away then I should just go ahead and do it. The more I talked about them, the more real they became.

I spent a long time thinking about this.

Why *did* I return, again and again, to the events in the train? I told myself that it had to do with reality. If I, as Simon put it, wished the rocks away, then I was cancelling out a section of my reality, like editing footage from a film.

There were, no doubt, excellent reasons for wanting to edit footage. But if a person went about editing everything that was painful, unpleasant or boring, it's quite possible that large chunks of life would be lost. A potential full-length feature film might be reduced to a thirty-second commercial extolling the virtues of a squeaky clean, well-waxed, dandruff-free existence.

How does one maintain the balance between relevant footage and seedy bits?

As the editor of my own life's film it was my decision, whether or not to retain this tiny segment involving the Moluccan. Returning to it again and again was a way of fixing the print in my mind, making it part of my mind's archive. But if I spent too long on it, then I risked sensationalizing that portion of the record. It was a question of creating priorities in the way that I filed away the experience. Depending on what I chose to maintain in the record I could make my life a film noir, a B-grade weepie, a horror classic, an epic or an art-house beauty. It was up to me. And that was all.

DUTCH ROULETTE

IT WAS THE LAST week of June and my twenty-fifth birthday was upon me. I had thought I would be depressed to be away from my family and been dreading it but it turned out to be quite a success. I got a card from Radzie, forwarded to me from Micki, to whose address it had been sent.

She had put the draft for a hundred and fifty US dollars into the envelope along with a birthday card covered in little spangled stars and sent it to Micki's address. Micki had forwarded it to Piet's address. Inside the card, in my sister's handwriting were the words *Shine on you crazy diamond!* quoting Pink Floyd's *Wish You Were Here* album. Tears of guilt and relief stung my eyes. I did not deserve the love of my family.

Then I told Simon it was my birthday and we went out together to McDonald's. We ate two Quarter-Pounders each and washed them down with chocolate milkshakes.

In the evening I went out to a movie with Piet. It was called *Thèmroq*, a French film noir in which the residents of a housing complex decide that they are tired of being civilized. They tear down the outer wall of their flat, and live like barbarians, on the seventh floor, in full view of the other residents. When anyone comes to complain, they are either absorbed into the lifestyle or cooked and eaten. The film ends on a sybaritic note, with more and more residents of the housing complex falling into line with this way of thought, repulsing government troops and locking the gates of the colony against all outsiders. *Finis*.

'It's the social security, huh?' said Piet, after the film. 'We get too used to living free of work. We begin to suspect what we have, what we don't have, who we are. Savages don't hate themselves, huh? They have complete belief in their own rightness. But the so-called civilized people, like the Westerners – or rich Indians or Chinese or etcetera – we have the luxury, you can call it, of hating ourselves and our comforts.' In Freudian terms: the father-figure of the state was being attacked for seducing the mother-condition of insecurity, poverty and neediness.

We had barely got home late that night when there was a knock on the bedroom door.

It was Japp. He had a key to Piet's house and had let himself in.

He looked as if he had spent the whole day sitting in the washing machine during its spin cycle. He didn't say anything when he came in, but reached mutely for the carafe of hot water on the mantle shelf to pour himself a cupful.

His hands were trembling. The blond strands of hair which fell in an unkempt fringe over his forehead were damp with sweat. The pupils of his eyes had shrunk to strangled pinpricks in the lifeless blue of his irises. When he could speak, the first words he said were, 'My Gott. It is strange to be alive.'

He told us that he had been sitting with Henk, the boyfriend of Ramona. Henk dabbled in the music business and had apparently recently agented a successful Dutch rock singer. He had just returned from the US. He had brought back a handgun with him, a revolver.

Japp said, 'So we woss sitting, you know, with Henk and Ramona and two others. And Henk brought the gun. So I looked into it, with its bullets inside. So I took them all out. And we woss all laughing, you know? It woss ffery funny, to be playing with the gun. So then I put three bullets back inside the gun – you know, leaving one space between each one, so that there woss a pattern. I said, *Today, we will play a little game of Dutch Roulette!!* And I spun the barrel of the gun. We woss all still laughing and joking. It woss nothing. Then I put the gun to my mouth and I' – he followed this with the action, using the first two fingers of his right hand to symbolize a gun – *'tok!* – pressed the trigger. And . . . my Gott. I felt my stomach drop out of my boots. Nothing happened – but effrything happened. I felt cold, I felt hot. I wanted to cry, to scream.' He shook his head slowly. 'But there woss no sounds inside me.' He held his forehead. 'I think I did cry, I don't know. My cheeks woss wet.'

He looked at Piet and myself, his face vulnerable and unguarded. 'I never knew that I cared so much about my life.'

He didn't stay long. 'I haff to go, I haff to walk around, to see all my friends one by one,' he said and left, looking confused and lost.

Piet was silent for a few moments.

Then he said, 'Japp is . . .' He didn't finish his sentence. He shook his head. 'I don't know what to feel about him, huh?'

Then he told me the story of Japp.

'It was when he was still my sister's boyfriend. They used to spend time here, you know, in my room.' He paused, remembering the scene. He shook his head again. 'One day, I came back and found the two of them – in my bed.' He looked at me, wanting me to react to what he had said. But I couldn't understand why, given the loose-weave texture of his life, this event had disturbed him.

'I can't explain it,' he said, the features of his face contorting. He looked around the room, feeling it enfold him in its security. 'It has something to do with this room, the fact that it is my room. And he was here, with my sister! Isn't that . . . I mean, don't you find that . . . sick?'

I didn't know what to say. Either Piet was a territorial being, in which case he would never have allowed Japp to use his room at all. Or he wasn't territorial, in which case it shouldn't have mattered to him what Japp was doing or where or with whom. I shrugged and said, 'No experience without desire, wouldn't you say?'

For an instant Piet glared at me, as if pained and hurt that I did not automatically see his point of view. Then he collected himself and said, 'Of course. You are right.' He made a wry face. 'We all have our own personal cobras to watch, huh?'

I nodded, saying nothing. Whereas at one time I would have found it easy to empathize with his problem concerning Japp, or would have at least tried to see his point of view, I now found myself on the opposite side of a fence, actually constructing a mental barrier between us so that I could defend myself against knowing or understanding his thoughts.

He was often over at Anneke's or working on his motorcycle late into the night so that I was already asleep by the time he came back to his room. I still could not understand what I felt towards him. Whenever we were actually in a room together, I felt like the audience of a play that has been going on for too long, waiting impatiently for the curtain to come down. When he was away, I'd be desperate to talk to him.

In Bombay we'd had so much to say to each other that two lifetimes would not have been enough to say it all. Now we could barely rub two sentences together without silences starting to build up.

GOING WITH THE FLOW

PIET AND HIS GROUP of friends, about twelve people, had been planning a trip to France. Piet told me that it would be good if I went too, because the focus of the trip was Maitreyi, a renowned French guru. The cars and passenger allocations had been made months in advance. There was no space for me, so if I wanted to go I had to make my own arrangements.

When I first heard about the trip I really did not want to go. I had lost my taste for mystical discourses ever since meeting Kay. But I changed my mind. One reason was the draft that I'd got from Radzie for my birthday. It allowed me to feel that I could at least afford the trip.

The second reason was that I had begun to feel that Simon, while urging me to find the means to come along, was politely suggesting that his mother would really prefer it if I went. The alternative was that I would be alone in the house with her and the younger boys. I believed that Simon was trying to tell me, as diplomatically as he could, that I might find it awkward if neither Piet nor he were around.

But the third reason was the clincher: Hans, whom I had met first at Kay's house and then a few times subsequently, said that he wanted to go but couldn't justify the expense of the trip if he travelled all the way alone in his car.

I had become so used to making decisions based on traffic lights in the ether that I took Hans's remarks as practically an order shouted from on high commanding me to go to France. I didn't need the incentive of wanting to see the French guru. I had entered that state of mind in which I did whatever seemed appropriate to the 'flow'.

Meanwhile I wanted to finish the poster for Willy before leaving for France. He had said I would get paid only once the design was printed and out on the market, which would take two to three weeks.

We had agreed upon a price of 300 guilders for the initial print run and then an additional 150 guilders for every thousand posters printed thereafter. It seemed to me that with this sale, my European quest would find a fitting conclusion. I needed only to sell another three or four in order to be able to buy a ticket back to Bombay.

Simon and I went to all the trendy poster shops looking for existing photographs from which I could put together four portrait heads of ABBA. I didn't especially like the group and Simon hated them so much that we had a hard time making our selection. I finally picked up two posters and a cheap promotional 'album' of photographs.

When we got home, I discovered that one of the posters was actually of John Travolta. It was pure coincidence, because the posters were taken out of numbered bins and this one had the number of the ABBA poster I had selected from the rack. But it was a clear and usable picture of Travolta, cheesing for the camera, one knee bent, his head supported on the fist of his right hand.

I told Simon about it and he agreed that this was a Sign from Fate that I must do a poster of Travolta, not ABBA. I called Willy and explained that I'd had a flash of inspiration and now wanted to draw a huge enlargement in monochrome of the star of *Saturday Night Fever*. Just his face. Willie agreed. I settled down to draw.

I had forgotten how much I actually enjoyed drawing. Even though this was merely copying something else, it was such a wonderful relief to find that I had not, after all, completely ceased to be an artist.

I felt like someone who had returned to consciousness from a deep coma. I enjoyed everything about the struggle, including the mistakes and the tedious length of time. I knew that I wasn't an artist of the wild-haired genius kind, spattered in paint, producing masterpieces in my sleep. I would always be a plodder, working slowly and methodically rather than in fits of creative frenzy. Being distanced from myself had taught me humility.

I had very little time in which to complete the drawing, so I remained locked in Piet's room, starting in the morning, toiling through the day and late into the night. I took breaks only to get myself Big Macs to eat in the evening. I didn't allow anything to get in my way, not even Simon. His joints were a distraction I could not afford and didn't want. Sometimes he came in to watch me while I filled slow inches with fine black dots, but the progress was too gradual to be interesting.

By the time it was done, there was one day left before departure. Hans was due to come by the next morning to collect me in his little almond green Deux Cheveux. Simon was scheduled to leave the following afternoon.

I delivered the drawing and was very grateful that it was well received. Then I practically ran all the way back to Piet's house from the station, to pack a small kit. The trip was meant to last one week. I had very little idea of what to expect. According to Simon, we would all be staying in a large rented villa and since it was paid for as a lump sum, it made no difference how many people occupied the villa at one time.

I threw underwear and two changes of clothes into a sling bag and the next morning set off with Hans. We went first to Amsterdam to pick up a week's visa to France for me, then to Paris, where we spent one night at the apartment of a former girlfriend of his, Antoinette. Along the way, Hans had revealed that he thought I might be an ideal soulmate for him. In Paris, he arranged our sleeping bags for the night in the front room of Antoinette's two-room student accommodation in a configuration which made his romantic intentions clear.

I had not discouraged him. According to all my current companions, if a thing was due to happen, it would. In which case, there was no point struggling, was there? Hans was pleasant enough, he was attractive, he was intelligent. On the surface, he was no different to any of the others of Piet's little group of friends. I could not find any logical reason for refusing his attentions. The fact that I was not actually attracted to him seemed to me to be a failing on my part rather than a presumption on his.

In Antoinette's bathroom I saw a reflection of myself for the first time in weeks, in the mirror above the sink. We had last met, my mirror-persona and I, in the washroom on the train to Holland. So much had happened since then!

We eyed one another in silence, as I brushed my teeth.

Well, my mirror-persona said to me. *What are you going to do?*

About what? I asked her.

About Hans, said the mirror-persona.

Sleep with him, I guess, I said, feeling impatient with these questions.

Even though you don't want to? asked the Mirror.

It would be unfriendly not to, I said to her. *I'm learning to flow, you see. I'm learning not to place my emphasis on who and why but on Just Being. He'll be sweet and it may even be quite nice.*

He had told me, for instance, that he had been without a girlfriend for a whole year now, following Antoinette's departure for Paris to study art.

It's a mission of mercy on my part, I told the Mirror. *I can experience the novelty of being Florence Nightingale and Suzy Wong both at the same time.*

With these arguments in place, I removed my contact lenses and stored them away in their case. I hadn't been wearing them since my arrival in Piet's house, but for the trip, which I was told would be sunny, it made sense to use them so that I could wear my sunglasses too.

As I took the lenses off, it seemed to me that the Mirror was smirking at me. As if she knew something that I didn't know. I paid no attention to her.

Within seconds of exiting the bathroom however a sensation I had never had before began to overwhelm my eyes. It announced itself as a mild smarting sensation, which, in the brief distance of five yards it took for me to reach the front room from the bathroom, became a major conflagration.

The surface of my eyes felt as if they had burst into flame, though my vision was unaffected. I had no idea at all what the problem was. Nothing like this had ever happened to me. I was too stricken to do anything but continue towards my designated sleeping bag, with my eyes screaming in pain.

Hans was practicing his lotus position with patient concentration when I appeared. I sat down and said, 'Hans . . .'

He opened his eyes wearing a friendly, dreamy expression, with the first words of romantic invitation already poised between his teeth.

I said, 'Hans – I don't know what's gone wrong! My eyes are . . .'

They felt as if their outer membranes had been flayed off.

I didn't have to worry about being believed because my eyes were pouring with tears. Nothing I did made them feel better. When they were open they felt as if they were being scraped by thorns in the air. When they were shut they felt as if the inner surface of my eyelids had been lined with sandpaper. Neither washing them in warm water nor holding ice to them in a hanky produced any relief.

They were tearing so much that I felt the need to drink glasses of water to replace what was being lost from my eyes.

In *The Clockwork Orange* there's a scene in which Malcolm McDowell's character is made to watch porno-horror films with his eyelids clipped open. In order to keep his eyes from suffering dehydration damage, an attendant nurse constantly drips saline solution over them. I did the same, using the storage solution that was part of my lens kit. For brief seconds the solution laved the surface of my eyes bringing slight relief. Even an hour later though, there was only a very minor change in my condition.

Poor Hans. There was nothing for him to do but to turn over and go to sleep.

Years later I would read that the condition was called 'snow blindness'. It affects people who are exposed to glare on snowy ski slopes as well as those who wear their hard contact lenses without gradually extending the wearing schedule in daily increments. I had stopped wearing without realizing that I could lose tolerance for them.

Hans had planned to leave early in the morning for Nice and we decided to keep to our schedule. I managed to fall asleep eventually and when I awoke my eyes were no longer aflame, though they felt worn out. So long as I didn't use my lenses I hoped there would be no permanent damage. Hans drove straight through till late in the evening, stopping only for snacks and pit-stops along the way, till we reached the villa where our friends were staying.

We arrived at the villa late in the evening, just as Japp and Simon were washing up after dinner, in the pantry. The rest of the party had retired. Rather than work out any complicated sleeping re-arrangements it was agreed that the simplest thing would be for me to spread a sleeping bag and sleep on the daybed in the formal dining room, big enough to double as a ball room. It was never actually used to eat in.

Alone in the darkness of the great white hall, with its tall windows and the chandeliers, I lay down.

There was no question of sleep.

My mind was swirling.

The sudden solitude of that unknown, unfamiliar villa was a relief from the kaleidoscope of people, places, conversations and ideas I had been immersed in for just under two months now.

I felt as if I had been living in a whirlpool above which now, after the long tiring drive, I was briefly suspended. There was a silence which went beyond the still, moonlit night, unbroken by any unnatural sounds.

It was as if the mind-waves in which I had been immersed ever since arriving in Holland had been switched off. I wondered where Piet was and looked reflexively up at the ceiling, as if by doing that I would be able to locate the beam of his psychic wave pattern. But there was a blessed nothingness. Perhaps the villa was inhabited by gentle spirits who calmed twanging nerves and silenced unruly minds. Certainly I felt more at peace than I had for two months.

I felt, for the first time since I had met Piet, a sense of weariness with all the heat and sweat I had been putting into maintaining contact with him.

What was it about, why did it matter? He was just another person, after all, just another conscious, thinking, feeling being, burdened with all the baggage that goes with the estate of being human. It wasn't a surprise to discover this, but I had to ask myself what justification I could offer for chasing after him the way that I had.

It seemed such a very long time since my mind had been this calm and well-equipped to assess my situation. In a cool and deliberate way I could see the whole story as if for the very first time, in its entirety.

This was the picture that I had glimpsed in miniature at the time of the energy transfer all those many nights ago in Bombay. I had never given myself the chance to examine it dispassionately. The moment it had appeared in my head, I had wrapped it in successive layers of padding. First there was the mystic layer and then the guru layer and then the romantic layer. Each one had seemed quite compelling in itself.

But ultimately, they had each been used to hide from myself the fact that what I really wanted was to run away from my life in Bombay.

I was too lazy and too effete to work out the logistics of such a flight on my own. It was only because a lever as big and as powerful as Piet had wandered into my life that I was able to use him, disguised as every other kind of thing, to prise myself out of the prison-setting in which I was so securely lodged, just like every other person of my class and cultural background.

Piet had only ever been a passive element in my struggle to be something other than what I was. I could see that now. I thought of him as a magnet but he had done nothing to pull me towards him. I had pulled myself away from my life, using him as an excuse.

But what next? Now that I could see this, did it mean that I was free of Piet? And by making this trip to Holland had I succeeded in finding something worthwhile? Or had I merely exchanged one kind of discomfort for another kind? Was I better off the way I was in Holland or would I be happy to go back to the way I used to be?

There was no answer to these questions. I looked around me in the dimness. The gentle spirits around me were ebbing away. I could not get any more information from them. I fell asleep.

CHESS

THE SUN AROSE BRIGHT and brisk. No one disturbed me in the dining-hall. Looking around me, I saw that though the building had been constructed on a grand scale, it was maintained modestly, as a private residence. Behind the day-bed where I had slept, for instance, there was a glassed-in bookshelf with a row of paperbacks, most of them in English. I was pleased to see a favourite book there: Rumer Godden's *Kingfishers Catch Fire*.

I went to the pantry where a note written in Dutch and stuck on the fridge suggested a scale of payment that might be left in a tin by the door, to maintain a minimum stock of bread, cheese and milk. I approved of the sensible way the group dealt with food. They enjoyed it without regarding it as something to be worried over. A similar contingent of Indians travelling and living together would have planned the eating arrangements as if for a military campaign.

I went upstairs to find the bathroom. It was the size of a bedroom. I couldn't remember the last time I had stepped into such an opulent facility. I felt tentative and uneasy, as if I had to introduce myself to the plumbing fixtures before using them. *Excuse me M. le Tap! Will it please your gracious self to be turned on?*

I looked at myself in the mirror over the sink and thought that my reflection looked quite uncomfortable today, in her elegant setting. *Mlle Du Miroir! May I disturb your shining surface by forcing my rough visage upon it?*

The bathroom was situated at the head of the sweeping staircase that led up from the entrance hallway to the first floor landing from which the doors to all five bedrooms in the villa were accessed. I had just entered the bathroom when Japp called out from the stairs, running up them three at a time, 'Wait! Wait! I have to use the –' He entered the bathroom like a typhoon, went straight to the toilet and yodelled 'Wharf! Whoo! Yah!' as he peed.

I started brushing my teeth. In the mirror, I could see his back.

He was looking uncommonly natty, as if by mistake, in a dark grey jacket, black trousers and a pale salmon pink shirt with fine grey stripes alternating with white. He wore everything loose, the shirt open at the throat and unbuttoned at the cuffs so that they flopped over his hands.

His hair was looking particularly unkempt, hanging to the shoulders now. He turned his head around to see if I was looking and our eyes crossed in the mirror. He grinned. I made a face back at him, while brushing my teeth. He was unshaven, but his facial hair was so sparse and so fair that it showed up only as a faint speckling on his chin and upper lip.

When he was done he came over, washed his hands and made faces at himself in the mirror. I had finished brushing my teeth and turned away in order to avoid giggling but didn't succeed.

He was quick to respond, taking it as a compliment.

He gave me a crushing sideways hug. Then he told me to wait while he brushed his teeth. He used a tooth brush which may or may not have been his, but was already out on the sink. He insisted that I stay right by him 'so that you don't go and commit suicide!'

We went downstairs.

'If you're looking for Piet,' said Japp, 'there he is!' He pointed to the terrace that stretched outside beyond the doors of the dining hall in which I had spent the night.

I said, 'I'm not looking for Piet,' even as my eyes sought him out and my pulse quickened.

The clarity of the night before clouded over. I could no longer be certain what I felt. Perhaps this confused, uncertain, shackled state of mind was what other people called love? I pushed the thought aside, telling myself that if this was what they meant then it was definitely not something desirable. My mind felt gluey and inefficient. I felt confined by this feeling, not released. Whatever name I could give to this feeling, it was not one I enjoyed.

He was reclining on a folding deck chair on the open front courtyard. He had his shirt off and was soaking up the sun along with five or six others similarly arranged about the chequerboard marble flags of the courtyard.

It was a very fine day. The sky was like a blue-domed sculpture gallery for clouds. The light was dazzling yet mild. The villa had been built upon a low hill and we could see the Mediterranean sparkling in the distance, the fruit orchards around us and the tapestry of warm earth and grass filling all the spaces in between.

Several chairs were still unoccupied. Japp and I drew two up to Piet. He opened his eyes at the sound we made and, seeing me, said, 'Oh! You made it!' He seemed genuinely pleased.

We talked about my journey, about their stay so far and about the French sage, Maitreyi. There was a chess table nearby, an almost-empty bottle of rosé wine left open on it and two glasses. Japp had lifted the table with one hand like a waiter holding a tray, the two glasses still balanced upon it and the wine bottle held in the other hand. In this manner he brought the table to where we were sitting. He waggled the bottle at me, but I declined the offer of a drink. He filled one of the glasses, handed it to Piet then emptied what remained of the bottle into the second glass.

'Do you play chess?' he said to me, taking a sip from his wine.

I said, 'Yes, but not particularly well.'

Japp took another sip of the wine and said, 'Mmm. Good wine!'

Piet nodded noncommittally and tossed off what remained in his glass. Japp savoured what he had, while pulling out a little drawer under the table in which a box of chess pieces had been kept. With one hand he began to set up the pieces, while in the other he held the glass of wine. Then he handed me the box so that I could set up my pieces. He had automatically chosen black for himself, gifting me the handicap of white.

When the pieces were set up, he lifted the wine glass to his mouth and tilted his head back, emptying the contents of the glass. Then he glanced at me, his head still tilted back in an awkward position and waved his hands towards himself, inviting me to lean forward. I did so, thinking he was going to tell me something, though his mouth, I could see, was still full. The chess pieces scattered as I bent over the table.

Japp put the glass down and grabbed my head with both his hands. In a quick, neat operation, he transferred the wine in his mouth to my mouth. I opened my eyes wide to show that I was startled. It seemed pointless to resist him or push him away. I could feel Piet watching this exchange but didn't turn to look at him. Japp said, wiping his face with the back of his sleeve, 'I wanted you to taste the wine.'

We played two games of chess in quick succession, both of which I won. During the second one Japp said, in a small voice, 'No, no – my manhood is at stake!' But I laughed in his face and won anyway.

I didn't stay the full four days in France and saw very little of Piet, Anneke or Kay while I was there. I spent much of my time alone in the villa, while the rest of the group went to listen to Maitreyi's lectures. They were in French, so I couldn't have understood them even if I had wanted to.

At the end of the second day Simon said he wanted to leave. He was in a tense mood, smiling in his tight, unhappy way. When he had a moment alone with me he said it was because of Kay. He said that Kay had insisted on joining the beds in Simon's room so that when Hans arrived there were four of them sleeping in one great continuum.

'It wasn't anything very specific, you understand,' said Simon, 'nothing that I can swear to – but I felt that he was sort of *touching* me. Just my arm, you know? Or my shoulder – I mean, it wasn't some very special part of me, you know? Just that he was touching me in a way that meant more than I would like.'

On the next night he moved out of that room and slept in one of the others. He said that Kay became cold with fury and had not talked to Simon since.

Later that day, in the evening, our whole group attended an entertainment at Maitreyi's estate. It was a flute recital by a young Indian musician. During the performance, I could see his eyes straying towards me. Aside from his mother, who had accompanied him, there were no other Indians around so I must have seemed like a friendly Asiatic.

After the performance which was very well received by the rest of the audience but which I had thought was tediously romantic in the way that mediocre bamboo flute tunes can be, I was introduced to the player and his mother.

The young man was dressed in a raw silk kurta, his shoulder hair oiled and slicked down. His mother wore white, in that way that suggested she was a widow. They both made formal namastés to me and engaged me in the kind of conversation whose only point was to establish my breed and pedigree.

I responded gracelessly, fumbling the namasté and speaking in monosyllables. I felt like an imposter, who just happened to appear like a fellow-citizen to them. I wanted to inform them very politely, that I was actually a tiger, not human at all and that I must not be caged within their suffocating categories of who-what-where. I must have succeeded because they very quickly turned their attention away towards those who wanted to hear them talk about the glories of Indian culture.

As I heard them speaking in their low, melancholy voices, as if continuously mourning the distance between themselves and their beloved native soil, I caught the familiar references to five thousand years of civilization, the wonder that was India, the privilege of higher consciousness, on and boring on.

I felt within me the sensation of grinding frustration that I remembered from childhood, as I recognized the difference between what people said and the visible reality on the streets of India, so removed from those descriptions of grandeur. I felt as if I had been running away, since childhood, from being sucked into the illusions that others around me accepted as fact. I felt as if I had never stopped running.

I thought, this was the source of all my resistance. Any shackles, even the bonds of friendship and affection led back, link by link, to these shackles of culture and ethnic membership.

I looked at the musician and his mother, so secure, so certain of what they were, of their cultural pride, their patriotism honed to piety.

And I felt envious of them.

At least they had their illusions.

GETTING NOWHERE

TWO WEEKS AFTER RETURN from France, I had a call from Willy to tell me that my poster was in the shops and selling well. He had money to give me. I was delighted. I returned from the visit with six hundred guilders and ten complimentary posters. We had discussed the next couple of designs I might do. Armed with the confidence of one successful poster, I returned home feeling heady with purpose.

The elation didn't last long.

Piet and Japp had returned from France the previous day.

This morning, by way of celebration, they had picked up an automatic hot-beverage dispenser from the pavement where it had been left outside the small supermarket that had discarded it.

Piet had just finished installing the chocolate-and-coffee machine in his room a few moments before I walked in with my posters, wanting to share the pleasure of my success.

But the pilfered machine had everyone's attention. It wasn't really a theft, said Japp. They had encountered it at a moment in its life when it was clearly awaiting dismissal to the Old Machines' Home. Piet and Japp's role had merely been one of assisting in its departure while adding to the beauty and convenience of Piet's room in the bargain.

They had filled it with milk powder, hot chocolate and coffee but the brew that emerged from the machine once it was all set up tasted vile. It required its own custom-formulated ingredients to work properly. Japp looked at the back of the machine, where the manufacturer's name and address were listed. Then he looked up the telephone directory, called the listed number and placed an order for two months' supply. To everyone's amazement it was delivered to the house that very day.

Piet entered a bogus signature with his left hand and within another half hour hot instant coffee and chocolate were available on tap in his room, for the modest consideration of only fifty Dutch cents, thank you!

Watching the coffee machine being made operational, my mood of triumph deflated like a punctured gas balloon. I went out for a solitary, aimless walk, wanting to sift through the debris in my brain for answers.

The theft of the coffee-machine was disturbing to me. I was reminded of the bus tickets en route to Kay's house in Amsterdam. When do innocent pranks turn into petty crime?

Then I turned the enquiry towards myself: While returning from France I had willfully sneaked across the Dutch border without a valid visa. I had smoked illegal substances in Germany. As for lies! I had lied to my family, my friends, everyone I knew.

Which was worse? Picking up a disused coffee-*aparat* from the street where it had been left untended? Or betraying the people who represented all my emotional capital in the world?

If there was no difference between me and my Dutch friends then what was the source of my unease when it came to coffee machines and bus tickets? There was no argument which could translate what I did as being less serious than the things they did. It seemed to me that I was attempting to do what everyone does, ultimately: justifying my own actions while criticizing others'.

I felt myself growing muddled. These questions had once been very easy to answer. Plus there were other problems. While the coffee machine drama was going on, I found myself standing apart from the rest of the crowd, asking myself how, in this kind of circus, I could possibly centre myself enough to produce two new posters.

Downstairs in the living room, there were the cats, the guinea pigs, the hamster and a now-pregnant dog underfoot. The pregnancy had caused the dog to wander around wearing the expression of not just a martyr but an angry martyr.

The other day she had gone into Piet's mother's room and savaged a goose-down pillow. Japp was visiting at the moment that the crime was discovered and had let me photograph him with the disemboweled pillow dangling from his mouth, goosedown spilling out of it like white blood.

Upstairs in Piet's room there was even less sanctuary these days. People kept dropping by to see Piet or to just hang out. It was not my room after all but Piet's room. My needs could not take priority.

The weather had turned sultry. There were parts of the house which accumulated heat like a kiln. I had noticed that I was gradually being covered in bright red itchy splotches. They itched in that eye-watering way which comes close to being a type of pleasure. They also left nasty dark pock-marks which refused to fade away.

Simon identified them as cat-flea bites. 'When the weather is hot, the fleas jump off the cats and jump onto any person who has the most similar blood.' No one else in the house was being bitten, which made me feel like the only mutant whose blood most closely resembled a cat's.

My mind felt like a ball of wool that has come unraveled. I could not see the end of the skein. I felt knotted, strangled, undone, diffused.

There was no-one I could speak to. Japp was out of the question. Piet and Simon might interpret my remarks as a criticism of their hospitality. I had no other friends. The last time I had spoken to Micki was shortly after my birthday but before the trip to France.

She had said then that she had a letter from my parents asking for news of me. What should she do? We discussed the matter but I said I wasn't ready to reveal my whereabouts. Just talking about home brought on a sense of suffocation and constraint.

We agreed that the best solution was to send a brief note back, to say that I was travelling and had no fixed address, but that I was doing some work for a poster company, to which they could send mail. At that time I had mistakenly believed that the name of the company I was going to show my work to was Verkerke Posters. So I had got their address from a poster lying on the table and given it to her.

Thinking back to that conversation now, I couldn't see myself calling her. What would she say except that I should leave? And how could I leave if the slender thread on which my future prospects hung was Melody Posters in Holland? Even if I left to go back to Germany, that wouldn't help, because I would still not have a place in which to produce work.

I got back from the walk feeling that I was wandering in a maze, as lost now as I was when I set out.

Simon asked what was troubling me. I told a half-truth by saying it was the theft of the coffee-machine. He gave me his unhappy smile and said, 'Oh, this is nothing! Our family is notorious. We take whatever we like, whenever we like.' It was clear that it didn't gladden him to make such an admission.

According to him, the operative principle was to 'collect' items which were not necessities. 'It wouldn't be, shall we say, cool to take things we actually need. So we take things that we don't need, just to prove that ownership of property is pure *maya*!'

I didn't argue with him but what he said only drove the corkscrew of guilt and moral unease deeper into me.

A DEATH

IN THE SECOND WEEK of August, Piet's mother made an astonishing announcement: she and the younger two boys were going to France for their holiday, to a nudist camp. She said she'd been looking forward to doing this for a long time now, and this summer she was going to do it. She would be away for two weeks.

Piet said, 'Now start the seven lean years!' I thought he was being alarmist, but he was right. From the time that his mother left the house, support systems started to fail. The house looked disshevelled and food stocks dwindled to nought.

Anneke came into her own. She invited Piet to stay over with her, so that she could feed him there. Both he and Simon took summer jobs at the Mercedes factory. I was alone in the house for most of the day. In the late afternoon, Simon would return from work and we would procrastinate about what to do about dinner before giving up and opting to go to the local McDonald's.

It should have been the ideal time for me to get the two commissioned posters done. With the two younger children out of the house, I could work uninterruptedly at the dining table. Then the hamster died. And everything fell apart.

Japp had been away in Amsterdam. He visited on an evening when Simon and I were sitting at the dining table chatting. Japp looked over to the hamster's cage on the low table in front of the TV. He noticed how active the little creature was.

'He's reelly ffery smart!' said Japp, going over to watch him leaping about, doing acrobatics on his exercise wheel, hanging upside down from the top bars of his cage and scampering about from one side to the next. Simon and I also came around the cage, to watch. He was in an extraordinary mood, practically spinning about, gnawing on the bars of the cage and doing hand-flips. He did everything he could short of speak to us to tell us why he was so desperate to attract our attention.

The next morning, he was dead. We had forgotten to feed him. While the other pets had gravitated towards the grandmother's house where they knew they would find food, the hamster was imprisoned in his cage. He had starved to death, a poor mute beast, surrounded by people who claimed to be fond of him.

Simon was the one to find him, on his way out to work that morning. He ran up, told me that the hamster had died and ran out again to catch his bus. I spent the whole morning sitting in Piet's room listening to a Ravi Shankar record and crying.

Talking about it to Simon later, I said, 'We killed him, Simon,' I said. 'We were responsible for a small breathing creature. We let him die a horrible death.'

Simon, despite being very gentle, wore the cap of inflexibility when he said, 'It was his karma. And it was *our* desire which resulted in his death. We desired it, by forgetting about him. Because he doesn't experience his death, you know? I mean the hamster can't anticipate. For him it's just CURTAINS! Like an earthquake or some plague. It's we who can experience his death as our loss, our regret. We feel guilty, we feel unhappy. So it's our experience. And if we don't *desire* to be more careful about the little animals we take under our roof then . . . we have the *experience* of his death.'

I said, 'A hamster's not a piece of rock or a block of ice. He could think and feel, even if only in a limited way. On his own, he could have provided for himself, made a little nest, reproduced and died. It was because of us that he was unable to *eat*, for god's sake! That's so basic, so fundamental! If you say that he experienced his fate because he desired it in some way, because of past life experiences or whatever well . . . we're *all* just hamsters then, of one sort or another! Sitting in a cage of reality, waiting to be fed or not fed, depending on the sweet will of Fate!'

Simon shrugged and repeated what he had said earlier: there's no reason to expect the answers to be pretty.

I could not concentrate on anything after this. There was no point making the effort to do anything, if the only difference between me and the hamster was that I could not see the bars of my particular life-cage. There was no point making the effort to run after poster companies or to make money or to have any goals or aims in life if at the end of the day some completely arbitrary event, such as the thoughtlessness with which we forgot to feed the hamster, could result in a slow and painful death. It was fatalism of the Oriental kind, compounded with the coldly analytical logic of the Occident.

I had no dollars left. My wad of six hundred guilders was already thinning out. My visa had expired, I didn't have a ticket, I was covered in flea bites and finally, I was starting to cough.

The coughing was because of stress-related asthma. I had been clinging to the idea that I couldn't be really unhappy because when I was really unhappy, I got asthma. Now I was starting to cough and though it was very mild I knew that if it got worse, I had no pills or prescriptions to control it. It was a physical confirmation that I was unhappy. My body was giving me notice that I must act to get myself out of the situation I was in or face the consequences.

I had no will to do anything about anything. I spent whole days just staring out of the window in the dining room, trying to scrape together enough energy to make myself a cup of coffee or butter a slice of bread. When one of the others was around, I came alive and talked. But the moment I was alone, I became like a torch whose batteries have died within it. I could no more recharge my own batteries than a car can fill itself with petrol.

One morning, Piet came back from his day job to say that he had made a plan to hold a study meeting in his room and since it may go on till late, could I manage to spend the evening out? Till about eleven-thirty, if possible? Japp had come by and I suggested to him that we go out to a movie together. We saw *Thunderball*. We had both already seen it so it didn't especially hold our interest. I told him that I couldn't get back till after eleven. We wandered about the streets. We had a couple of beers. We wandered some more.

I explained to Japp that I was extremely depressed.

He said, 'Oh yah – dot happens. In Piet's company, dot happens.' I explained about the hamster and experiences which happen without desire. He nodded sagely. We wandered some more. We wandered all over town, on foot. He showed me where the city jail was. He sang a loud raucous ballad about nothing in particular. We bought cigarettes from a vending machine. And we wandered some more.

By the time we got back to Piet's house, it was three in the morning. Piet's study session was long over and he was once more away at Anneke's place. I told Japp that I was tired and wanted to sleep.

Japp asked if it was all right if he slept on the horsehair sofa. I said, of course it was.

We settled down in our separate corners of the room, but after a few minutes of silence in the darkness lit only by the fish-tank, Japp said, 'Are you there?'

I said I was.

He said, 'I would like to say something to you.' I told him to go ahead.

'I need to come there,' he said, 'to where you are.' I said he could.

He swarmed into the bed with little shrieks and yelps. He was an extreme contrast to Piet. He engulfed me completely. His mouth was like a warm mushy lake. His arms wrapped around me like twin pythons. His legs were like young saplings. In *Shogun* mention had been made of the 'turtle-headed mace' some warriors had in their personal armoury and Japp was certainly one of them. Merely to coax his equipment into a latex jacket took an enormous struggle because it seemed not to fit. He was noisy and immoderate, like a force of nature. I was glad that I didn't want to oppose him.

Dawn had already appeared on the horizon at this time.

A couple of hours later, perhaps at nine o'clock, the door opened and Piet came in, with Anneke. The sudden noise caused Japp to jerk awake and I, who had fallen asleep at the margin of the bed, fell out, completely naked.

It was like a scene from a classic farce, except that there was no music or laughter. Everyone behaved calm and apparently unconcerned. I reached for my nightie and put it on. Japp rumpled his hair and stretched. Piet collected a book from his desk, Anneke smiled politely, nodded and then the two of them went out again.

If I could have skinned myself alive with a blow-torch I could not have produced a more violent distress than what I felt immediately after this incident.

I had often wondered before this how other people survive the shaming and embarrassing incidents that one reads about in books and news reports. Now I knew. My mind went blank and for however long it took to restore normalcy, there was a buzzing sound in my ears in the place of thoughts.

I continued to live in the house. Piet and I continued to be, on the surface, friendly. Without discussion, I began to sleep downstairs on the sofa in the living room. I still had the key to his room and my suitcase and belongings remained inside there, but I knocked before entering and did not presume to use it as my own space. The three of us, Piet, Japp and myself even spent a couple of evenings together, as before.

Under this smooth surface, the bond that had kept me connected to Piet in all these months was now finally and completely smashed. Nothing needed to be said. By repeating in awful burlesque the scene between Japp and Juliana, I had managed to do the one thing, perhaps the only thing, that could destroy Piet's regard for me, forever.

Simon, when I told him about this event, said I must understand that it had nothing to do with me. It was part of the delicacy of his friendship with me that he never asked me to define my relationship with his elder brother.

He regarded the whole event as a function of Japp's disordered personality. 'You are under his influence,' said Simon. Japp's peculiar gift, explained Simon, was to inspire weird behaviour in others.

'He's not completely normal, you know?' said Simon. 'Did he tell you that the army wouldn't take him because he was mentally unstable?'

I told him about Japp's story concerning the encounter therapy group. Simon said that Japp was lying. Neither did he drop the woman, nor did she kill herself. According to Simon it was in Japp's nature to bring out the worst in everyone, even himself.

I thought it was sweet of Simon to be willing to make excuses for me, but I knew that he was wrong. I had an attachment to Piet that I could not afford to maintain. Once it had lodged inside me, I could find any number of justifications for leaving it in place, but was helpless to remove it. The only way it would come out was to be torn out and that's what had happened.

I did not feel in any way relieved but decided that I had to forge onward without pausing to heal wounds and recover composure. All that mattered now was to complete my posters and use the money to buy my ticket home.

The next day, while I was setting up the paper to start work on the first of the new posters, Japp came over. He seemed in a pleasant, calm mood. He asked how my depression was getting along. I said that I was doing all right, considering that I finally felt confident about getting my posters completed.

He said, casually, 'Yes but – Ma is coming back, you know! In two days.'

I knew this. I had asked Piet whether I could use his room to draw in during the day and sleep downstairs at night. He said, sure that was fine. So I said to Japp, 'And so?'

'Oh . . . nothing,' he said, in that portentous way he had. 'Just that she said she don't want to see you around no more when she came back!'

My fragile composure fell to the floor shattered into a million splinters.'What!' I said, stammering. 'I – I had no idea . . .'

Japp was very definite. 'No, no! She was against it from the very beginning!' She hadn't wanted an extra mouth to feed, she hadn't liked me when she met me, and she had thought I was an inconsiderate oaf who did nothing around the house to help, drifting about in my nightie at all times of day.

And though she didn't care about the private lives of her children, what about the suspicion, voiced loudly by the grandmother, that Piet did not, as he claimed, sleep on the horsehair sofa, but in the bed with me?

Japp looked at me, with his pale, goldfish eyes and his mild, manic smile.

No doubt he had been the agent which had helped winnow fact from fiction.

I had managed to avoid thinking about how I must appear to the other people in Piet's house, in part because it suited me, but also because I believed that they were genuinely disinterested in such matters. Now, suddenly, I saw that I was hopelessly off-target. I had been abysmally stupid and insensitive. I had ignored every obvious signpost pointing me in the direction of common sense.

Losing my connection with Piet was a private failure. Anyone might fail in that way. But to have alienated the family to the extent described by Japp suggested failures at the level of very basic social skills.

I had managed to avoid identifying with their views and by keeping myself aloof had managed not to admit any shame or guilt to my consciousness. Now, suddenly, Japp smashed through the force field I had maintained around my awareness. I had no energy left to put it back up.

I was flooded with uncontrollable embarrassment. 'I don't know what to do!' I said, finally.

I don't think Japp realized how powerfully his words had affected me. My face must have looked as impassive as before.

'You can move in with me,' said Japp, tranquilly. 'Of course, it's not reelly my place, where I live, but you can stay there. For some time at least, huh? At least so that Ma doesn't see you first thing when she comes back?'

'Oh – can I?!' I cried. I felt nothing but a sense of reprieve. All right, I deserved to be stepped on and wiped off the face of the Earth. But staying at Japp's place would buy me a few days' grace in which to review my misspent life. I couldn't think of anything beyond the span of time that connected the present with the moment of Ma's return.

That evening, I discussed it with Simon. I didn't ask him right out whether he knew that his mother didn't want me in the house saying only that I felt it would be best to move out before Ma came back.

Simon was distraught. 'Not with Japp!' he said. 'It won't suit you! He lives in a building which isn't safe! He's not safe himself.'

He said it was just another of Japp's lies. He, Simon, had not heard his mother expressing any extreme disapproval concerning my presence. But my mind was made up. There was no going back on my decision. We worked out schemes for staying in touch, since there was no telephone in Japp's digs. There was a toilet but no bathroom, so in any case, Simon pointed out, I would need to come back to use the shower. He continued to assure me that his mother would not object to anything.

I told Piet that I was moving out to Japp's room. I asked if it was all right with him for me to leave my suitcase in his room till I was ready to leave Holland, which should be very soon now. He nodded and said that was fine. He asked no questions, from which I assumed he felt relieved. I was glad that I had found a way to leave of my own accord rather than force him to ask me to go.

LEARNING TO BREATHE

THE MOVE TO JAPP'S house took half a morning and two trips. On the first one I carried my sling bag across and on the second I took my stock of art materials. The idea was that I would be working industriously while I was in his room, which was in a derelict building that Japp's 'landlord' was claiming under squatters' rights.

No one could be moved out of it, but as a condemned building, it wasn't in the best condition. All three floors were occupied by people similar to Japp, in that they needed temporary accommodation while they worked out the details of their lives. They paid the landlord a small consideration for the privilege of remaining where they were.

The room had two windows, two doors and an old-fashioned iron wood-stove with a pipe climbing up to a hole in the roof. The outer door led to the landing and stairs, but it didn't have a lock and didn't shut completely.

Outside this door, on the landing, was a deep white porcelain sink of the sort that one might find in a laboratory. On the first floor landing was a toilet. The inner door led to another room which was smaller and had no front wall, so that it was like an unfinished balcony. That room was filled with construction materials and served no function.

In the way of furniture there was only one winged armchair and a wooden stool. Covering the floor were two afghan rugs of a vintage which made Piet's rug look new. The sleeping area was defined by two sleeping-bags spread one on top of the other to form a mattress with sheets and a blanket drawn over them. In a corner stood a midget pedal organ, even smaller than the one in Piet's room.

On the wall was an original oil painting. It was surprisingly elegant. It could have been a one of Gauguin's minor studies. Japp said that he had found it at a flea market and thought it looked like a masterpiece except that no one else had discovered it before him.

It showed a brown-skinned nude sitting in the foreground, with palm fronds behind her. It was an utterly banal subject but painted with a cool, knowing touch, the whole composition in short strokes and thick paint, so that it looked like the vision of a short-sighted artist who has removed his spectacles to dash off a quickie in the middle of some frangipani-scented afternoon.

'Home, sweet home,' said Japp spreading his huge arms and twirling on his toes.

We spent a week together. During that time we lived like castaways on a desert island, waking when we pleased, eating out of the single plate, going out at midday to buy a bit of breakfast which meant in practice that I would buy one line of foods while Japp filled his WWII jacket pockets with another line of foods for which he did not pay.

He could be unpredictable. We were walking along a canal road once when he grabbed the collar of my denim jacket, held me up above the surface of the road, said, 'Maybe for you it will be an interesting experience to enter the canal for a few minutes, huh?' I didn't struggle, knowing that it was useless. Then he put me down and said, 'But not today.'

He was affectionate in the way of a Great Dane puppy, liking to sleep completely entwined.

Once, when I resisted his attentions, he said, whispering, 'But maybe it's important for you to know what it's like to be, you know, forced?'

I whispered back that it wouldn't really be force, because I was, after all, only denying access temporarily. If he was very keen, then I wouldn't resist him. But I would rather he wasn't keen for the moment.

'Yah,' he whispered back. 'That is a point. Goot night!'

At the end of the week, he went away to France, wishing me a fond farewell. I told him that I would probably be gone by the time he came back.

That day, the day he left, the rain returned in earnest. The room was open on all sides because neither of the windows had glass in their panes and neither of the doors could be completely shut. My cough, which had been on standby for two weeks worsened to the point that I was breathing in short gasps. Bitter grey water rattled down from the low sky.

I had been back to Piet's house a couple of times, to shower and to wash clothes. I gave back my key to Piet's room, but Simon insisted that I should keep the front door key ' . . . just in case'.

Japp's room had no heating facilities aside from the wood stove. He had left a few shards of wood for me to feed into the stove. I had avoided doing it however because I didn't feel confident about getting a fire going without setting myself alight in the bargain.

In the evening, I bought a takeaway nasi goreng from a fast food Indonesian restaurant in the market. The pale heat of its peanut sauce was comforting to eat. There was a portable radio in the shape of a dinner plate, hanging from a hook on the front door. It belonged to the landlord, said Japp, from whom he had it on indefinite loan. I turned the radio on for company but it echoed tinnily, making me feel even more adrift in the universe than ever before.

I had not seen any of the other residents since moving in with Japp and didn't know who they were or what they looked like. The landlord, whom I had met a couple of times, didn't live in the building. I tried to read a collection of Somerset Maugham short stories that Japp had in his room but felt too spooked by the silence to concentrate. Darkness enfolded the building, the front door would no longer shut completely and the wind was hooting softly through the window sashes.

I told myself that I must sleep.

I brushed my teeth in the laboratory sink, washed my face and arms in the ice cold water and used a torch to go down to the first floor landing to the toilet. Then I came back up, steeled my resolve and turned the single light off before cocooning myself in the blanket.

The air in the room thinned out, the temperature fell and the sound of the rain was cold and menacing, like a snare drum played on the inner membrane of my spirit. I appeared to be entirely alone. Not just in the building but in the street, in the city.

I started to feel afraid.

This darkness, unlike at the French villa, was an unfriendly one. It was seething with spirits. I saw moving flashes and creeping forms, my ears fashioned murmurs out of the random noises of the night.

It had been a long time since I'd felt such a simple, raw, skin-rippling fear. It wasn't of anything tangible or specific. Instead, like all the night-fears of childhood, it was irrational and had no antidote.

But, worse than the cold, the rain, the uncertainty about my immediate future and the fears, was the cough.

It began slowly but implacably to overwhelm me.

Anyone who has asthma knows this terrible feeling, as if the inner lining of one's lungs has grown a fine pelt of fur. And somewhere within the suffocating folds of the fur is a troupe of miniature carol singers who not only tickle and tease those delicate linings, but sing in chorus with every intake of breath and every exhalation.

Whee-whee-whee IN, *whee-whee-whee* OUT.

There is something so unbearably annoying about this involuntary singing that it makes the sufferer want to scream. The lack of air makes one dizzy with sleep, but so long as one is lying down, one's lungs are being compressed and even a trickle of air down one's windpipe becomes an impossibility.

I knew I had to sit up, but the cold air of the room was literally thick with spirits. They were swarming, they were pinning me down, paralysed with fear, to the sleeping-bag mattress. If I sat up, I felt it would be like immersing the upper half of my body in their slimy, phantom substance.

I ran through combinations of the Lord's Prayer, the Magnificat, 'The Lady of Shallott' and even, when pushed to the limit, the multiplication table to keep them at bay. But I was too tired and demoralized to hold my mind steady against the romping ectoplasms. I felt them starting to bite chunks out of my sanity, slashing through my composure, stabbing in towards the warm core of my being. They were winning. They were bringing their darkness in with them. They were blotting me out.

That was when the asthma saved me.

Beginning with a spasm that I could not control, I found my body jerking itself up from the bed, of its own volition. There was a profound silence inside my head, as if with my last exhalation I had also expelled every last thought. I rose out of the womb of sleeping bags, taking the blanket with me for warmth and crossed the room to where the light switch was.

I don't believe I was completely conscious. I had turned on the light and sat down in the winged arm chair before I really knew what I was doing.

Inside my head, on the panoramic display screen which normally provided me with a nonstop jabbering stream of images, thoughts, ideas and internal memos, there was now only the one, compelling message spelt out starkly white against vast blackness: BREATHE.

Breathe NOW.

Doing that was not easy by any means. An asthmatic fit cannot normally be brought under control without drugs. Gradually, however, I could take in a mouthful of air and hold it down and let it out, and then another mouthful of air and hold it down and let it out.

It may have taken an hour before I got even one clear breath without coughing. But very slowly, like someone climbing out of an endlessly deep tunnel on a ladder made of air, I was coughing less and less. The wheezing took a little longer to slow down. The choir of singers was still audible, though softer and less insistent.

I had been breathing quietly and steadily for almost twenty full minutes at a stretch before I noticed that I was no longer scared. I looked up and around me. I was alone in a room in a derelict building, in the middle of a cold, rainy night. And that was all. There were no creeping fears, no tinglings, no invisible nippings at my fingers and toes.

I looked around me, at the bare room and the drizzling blackness beyond the windows and thought, *I'm okay.*

I remained like this, breathing quietly and thinking placid, friendly thoughts about myself.

Piet, if he could have been an audience to these thoughts, would perhaps have dismissed them as irrelevant because my fears were irrational to begin with.

But he was *not* an audience.

Neither was anyone else.

I felt that my mind was cleared of all the unwanted passengers who had been clogging my gangways for so long.

Not just the more recent ones like Piet or Japp but all the earlier ones as well, including many people whom I loved and many others whom I didn't.

My sister, my brother, my parents, my sister-in-law, even some of my friends. There seemed to have been so many people in there trying to control of the ship of my destiny, telling me which ports I should visit and which cargo I should load, when to speed up and where to drop anchor.

Some did it gently and others were rough, but in the end they were just passengers, whereas I was the Captain. I was the ship. I was all my crew.

I felt calm and in control. Yes, there were many of me. Yes, we were sometimes confused and contradictory. Yes, we behaved in foolish and thoughtless ways for which we would have to face the consequences. Yes, there would be storms and whirlpools over which I would have no control.

Still sitting up in the chair with the blanket wrapped around me and the single light blazing, I fell asleep.

EXIT

THE NEXT MORNING DAWNED grey. I washed in the sink and ate the previous day's leftovers for breakfast. Then I heard the bell ring. There was one doorbell for the whole building, at the foot of the stairs. Anyone who felt like it could open the front door and come in, if they wanted to. On the off-chance that Simon had come to visit me, I leaned out to see who it was.

It was Freddie. He had called for me at Piet's house and had got Japp's address from there.

I threw on my flowery nylon housecoat and went down to open the door. Freddie was dressed in a three-piece pearl grey suit, looking uncomfortable to be seen on the doorstep of that ramshackle building. His expression was as good as standing in front of a mirror. He said, 'I came to find out if you would be interested in doing me a favour – but now I see that maybe I can do *you* a favour also?'

His proposal was a simple one: he and Jini were planning a week's holiday in England. In their absence, Freddie's brother Mies would look after the shop and stay in the house. He couldn't manage on his own, however. If I was willing to help out in the shop – and since it seemed that I had an accommodation problem – maybe we could both find solutions by my moving in with them? Just for a short period until he and Jini had returned from their holiday?

I just smiled. This was a dream, surely? But it wasn't.

I dressed quickly and went across to their shop. The idea had been Jini's and she was keen to make it work. By evening, I had collected my possessions from Japp's room and shifted to their house.

They lived with their one-year-old son Paul, in a suburb north of Utrecht.

They had an elegant two-bedroom house decorated in the Western style with a sprinkling of Eastern artifacts. A tiger skin sprawled across the living room wall, while collections of jade elephants glowed discreetly behind glass. There were gilded Thai apsaras ascending one wall and a butterfly case of winged insects displayed against another wall. There were hair ornaments from Java, Kashmiri filigree brooches from India and Mexican bolero pins.

Cane furniture and coarse white cotton complemented polished rosewood and glass. Broad-leaved tropical plants stood in their corner like well-behaved vegetarian pets. The master bedroom was carpeted from wall to wall in pale cappuccino. There were white chiffon curtains and a sunken double bed. All the brass was polished, all the crystal gleamed.

It was very strange for me to be inside this kind of home once more.

Jini's proposal was that I should start working right away at the shop half-days, combined with light *au pairing* in the house in the evenings. That way, she said, I wouldn't feel obligated to them and, by starting at the shop before she left for the holiday, I would become acquainted with the work.

Behind the main building of their home was a low-roofed workspace, partially self-sufficient. Freddie was planning to make it into a studio for restoring antiques that they brought in from their travels. The room had a toilet and sink to itself, rudimentary floor-cladding, a desk and light, but no heating or bed.

A sleeping bag was adequate however, given that the weather had not yet settled into autumn.

I made a terrible *au pair* and was only slightly better as a shop attendant. It must have been a sign of Jini's desperate need for someone that she didn't throw me out immediately. She and Freddie went away for two weeks and after they came back, I remained with them another ten days before leaving.

Very little went wrong aside from one incident involving the police.

I had stayed in touch with Simon and had given him my new contact numbers.

One day, he came into the shop with a conspiratorial look on his face and saying, 'Hi, there! I have some interesting news for you.' When I stepped outside with him he said, 'The police have been visiting our house! They were asking for you.'

Both of us jumped to the conclusion that they were following up on the lapsed visa.

Simon said, 'My mother was very good. She said, "Oh no – we don't know where that person is now, she went away somewhere for travelling. Maybe if she comes back, I'll tell her you were asking."'

Simon knew that I was not capable of being relaxed about police enquiries so he added, 'Don't worry. I was downstairs when they were talking to my mother and they didn't seem very concerned. It was just like a routine enquiry. They were not looking inside cupboards or under the stairs.'

In the days after Simon's visit, I felt like a character in a spy novel, wondering when I would hear the midnight knock. Finally one morning while I was in the shop, two young, uniformed policemen strolled in through the door.

I nearly threw up in panic. I was absolutely sure that they had come for me. But they appeared relaxed, claiming that they were checking out exotic gifts suitable for fiancées.

Jini had not yet left on holiday, so she offered them a cup of coffee, which they accepted. I cursed her silently for detaining them in my presence. Chase scenes from the movies played out in my head, none of them lasting very long, because I have never distinguished myself as a runner.

Were visa offenders tortured before being sent home in chains, I wondered? Were they thrown into tiny bamboo cages and made to eat boiled rats? Simon had tried to calm my fears by telling me that the

Dutch police were cool dudes. 'They grow their hair long and wear earrings!' he said. 'They won't be too nasty.' But how nasty does nasty have to be before it becomes 'too' nasty? I didn't want to find out.

While I was thus preoccupied, one of the policemen glanced across at me. No doubt he was distracted by my efforts to look invisible. He said something in Dutch and when I shook my head, staring down at the plaited banana fibre matting on the floor, he said, 'Where are you . . . fon?'

'India,' I said, thinking, *here it comes!* I had to admit, though, that what I could see of him, in the reflections winking at me from tiny glass mirrors in the embroidered cushion close at hand, was the very definition of non-threatening. He had dark hair curling down around his ears and a Frank Zappa moustache. The thought crossed my mind that it may even be fun to be arrested by such a person. I could write about it years later, when I was released from labour camp in the Friesian Islands.

He gestured at the framed miniature paintings on the wall behind him, speaking in carefully phrased English. 'Dese . . . dese paintings . . . dey are . . . foor sale?' I was surprised enough at this question to look up to see what he meant. Maybe this was the procedure for trapping visa offenders in Holland? Soften them up with questions on art and culture before pouncing?

I said, in what I hoped was the voice of one who has more visas than she knows what to do with, 'Yes.'

'And dey are . . . fon . . . which country?' The other cop had not been paying much attention, sipping his coffee as if meditating on handcuffs and other restraining devices.

I said, 'India.' I considered turning myself over without a struggle. Perhaps they would let me off with a light reprimand. *Neffer do this again*, they might say, wagging admonitory fingers at me, while I and other unwanted visitors sat in our transporter ship, chained to our oars.

Pony-tail smiled broadly and said, 'Ah . . . the paintings too are fon Eendia! Chust like you!'

I raised my eyebrows, thinking that this conversation was taking a strange turn. I felt I should stop it in its tracks. 'Yes,' I said, 'except that I am *not* for sale!' The little joke was a hit. Both cops laughed uproariously. A few further pleasantries later, they left. No discussion of visas.

When I described this exchange to Simon, he said, 'What did I tell you! You worry too much! Forgetting to *watch the cobra*!'

I told him that my bourgeois upbringing made it impossible for me to face the idea of arrest and deportation calmly. He told me that this was a good reason to give up the bourgeois upbringing. I said that it seemed to me I had gone quite a distance in that direction by staying in Japp's room. He laughed, agreeing that Japp's room was as good a 'de-bourgeoisizing machine' as I would ever find.

His girlfriend was still playing the field and he was still at loose ends. He came over in the afternoons, when my duties in the shop were over. We wandered the streets, inspecting the tulips blooming in private gardens and awarding prizes to God whenever we saw a particularly accomplished sunset.

On weekends, we went sightseeing. We visited the Rijks Museum in Amsterdam to worship in front of the Rembrandts. We spent an afternoon at the Evoluon, a museum of science and technology shaped like a flying saucer, swarming with school children. We played with early computers and visible light. I listened to my voice distorted to sound like a man's. Simon tried his hand at playing the Moonlight Sonata on a futuristic instrument made of brass panels and light energy. We had a happy time.

I had called Radzie in the US soon after moving in with the Hopps. It felt like the first phone call from space. She was warm and loving, assuring me that no one was angry with me, either in Bombay or anywhere else.

She had heard, just that week, that between Prashant and Gai, they had found a paying guest accommodation for me. It was in Colaba, near all my familiar haunts. It was near Prashant. My desk had already been shifted across. ALL WAS WELL.

I called Bombay then and spoke to everyone at home. My mother was visiting from Calicut and scolded me while telling me that she never thought she would hear my voice again. Dates were discussed.

'So!' said Simon, when I told him that my departure was a certainty. 'Are you going straight into a marriage?' He knew about the complications that had played a part in triggering the trip.

How far away those anxieties now seemed.

I said to Simon. 'I needled my brother into saying things which angered me enough to come on this trip. It had nothing to with him, right? It had everything to do with my desire to run away from my life for a while. Just for five months. He was a catalyst. He pushed me into doing what I wanted to do anyway.'

'And what about your "exit" at thirty?' he asked. 'Still hoping to buy a ticket on the QE II?'

I laughed and said, 'I'll send you a postcard when I'm on board, I promise!'

Japp had returned from France a few days before I was due to leave from Holland then had gone away again, to spend time with his parents. He left a bouquet of flowers for me at the house. He told Simon a story about how he had set fire to a mound of excelsior lying in a rubbish tip. Then he had called the fire brigade to say that there was a fire raging on the corner of such-and-such a canal. Then he had gone back to mingle with the crowd that came to watch the fire.

The late hamster had been replaced with a new hamster and the dog had given birth. But Henk's thoroughbred Dobermann (Doberfrau? I wondered out loud to Simon) Suzie had also just given birth, to eight thoroughbred puppies. Suzie was a worthless mother so her brood was brought for wet-nursing to poor tailless Mouse of the long-suffering eyes. Her own puppies were sent back to the reincarnation bureau by the vet.

'And so it goes,' said Simon, sagely, 'so it goes.'

I finished three posters but didn't have the time to take them to Melody, so I left them with Freddie to do with as he pleased. I had not fulfilled my plan to earn my way out of Holland. But I had decided that it was enough to know that I *could have* supported myself on my work, based on the experience with the Travolta poster.

I had called one of my uncles in London. Radzie had sent an air-ticket for me to their address. I booked a ticket out to England on the ferry from the 'Hook of Holland'.

I had been over to Piet's house. I gave them a signed copy of my Travolta poster as a gift. Simon came with me on the train to see me off at the ferry.

I said that I would return to Holland as soon as I could afford the journey on my own money, maybe in the following year? Simon said he was glad to hear that because he felt he had been the one to benefit the most from my presence in the house. I told him that of all the experiences I had had on the trip his friendship had meant the most to me. He had been steady, good-humoured and caring. I would not have made it through my particular tunnel without him.

We agreed that probably the best part about the friendship was that it was just that: a friendship. Nothing more. 'It's strange, huh?' he said. 'We say, "nothing" more and yet it's much more. Than the other thing.'

I had two aerosol cans of fluorescent orange paint with me which I had planned to use on one of the posters but hadn't, in the end. They had been expensive to buy and I had been unwilling to let go of them. But all the way to the ferry, they had been weighing down my hand luggage. I took one of them out now and gave it to Simon. When it was time for me to go past the final barriers, through a gate to the other side of a chain-link fence, we hugged and promised to stay forever in touch.

From my side of the barrier I waved to him and he waved his aerosol can at me. Then he sprayed a small patch of paint onto the cement at his feet, and called out, 'To mark the spot where we'll meet again next year!' Then he moved out of sight on his way back to the train station. I turned and followed the other ferry passengers.

There was one last obsessive worry and that was about the lapsed visa in my passport. Maybe there was yet a hurdle to clear, at the very end, right at the finish line? But Simon had said, 'So long as you're on your way out, they won't stop you!' Sure enough, the immigration officer barely glanced at my passport. He stamped an exit date on the visa page and I boarded the ferry for England.

A couple of days later, in early September, I was on a plane back to Bombay. My mother was at the airport to greet me when I arrived. So was Prashant. No one scolded me or ticked me off.

I didn't say much about my trip to anyone and no one asked me. My explanation for my disappearance was that I got stuck trying to work my way out and as a result was too hassled to do anything, even write letters. I had the copies of my Travolta poster as proof that I had actually got something done.

I still had very little money and no immediate prospect of earning more. I was still just a paying guest in someone else's house, though on my own this time and more self-reliant. I still had my desk, in the new place. Most of my personal belongings were the same that I had had before. I was still overweight though not quite as much as when I started out on my diet.

For a while I and Prashant stayed together. We still went out most evenings and I still spent nights over at his room in Jujube Towers. At my request, we were friends, not lovers. I said I didn't want to talk about anything and if he didn't want to see me any more right away, I would understand. It was his choice. He said he'd prefer to try it out. We agreed upon the period of a year. If in that time I hadn't found my way around the blocks in my emotional plumbing, we would formally stop spending time with one another.

One year after I returned, upon the designated date, we spent a final evening together and said a peaceful, dry-eyed goodbye. He was, by that time, glad to move on. He got married soon after, had two children and is, as far as I know, happy and contented with his life.

The real changes, most of them, were within me.

The sense of being in some fundamental way a loner and an outsider to humanity never left me. But I don't feel oppressed or caged in by circumstances in the same way as I used to. I don't test the bars, I don't try to run away.

I draw and I write. I breathe.

Sometimes, when the jungle is quiet, my whiskers feel shiny and I purr.

ACKNOWLEDGEMENTS

Warm thanks to Thomas Abraham and Poulomi Chatterjee for having faith in me and in the second edition of this book.

To Bhavi Mehta for the glorious breakthrough, after close to a year of struggle, in finding the perfect photograph for the cover.

To Rajdeep Mukherjee of Picador Books for the first edition. And to Mary Mount, my editor for the first edition.

To several members of my long-suffering family who have had to put up with being featured (or not) in this book.

And finally, to G.v.d.E., the brother whose kindness and continuing friendship enables me to look back with gladness.